Early Formal
Education

KH

Library of Congress Catalog Number: 2009036902
ISBN: 978-0-202-36329-5
Printed in the United States of America

Library of Congress Cataloging-in-Publication Data

Conference on Pre-school Education. Chicago, 1966.
   Early formal education : current theory, research, and practice /
Robert D. Hess and Roberta Meyer Bear, editors.
         p. cm.
"Papers ... presented at the Conference on Pre-school Education, held in Chicago on February 7-9, 1966 ... [and] sponsored by the Committee on Learning and the Educational Process of the Social Science Research Council."
   Includes bibliographical references and index.
   ISBN 978-0-202-36329-5
   1. Education, Preschool--Congresses. I. Hess, Robert D. II. Bear, Roberta Meyer, 1942- III. Social Science Research Council. Committee on Learning and the Educational Process. IV. Title.

LB1140.C632 2009
372.21--dc22

                                                        2009036902

7/5/11

Early Formal Education

Current Theory, Research, and Practice

Robert D. Hess and
Roberta Meyer Bear

editors

ALDINETRANSACTION
A Division of Transaction Publishers
New Brunswick (U.S.A.) and London (U.K.)

PREFACE

IN February, 1966, the Committee on Learning and the Educational Process of the Social Science Research Council sponsored a conference on early education. This volume is the result of that Conference. It is more than a publication of papers presented; a number of the chapters have been rewritten, expanded, or greatly revised as a result of the Conference and subsequent discussions. One chapter is included which was written after the Conference in response to the formal papers and discussions that had been scheduled. One Conference presentation is not included here: Fred Strodtbeck elected not to prepare a written paper.

The conference was planned by an ad hoc committee of Lloyd Morrisett (chairman), Alfred Baldwin, and Robert Hess. Members of the Committee on Learning and the Educational Process chaired the Conference sessions. The discussion was recorded by machine and by several graduate students of the University of Chicago: Janet Berstein, Gene Fox, Rae Isenberg, Boaz Kahana, Nancy Kohn, Jane Lathrop, Richard Logan. The discussions have been summarized in the concluding chapter of this report.

The Conference and the preparation of the manuscript for this volume were facilitated by the assistance of administrative staff from the Urban Child Center of the University of Chicago, particularly Mrs. Ruth Vogeler, Administrative Assistant, and Mrs. Nellie Hickman.

Financial support for the Conference was provided by a grant to the Social Science Research Council from the Fund for the Advancement of Education.

ROBERT D. HESS
ROBERTA MEYER BEAR

CONTENTS

XIV.   Early Learning and Personality: Summary and Commentary, *Eleanor E. Maccoby*   191

XV.   Some Educated Guesses about Cognitive Development in the Pre-School Years, *Sheldon H. White*   203

XVI.   Some Problems in the Evaluation of Pre-School Intervention Programs, *Joseph Glick*   215

XVII.   Issues in Early Learning and Pre-School Education: A Summary of the Conference Discussions, *Roberta Meyer Bear*   223

         BIBLIOGRAPHY   231

         INDEX   265

ROBERT D. HESS

EARLY EDUCATION AS SOCIALIZATION

Robert D. Hess (B.A. 1947, University of California; Ph.D. 1950, University of Chicago) is Lee Jacks Professor of Child Education, School of Education, Stanford University.

THE future of any society lies in its ability to train, that is, to socialize its young. The stability of its institutions and political systems, the productivity of its industrial resources, and the creativity of its intellectual talent reflect the degree of success of the adults in the society who have been given responsibility for shaping and developing its youth. If these teaching functions are not being adequately performed, through failure of the agents or as a result of new demands created by new values, or social, economic, or political change, pressures are likely to emerge for modification of the socializing procedures or for a change in the agents who are allocated responsibility for socialization.

From this perspective, the contemporary preoccupation with extrafamilial "pre-school' education in the United States reveals a profound mistrust of our present methods of socialization. In particular it seems to express a growing skepticism about the effectiveness of the family as a socializing agent. The extension downward in age of the beginning of formal schooling changes and emphasizes the role of the school. Vis-à-vis the child, the school becomes increasingly instrumental as the direct agent of socialization. Vis-à-vis the family, there is an enlarging of the arena of the child's life with which the school is concerned and a marked gain in the potential impact of the school as a source of values, skills, and orientations.

The current growth of programs in early education and the large-scale involvement of the schools and federal government in them is not a transitory concern. *It represents a fundamental shift in the relative roles and potential influence of the two major socializing institutions of the society—the family and the school.*

1

The decision of the Committee on Learning and the Educational Process of the Social Science Research Council to call a conference on early education was thus both timely and significant. It illustrated the growing concern on the part of social scientists (as well as other professionals) over the process of education in this country. This concern is an acknowledgment that education is socialization into modern society and as such is a critical process deserving the attention of all members of the society, especially those with special training, experience, and competence in the study of early learning and development.

The recognition that early education is basic socialization was evident in the comments by the participants in the Conference sessions. Although the discussions focused on education and related mental operations, the members of the group recognized that distinctions among "personality," "mental behavior," and "education" are not particularly meaningful, particularly at the early stages of development. During formative periods in the child's life, the effects of both cognitive and "non-cognitive" experience are likely to be diffuse and general. Even in a pre-school setting, such corollary experiences as success, failure, approval by the teacher, or awareness of peer approval have consequences for social and emotional development, though they take place in activities intended to be purely cognitive. In short, early education is necessarily interlaced with development in other areas and may best be conceptualized as basic socialization. At these early age levels, the term "education" may be inaccurate. It may mislead us into the illusion that programs can be designed for the very young with sufficient focus upon cognitive content that we may ignore their consequences in social and emotional areas.

In a society in which early socialization—and training of all kinds —takes place primarily in the home, the parents hold legal responsibility for decisions about most of the experiences that the child encounters. They have virtually exclusive right to plan the pre-school program. Psychologists, social workers, ministers, and other professionals typically have only an advisory, consulting status, and that often indirectly, through colleagues who specialize in the application of psychological knowledge and theory to emotional and developmental dysfunctioning. Except in extreme and atypical cases, the parent exercises the options that determine the nature of early training. For legal, moral, and psychological reasons, the professional can play only a supplementary role, even when the behavior of the parent is clearly to the child's future disadvantage. When the process of education—or the technique of socialization—is institutionalized through the school, however, the community, through some form of government, assumes responsibility, often in a direct way and without necessarily involving the parents in planning. The decisions made and the programs developed are applied to all. When this occurs, the locus of decisions about what to teach and how to deal with the developmental problems of 3- and 4-year-olds shifts from parents to non-family sources.

The training of children under these conditions becomes a matter for public debate and public concern, and an array of questions comes quickly to mind. For example, are children of 3 years of age to be taught to read, and if so, are they to be taught by machine or human teacher? Is the 4-year-old to be coached in pre-mathematical concepts as preparation for an increasing concentration upon mathematics in elementary, secondary school, and college? How much of the curriculum is to be allocated to the development of social skills? What part to verbal facility, to peer interaction, and to other talents which assist the individual in the exercise of his cognitive abilities? What is to be the nature of moral training, of sex education? How does one teach the principles of human interaction that are basic to a society of civilized and educated men? Where and by whom will these decisions be made?

Or, indeed, is there need to be concerned? Is the experience of the 3- and 4-year-old child only of minor significance to the development of his adult behavior and capabilities and thus deserving of little attention? Is any adult—parent or teacher—as competent as any other in the early phases of human teaching? If not, how shall the teacher (the parent substitute in a literal sense) be selected? What qualities do we look for in teachers? What training do they receive? Is it important that there be serious attempts at formal education during the early years, as some believe? Or are the developmental processes and the genetic component in intelligence so overriding that we may offer an adequate program merely by providing competent custodial, group baby-sitting care? Is there an age range within which stimulation of varying kinds can be effective as preparatory experiences for later learning? Or is an organized and preplanned program of shaping and conditioning the most effective and shortest route to producing the sort of mind and personality the society will need for the next half-century?

Some issues emerge as particularly central to the concerns of the Conference. One critical question is whether the pre-school years deserve the fiscal resources and professional talent now allocated to them. This can be answered only when we know more about the relative vulnerability of the child's cognitive processes to intervention, either benign or destructive, at different age levels. What evidence can we

muster that a greater impact is possible at the pre-school than at subsequent ages? While there are some data concerning the relationship
between early and later achievement, there is little about the relative
effectiveness of intervention at, for example, age 3 versus age 13 in
terms of behavioral change in areas affected by education. Not only
do we not know the relative gain to be expected from intervention at
pre-school as compared with the school years, we know little about
the ages during the pre-school period that are optimal for shaping or
changing various kinds of behavior. This question is of theoretical as
well as economic interest.

Another issue in early education is whether socioeconomically disadvantaged children can successfully be socialized or educated in isolation, that is, without involving their family and community reference
groups. The notion underlying many contemporary programs for disadvantaged children is that such treatment compensates for deprivation
of stimuli in the child's experience. This idea implies a physical growth
or malnutrition model in which the enriched curriculum makes up the
academic calories lacking in the cognitive diet of the home. This is a
conception which has given rise to widespread efforts to transport children to museums and zoos, even to moving them in as guests for a
week or two with middle-class suburban families in order to provide
experiences not available in the slum community. Programs which have
been based upon this model may have done the field, and the children
involved, a disservice. Stimuli of various kinds, usually called enrichment, have been heaped upon children with little theoretically based
planning or programming and little understanding of how they might
affect the child and his family.

The cultural distance and status differential between home and
classroom are considerable. In order to be effective, the school must
function not only as a socializing agent but as a *re-socializing* agent.
As such, it must find ways to deal with those subcultural influences
upon learning styles which act in opposition to the learning and teaching climate of the classroom. On this point, imagination and social experimentation are badly needed. Should we, perhaps, attempt to educate families as units, or to deal with even larger segments of the
disadvantaged community?

A third point is not so much an issue for debate as a question:
What are the mechanisms of exchange that mediate environmental pressures into cognitive behavior? The association between learning and
environment, typically conceptualized in terms of social class and culture, is one of the most familiar findings in educational and developmental research. The concepts of social class and of cultural variation

within society have been particularly useful in understanding some of the relationships between social experience and education. Although many of the details and elaborations of this association have yet to be worked out, the correlation is established beyond dispute. Contemporary interest in this topic has shifted to the attempt to analyze process and to understand *how* social class is translated into behavior. For this purpose, the concept of social class and ethnic culture must be further refined and the behavior involved examined in greater detail. Social class is not, strictly speaking, a variable. It is a statement of probability —the likelihood that certain specific experiences will occur or have occurred in an individual's history and that they will have a more or less predictable effect upon his social, economic, emotional, and cognitive behavior. While this concept applies with particular relevance to the education of urban working-class children, it obviously states a more general problem: How do we conceptualize the effects of extra-laboratory experience in ways that will permit the planning and development of programs of education which will be effective?

Another issue of both practical and theoretical moment is the relative role and usefulness of man and machine in the teaching process. By this I do not intend to raise the question of whether teaching machines are effective. Rather, the question is whether a human teacher is needed for certain cognitive and psychological processes to occur in the pre-school child. What processes might be fostered by the human teacher that cannot be replaced by the machine? What about the role of that complex set of processes called identification? Does the term *identification* include subtle teaching which cannot be accomplished by machines, no matter how complex and well-programmed? Is there an age at which the human teacher is particularly important? Are there instructions and concepts which the human teacher cannot delegate to a machine at any age? This problem is basic to learning and to teaching.

It is not irrelevant, of course, that the primary energy and motivation for the surge of interest in early education had its origins in concern cver the educational consequences of discrimination. Project Head Start, with the accompanying funds for assessment and research that it brings to the field, will probably be the most significant influence upon early education in this decade. The connection between early training and programs to deal with cultural disadvantage was predictable from the ideas presented in Allison Davis' brilliant discussion in *Social Class Influences Upon Learning*, published in 1948. Had this book been taken more seriously, it is conceivable that the turmoil of recent summers could have been mitigated. Some of the current descriptions of the slum family and the effects of discrimination and poverty on children are echoes (often apparently unknowingly) of Davis' portrayal of twenty years ago. It has taken fifteen years, a Supreme Court decision, and a civil-rights revolution to stimulate action which led to the availability of more adequate resources in education for young children in disadvantaged areas. Perhaps because we tend to be ideologically uninvolved in our professional activities, social scientists—especially child psychologists—have been singularly insensitive to the social and educational disadvantage suffered by minority groups in this country. As a result, the energy for action, for research decisions, and for plans for programs has come from foundations and agencies of the federal government.

The influence of scholars in these activities, however, has not been entirely absent. Several psychologists were working in the areas of early education and cognitive development in disadvantaged children before it became popular in academic circles. Most of these people were present or represented at this Conference. The work of such professionals and the support of the officials of several foundations provided a basis of theory and experience without which federal programs in early education would not have appeared at this time.

The present state of early education is such that quite diverse philosophies and efforts are exercised concurrently, often in the same city, with little or no exchange of ideas, methods, or results. Despite an apparent communality of interest, the research and action programs created and pursued to date have been relatively isolated from one another. Several points of view offer different types of focus. This fragmentation of effort in the field is aggravated by the fact that little of the research conducted in the past five years in compensatory education has been published in scientific journals. The sociometric circles of conferences, mimeographed reports, consultation, and related activities have provided what little dissemination of information there has been.

The Conference on Early Education was planned to provide opportunity for a confrontation of ideas, philosophies, and research findings. It brought together scholars with various types of involvement in early education, and of different theoretical convictions about the nature of the learning process. The Planning Committee hoped for an exchange of views among the advocates of several approaches: those who focused upon deficits and lack of specific skills in pre-school children from disadvantaged homes; those who represented the developmental-cognitive approach in the tradition of Piaget; experimenters who test the theory that achievement motivation and behavior is learned and that it can be taught in nursery school; researchers who emphasize learning during the early months rather than the early years; those who are concerned with the impact of social structure and socialization upon early cognitive functions; others who are experimenting with restructuring the environment of young children; proponents of the Montessori philosophy and methods; language specialists, and scholars in early mental development.

One of the contributions of the Conference was to bring together a number of the most active persons in the field to encourage a more explicit statement of the concepts, theories, empirical data, myths, and flights of intuition upon which they are proceeding. Along another dimension, it included researchers who have attempted to test theory in experimental educational programs and researchers who have conducted their work in more traditionally academic settings.

The Conference convened only a few of the social scientists engaged in current research and experimentation in early education. In this expanding field, new organizations are being formed to deal with problems of research, instrumentation, training, and dissemination on a more adequate scale. Perhaps a future conference will deal with some of these emerging features—particularly with the regional centers emerging as part of the evaluation and research program of Project Head Start and the national program for research in early education which has been organized with the cooperation of a number of universities under the sponsorship of the U.S. Office of Education. As the field expands, the magnitude of its potential influence enlarges; in a real sense, this SSRC Conference faced the future of the field rather than its past.

Twenty years ago a book by Warner, Havighurst, and Loeb was published which bore the title *Who Shall Be Educated?* A current sequel might appropriately be called *Who Shall Educate?* As the responsibility for socialization shifts from the family to the school, decisions as to who will plan and administer the educational process become critical, at least to those who believe that early experience is salient in the development of personality and of cognitive behavior.

The question of who shall educate has usually not concerned child psychologists in the past. The problems which occupied our time were not, or did not appear to be, as urgent or as closely allied to basic national problems and goals. Now that we are being solicited for solutions, answers, and techniques, how much confidence have we in the knowledge and theory accumulated in the history of our professions? How shall we shape the relationship of our work to these emerging national instruments of early socialization?

As early education becomes the object of concern on the part of funding agencies and a growing number of social scientists, especially child psychologists, it seems likely that the character of the field may change substantially. In its present structure, pre-school education seems peculiarly vulnerable to influence, primarily because it lacks bureaucratic organization and has few ties to large, powerful, invested professional interests. Vulnerability to influence is not necessarily an advantage; pre-school education may be more easily affected for good *or* for ill than other areas of education. Indeed there are signs that the open-ended quality of this field is decreasing rapidly through the impact of Project Head Start, which has funded large-scale pre-school summer and year-round programs through the public schools. If social scientists want to establish ties with this important emerging field and contribute to its curriculum, to the training of its teachers, and to other critical aspects of its formal programs, they must act quickly to take advantage of an opportunity that is not likely to occur again.

Perhaps the most important issue to be raised here is one of value and strategy: what response will the community of social scientists offer at this point of emerging concern with the training of young children through formal societal institutions? Can we establish lines of interchange which will allow research to be applied to field conditions, without sacrificing our basic objectives of inquiry?

Perhaps a brief Conference was inadequate for the thoroughness and candor of exchange it was intended to generate. Its most useful contribution may be illustrated by the paper written by Joseph Glick after the Conference (which is also included in this volume). His comments were stimulated by the exchange and represent an important point of view which was not expressed adequately in the Conference itself.

This resulting volume of papers, some of which have been considerably revised since the Conference, is not a source of instructions or formulae, or guidelines for pre-school education. Nor was it intended to be. The orientation of the Conference was toward issues, and its purpose was to aid in identifying problems which are related to practice as well as theory.

In these sessions we hoped to explore the area of overlap between the theoretical and the real. The extent to which the Conference addressed itself to issues and realized its goals, the reader must judge for himself.

THE EFFECT OF EARLY STIMULATION IN THE EMERGENCE OF COGNITIVE PROCESSES

William Fowler (B.A. 1946, Dartmouth College; M.A. 1952, Harvard University; Ph.D. 1959, University of Chicago) is Associate Professor of Psychology and Education, Ferkauf Graduate School of Humanities and Social Sciences, Yeshiva University; Mr. Fowler was Assistant Professor of Education and Human Development and Principal of the Laboratory Nursery School, University of Chicago, 1963–66.

SOME two thousand years ago Plato drew us a sketch for a "great society." Central to its realization was the proposition that young children be removed from the untutored care of parents to institutions staffed with trained personnel.

In their time, Rousseau, Pestalozzi, and Robert Owen were all stricken with the impoverished lot, depressed condition, and blinding ignorance which prevailed among the masses (Raymont, 1937). Their efforts at reform were wrung with a powerful belief in the value of better education as almost a panacea to society's ills and man's freedom.

Another epoch of social and educational reform has descended. Our blueprint for the "great society" calls for extension of the professionalization of motherhood through the placement of more young children and infants of the poor in daytime schools and nurseries. Once again we turn to educational innovation and reform as the central hope for curing poverty.

Societal problems painfully similar to our own have existed before —what is "cultural deprivation" but this generation's term for ignorance? If we build the same old dreams with the same old schemes, are we not doomed to live in the same old mire?

The magnitude of influence which societal structures and cultural modalities exercise upon educational aims and methods, in the home or in the school, is difficult to measure and dangerous to overlook. Societal conditions may set the major mold within which socialization and educational practices must operate (for example, Barry, Child,

9

and Bacon, 1959). We need only to travel to our closest neighborhood for an illustration of the power of social structure over educational aims, a product of 300 years of educational progress: an American Negro ghetto school.

Despite the pervasive problems of context and the application of knowledge, there are a number of major signs of advancement in the state of our knowledge. Above all, the scientific method, accompanied by principles of logic and secular reasoning, increasingly dominates the world's orientation toward education.

An enterprise on the order of Project Head Start, in which literally thousands of pre-school programs have sprung up overnight all over the United States, is a vivid witness to the educational technology of our era. In company with this movement, there appears to be a marked and perhaps inevitable tendency toward the development of "canned programs," often in the form of kits and instructional guides and pamphlets (Hess, 1965; Project Head Start, OEO, 1965), devised in some research laboratory setting or school, to be distributed to hundreds of schools and teachers.

If, as it now appears, the world is destined in no more than a generation or so to find itself institutionally caring for and cognitively cultivating its children from the cradle on, what evidence has been amassed to justify our current high expectations for cognitive learning in early childhood?

This paper will review longitudinal studies within the framework of problems key to evaluating progress in the intellectual education of infants and young children. Problems of educational method and aims will be interwoven in considering the subject and measurement of early education and development. We shall also touch on problems of critical periods, cognitive sets and styles, and of structure and method relative to their influence upon creativity, socio-emotional, and cognitive development.

The Global Approach to Early Learning and to Measurement

An enduring problem is the question of the role of biological factors in development. Sometimes hibernating but never buried, some of the liveliest debates of the 1920's and '30's took place under the banner, "maturation vs. learning," with the Iowa child welfare laboratories in the forefront of the environmentally-oriented groups (Anastasi, 1958; Fowler, 1962a; Jones, 1954; Swift, 1964; Wellman, 1945).

Method variables were handled in several ways: early group experience in a nursery school was compared to exclusive home care; the effects both of foster home placement upon orphaned children, and of rearing children (including identical twins) in environments differing in a variety of social variables, were examined.

The collected findings of studies of this kind have been open to continued debate. In general, contemporary thinking is less polarized in terms of a simple dichotomy between heredity and environment. The interactionist orientation, recently elaborated by Hunt (1961), attempts to bridge extreme positions: the phenotype is a product *created* in the course of development through the *cumulative interaction* of the genotype and environmental stimulation. The fact is now widely accepted that environmental stimulation is an indispensable agent for a human organism to develop whatever potential with which he may be biologically endowed.

Looking at the old controversy from the vantage point of greater information and evolved concepts, we can now see a number of nets in which the thinking and methodology of the era was snared: the experimental approach at the time was severely limited at both ends of experimental design—in the treatment variables and in the measurement processes. Nursery school and related training experience as marked by social indices such as amount of formal education, number of siblings, ethnic background, foster home placement, etc., are too global with respect to the specific types and extent of intellectual stimulation a child is exposed to.

At the opposite end of experimental design, traditional IQ measures have been constructed more empirically than logically, the rationale for item selection restricted to two central criteria, age progression and internal consistency (Meyers and Dingman, 1960). Using these criteria leaves all kinds of abilities bunched together in a single category. In short, our measures have been too diffuse and thinly defined, resting on the dubious assumption that as long as they met the above criteria, we would somehow obtain a stable measure of basic intelligence ("g") and mental age.

Short-term Experiments

In this first of three categories of research we shall examine, a relatively tight experimental focus on different forms of learning under varying conditions allows a seemingly infinite number of problems, variables and conditions to be manipulated.

A recent series of experiments by the Kendlers (1962, 1963) illustrates this orientation and its chief limitation. According to their findings, children under 5 generally do better on a discrimination learning problem in which the child must learn the second of two discrimination tasks on the basis of shifting his choices to a new stimulus dimension (for example, brightness to height). This is called a non-reversal shift. Children do less well when the second discrimination task requires switching to the opposite end of the same dimension (for example, brightness). This is termed a reversal shift. Older children, when placed in an open choice situation, gradually increase their preference for reversal shifts.

The Kendlers account for these chronological changes on the basis of increasing language mediation control with development, as compared with the stimulus-response unit control which is supposed to prevail in discrimination learning in young children and lower animals.

There are distinct disadvantages inherent in the use of a short-term training series with different sets of subjects at different ages. It is not only that development may not follow a linear course, as Wohlwill (1960) points out, but there is no control over the variety and volume of stimulation a particular child has experienced cumulatively. We may contrast the Kendlers' work with an earlier, classic study to illustrate. Ling (1941) presented a series of training tasks on geometrical form discrimination with three-dimensional objects (crosses, circles, triangles, squares and ovals) to infants between the ages of 6 and 13 months of age. By pursuing her training series with each infant through several *hundred* trials over a several months' period, Ling was able to teach what she defines as a rudimentary concept of abstract form. The infants *all* learned to discriminate between forms, in the face of perceptual changes in relative position, size, spatial orientation, number and even of *reversal shifts* along several of the same stimulus dimensions.

Since Ling's infants, in keeping with developmental norms, had virtually no language facility available, it seems necessary to postulate some other form of cognitive learning potential or mediational processes at much earlier periods of development; the contrasting experimental approaches underscore the value of longitudinal training studies as a primary means of evaluating the educability of infants and young children. Developmental norms established without reference to cumulative, longitudinal educational efforts of this order can always be held suspect.

The Maturation vs. Learning Bias

The theoretical framework within which this second major class of research has been historically cast, following the influence of Gesell's stress on biological forces in development, has tended to obscure some valuable findings which bear directly upon the educational potentialities of the early years. The method here consisted of providing one of two identical twins or groups with several weeks of training in a particular area, such as language facility (Strayer, 1930) or motor skills (Hilgard, 1932), while the control twin or group remained in a supposedly normal or deprived environment. At the end of a specified period, the control child was exposed to the experimental training while the earlier-trained child was placed in the control environment.

These studies generally demonstrated the role of maturational factors in development: control children often progressed to equivalent skill levels in shorter training periods although started at older ages. The interpretive framework attributed the control children's advantage primarily to maturation, but the learning readiness of control children was not simply being allowed to ripen biologically by a few weeks of age in an environmental vacuum; they were living and learning in a basically normal environment, experiencing most of the usual caretaking and other stimulating operations except the specific one under control.

A more significant point for the purpose of evaluating educability, however, is the fact that the amount of learning gained by *all* children, experimental and control, was always a direct function of specific training, with the advantage shown by controls *never* large.

The maturational-developmental orientation of these studies leads to two central misconceptions which have dominated educational practice for many years. The first misconception is that child growth and development can occur outside the context of experience; hence the tendency to ignore the role of general experience in the foregoing experiments. The second and closely related misconception is that learning can be studied without reference to the cognitive levels and styles of the individual, attained as a cumulative and interactive function of idiosyncratic life experiences. Matching groups of children for age, sex, and even IQ, provides grossly insufficient and even distorted information on cognitive readiness to learn in particular areas of knowledge.

Learning and educational experiments should take one or both of two forms: they should either experimentally control the type and amount of stimulation from birth, and/or they should provide some reasonable measure of the patterning and organization of cumulative competencies acquired by experimental subjects, including a statement of the relationship of the learning tasks to these abilities.

Some Developments in the Measurement of Cognitive Processes

Before coming to our third class of studies, longitudinal research, we shall briefly review some recent developments in measurement which have implications for experimental work in early-childhood learning and education.

Awareness of the limited value of IQ tests as measures of cognitive abilities has finally reached a stage where dissatisfaction is being transformed into action. A large program has been underway now for some years (Meyers, 1960, 1962, 1964), guided partially by Guilford's model of the structure of abilities (1956, 1959). Meyers has identified four different abilities at three early age levels (2, 4, and 6 years) for both normal and retarded children: hand-eye psycho-motor, perceptual speed, linguistic ability, and figural reasoning. These factors, along with others, have been discovered through factor analysis of existing instruments and new tests designed specifically to reflect hypothesized domains of ability.

Despite this new endeavor to merge mathematical techniques with logical reasoning, the instruments used tend to be somewhat more descriptive than cognitive; there is little in the way of analysis of the cognitive structure and sequence of ability patterns; and the choice of tasks does not always appear to represent a wide or thoughtfully chosen array of content areas. But the thorniest problem which Meyers does not seem to handle is a problem intrinsic to the difficulty of standardizing any new instrument. Standardization involves selecting and scaling a pattern of test difficulties with the aid of selected populations, but populations are expected to vary unevenly in abilities as a result of their different combinations of experience. Any test standardization which is carved out of the performance pattern of unknown populations is, in effect, basing its factorial picture on spurious correlations.

A second major orientation toward the measurement of intellectual functioning stems from Piaget's theories of cognitive development. Under this aegis, Church (1964), Kohlberg (1958), and Uzgiris and Hunt (1964) are constructing scales for assessing six sequential stages of development of the infant's sensori-motor intelligence during the first 18 months of life. Kohlberg (1962) is also developing a scale for measuring cognitive complexity from the concrete to logical and abstract levels. These instruments assume and are constructed on logical and transformational principles of cognitive development rather than the linear or additive notions of the traditional Binet-type measures.

This system of test construction appears to be an improvement because it advances hypotheses on the nature of internal mediating processes of the child, but it still leaves us with a single index of intellectual competence at any given phase of development, and the same assumption of "g" or general intelligence seems to underlie the construction of these cognitive scales. Thus, they may obscure the intraindividual differences in competence levels across different information categories, which have been found in several studies (for example, Uzgiris, 1964).

In a third orientation toward measurement of cognitive abilities in early childhood, I am in the process of constructing cognitive tests and scales organized around specific classes of information and modes of functioning. The conceptual framework established employs a gradient of cognitive complexity based on the level of abstraction involved, following concepts of conservation, reciprocity, and hierarchical classification which Piaget and others have identified with cognitive development. Complexity is also scaled by the number and intricacy of the elements and relationships inhering in a specific reality structure. The role of cognitive style variations in the level of complexity of cognitive functioning attained is also being explored. One outcome of this long-range endeavor would be a set of measures founded on logical principles of general cognitive functioning yet anchored in particular domains of reality to provide more accurate assessment of intraindividual patterns of competence.

A number of investigators have for some years been exploring and developing measures of cognitive styles as a major source of influence upon cognitive abilities and as variations in their own right in type of intellectual functioning. (Gardner, R. W., Holzman, Klein, Linton, and Spence, 1959, 1960; Kagan, Moss, and Sigel, 1963; Santostefano, 1964; Santostefano and Paley, 1964; Witkin, Dyk, Faterson, Goodenough, and Karp, 1962). This approach suggests another important alternative to the concept of an overriding, unitary direction and order in the development of cognitive functioning, through postulating a multiple typology of directions in development. On the other hand, it may prove possible to define these stylistic differences as persisting individual differences operative on *intermediate* levels of cognitive organization, while relating them to a developmental hierarchy as Kohlberg (1962) and Santostefano (1964) have done.

While most of the research on cognitive style has been conducted on older children and adults, Sigel and associates (Sigel, Jarman, and Hanesian, 1967) have recently observed that 3- to 5-year-olds tend to use preferred styles of categorization in their manner of grouping objects in a sorting task; Sigel has also found that lower- and middle-class children differ in their ability to group pictures, but not in their ease of grouping the actual objects. This is a promising line of measurement for probing variations in modes of cognitive functioning in children.

In addition to the fo   *Early Formal Education*   of measures of intellectual functioning under development there are, of course, large numbers of particular measures being devised in conjunction with various experimental and applied educational projects (for example, Caldwell, 1965; Deutsch, 1965). There is also a widespread emergence of interest in assessing the mediating role of language development, which has led to the construction of specific measures of language functioning and style in a variety of contemporary studies, especially on the socially disadvantaged pre-school child (Bereiter, Osborn, Engelmann, and Redford, 1965; D'Asaro and John, 1961; Luriia and Yudovich, 1959; Olim, 1965; Smilansky, 1964). Except for the now widely used Illinois Test of Psycholinguistic Abilities (Kirk and McCarthy, 1961) which itself confounds associational, coding and decoding processes, however, there is little consistency evident in either theoretical or empirical organization and selection of measures from project to project.

Longitudinal Studies of Early Stimulation

The third major class of investigation is longitudinal designs directed at studying the effects of systematic stimulation upon early and later development. Ling's (1941) infant learning experiment is a promising but still truncated instance of the all too rare, controlled experimental investigation in this category. Most longitudinal research on stimulation has been descriptive and focused on so-called "gifted" children. Yet these studies remain our best source of information on the complex learning potentials of young children. In an earlier survey of cognitive potentials, this reviewer brought together studies from a variety of content areas showing progress in many skills (reading, writing, computing, drawing, music, and motor processes) induced in 2- to 4-year-old children in different kinds of programs under differing degrees of experimental control (Fowler, 1962a).

In these studies there is the same melting of variables in the two big pots of experience and global ability; but, unlike the IQ research series, there is also frequent documentation of educational specifics, which describe in some detail programs and methods of teaching together with an accounting of specific achievements.

Accordingly, the role of early stimulation emerges as more than of fleeting interest. In *no* instance (where documentation exists) have I found any individual of high ability who did *not* experience intensive early stimulation as a central component of his development. It is, therefore, essential not to write off the studies of "giftedness" as of no relevance to early education because it is biased evidence. The unvarying coincidence of extensive early stimulation with cognitive precocity and *subsequent* superior competence in adulthood suggests that stimulation is a necessary if not sufficient condition for the development of high abilities. The fact that a family social psychology of high and persisting expectations for achievement is so frequent and that high achievement and superior social and personal adjustment throughout later development are the rule, arouses further interest (Miles, 1954). Giftedness is also highly associated with social class (Miles, 1954) and gifted children are recruited most heavily from first-born children (Altus, 1966).

Such findings become even more salient when juxtaposed to the disproportionate distribution of high ability and achievement typical among different ethnic groups. Among Jewish cultural groups, high intellectual and verbal ability appears in much greater proportion than found in average United States populations (Terman, 1925). This contrast with the deflated abilities found consistently in Negro populations (Anastasi, 1958) together with the endemic deprivation and higher incidence of psychopathology associated with Negro groups (Faris and Dunham, 1939; Rose, 1955), suggests that very large numbers of potentially superior as well as average achievers are lost to our society. Deprivation should be measured relative to ultimate potential; it may be just as extreme for the potentially bright to endure average conditions as for the potentially average to live through conditions below the stimulation "norms" of the affluent half of our society.

Perceptuo-cognitive Learning

Perceptual and motor learning are often treated as distinct processes, where the role of cognition has been largely ignored. But both perceptual and motor processes might better be described as phases of the total means-end action system intrinsic to the organism's functioning. Perception involves relations with the world through the sensory apparatus, and no learning can occur outside of these channels. On the other hand, learning may or may not require the involvement of motor acts, as Lenneberg's (1962) studies on language comprehension of a mute child seem to show.

There may well exist different kinds of learning operative at different levels of development, based on the involvement or non-involvement of language or other mediational process as Piaget's (1952) theory asserts and a body of evidence recently summarized by S. White (1965) suggests. Yet this division between major levels, if it exists, seems better defined as one between non-verbal and verbal-symbolic learning, rather than between perception and cognition, or between motor learning and cognition.

An extensive series of studies by Welch in the 1930's was based on just this assumption. The learning of concepts and abstract classificatory hierarchies was defined operationally as perceptual discrimination between objects on the basis of variation along one or more dimensions, such as size (1939b, 1939c), form or area (1939a); or defined as the grouping of objects according to attributes (1940a, 1940b, 1947). Children from 12 months to 4 years of age were successfully trained over a period of months to make discriminations of size, form, and area many months in advance of control children.

Ling's (1941) work on form discrimination learning in infants may also be classed here.

In the USSR there appears to be in progress much research on early concept learning. Among these are a series of studies under the direction of Koltsova (1962), who has been able to induce object-label learning and genus-species concept learning in infants from 1 to 2 years of age. Ricciuti's (1965a, 1965b) observation of selective ordering and primitive categorizing behavior with geometric forms in 1- to 3-year-old children lends further support to the possibilities of classificatory learning in the early periods.

In these experimental studies, as well as in contemporary research projects on deprived children (Bereiter *et al.*, 1965; Caldwell and Richmond, 1964; Deutsch, 1965a; Gray and Klaus, 1965; Strodtbeck, 1964; Weikart, Kamii, and Radin, 1964) concept learning or the learning of classificatory operations and systems are treated in a generic sense. Objects employed range from those common to the everyday social scene to geometric forms, but there is seldom much attention devoted to imparting knowledge in careful sequences through a limited set of classificatory types—except for learning simple concepts like those of color, size and form. Thus, while Welch trained children initially in limited dimensions of form and area, when he undertook genus-species learning, he tended to throw together examplars from a variety of miscellaneous types without regard to the closeness of their associative links in number and similarity of attributes. Nor has anyone followed through a conceptual system in any depth of complexity. Bereiter (*et al.*, 1965), Moore (1963), Montessori schools to some extent, and myself are conducting programs where concept learning sequences are programmed, although others, such as Deutsch (1965a), Gray and Klaus (1965), Caldwell and Richmond (1964) and Weikart (*et al.*, 1964), are giving considerable attention to the dimensional details of simple concept learning. Many contemporary projects still suffer from diffuseness, both in curriculum and in measurement. This may account for the second-year relapse in IQ and language gains reported for example, in the Ypsilanti project (Weikart *et al.*, 1964).

In my earlier study on disadvantaged twins (1965a) experimental twin members generally increased the number of well-formed classificatory concept responses, on a modification of Welch's measures, compared to the control twins increasing the number of minimally formed responses. The experimental twins also generally made greater gains on a variety of other measures of cognitive development. Results were mixed, however, in face of an intensive eight months' program based on teaching toward abstract principles across content areas. Since that experiment, I have been developing the more refined model of conceptual learning mentioned above (Fowler, 1964, 1965b). Using this model, the teachers (Mrs. Benedict, Miss Brindley, Mrs. Franklin, Miss Labow, Mrs. Schreiner, and Mrs. Semkoff) and I developed in the University of Chicago Laboratory Nursery School a variety of research and exploratory projects on concept learning in such areas as animal life, language, mathematics, and reading.

The pivotal notions on which the model is based are those of analyzing and defining dimensions of stimulus object structures, ecological structures and classificatory systems. Once a total system, such as a transportation system, is defined in terms of the patterning and levels of its component structures and elements, an instructional program is devised in which the presentation is programmed according to perceptual-conceptual sequences of cognitive complexity. Developmentally, these sequences may be seen as progressing from sensori-motor and concrete, infralogical levels to increasingly symbolic and logical, but more varied forms of functioning. Built into the model are a number of cognitive learning tasks and style orientations, selected motivational systems, principally play and problem-solving game orientations, and a defined social structure of the small-group learning situation.

Motor Learning

In view of the stress on sensori-motor learning in the nursery school, it is surprising how little research has been done to measure just how and to what degree sensori-motor processes feature in the functioning of the infant and young child. A number of Koltsova's findings (1960, 1962) bear directly on this question. She finds (1960) that children whose instruction in a verbal task—"Show me the book"—is accompanied by demands for a wide variety of motor acts, learn to generalize in a test situation to a criterion of 80 to 90 per cent compared to no generalization for children presented with only one or two motor acts. And she finds (1962) that classificatory concept labels of a genus-species type are learned more readily when accompanied by conditioning in tactile, visual, auditory and kinesthetic-proprioceptive modes than when acquired on a verbal level alone.

Lyamina (1958), on the other hand, reports that children of this age learn object labels more easily when *not* engaged in motor activities with the objects. She found considerable conflict for children in coordinating behavior in the two spheres until walking and other motor learnings are well-mastered, a finding which corresponds with Shirley's (1931-33) earlier work. Luriia (1961) reports that children of less than 16 months of age cannot inhibit a motor act on the basis of verbal instructions alone. Once the activity is launched, instructions to stop usually result in increasing the rate of performance. There is need to reconcile such divergent findings, in view of our current emphasis upon language learning and the prominence which nursery school practice and Piaget's theories accord to the sensori-motor bases of early concept learning, as well as the traditional stance of the S-R learning model.

The earliness at which motor skills can be influenced by environmental stimulation is illustrated by the careful studies of visually-directed reaching in infants under 6 months of age by B. White and associates (1964, 1966). In addition to observing a series of stages of development of visual-motor schema, White has found that by manipulating the objects and conditions proximal to the infants in the crib, the rate of this development can be accelerated (1966; see also B. White, Chapter XII of this volume).

Longitudinal research on the acquisition of cognitive motor schema is rare. Klatskin (1952) in her study of 316 12- and 13-month infants in the Yale rooming-in project found that Catell norms were significantly higher than control scores for gross-motor, but not fine-motor, problem-solving and vocabulary items. The differences were presumed to be a function of the permissive or flexible infant care with which the rooming-in children were reared.

Most other work on motor learning was carried out some years ago, and the tasks presented were of a simple order with a low ceiling of cognitive complexity (Gesell and Thompson, 1929; Hicks and Ralph, 1931; Shirley, 1931–33). The small advantage commonly gained from specific training over maturation and general practice is hardly astonishing. When more complex maze performance training was undertaken, the advantage of specific training appeared to gain in proportion to the complexity of the tasks presented (Mattson, 1933). This principle is dramatically illustrated by McGraw's (1935, 1939) classic co-twin control study on gross-motor learning. At age 2, following two years of intensive, daily training in a variety of complex cognitive-motor skills (swimming, climbing, roller skating, tricycle riding, and others) the experimental twin was clearly superior in all skills—as well as in self-confidence and general motor coordination—to his fraternal control twin who had experienced only two-and-a-half months of guided stimulation. Four years later (without intervening training) the experimental twin was found to have retained his general advantage in attitude and coordination and in specific skills which (1) had been earlier well mastered, and (2) did not present new learning problems arising from changes in body proportion due to growth. McGraw's experiment is one of the best controlled longitudinal studies on the role of systematically graded early stimulation reported in the literature.

Recently, however, Dennis and Sayegh (1965), working with retarded 7- to 18-month-old institutionalized infants in Lebanon, succeeded in improving the sitting performance and Catell developmental age scores of infants by providing one hour per day of sitting and other activities over a 15-day period. This would seem to indicate that children environmentally deprived below social norms for simple type activities can sometimes benefit from even fairly short-term specific compensatory training experiences.

Music and the Plastic Arts

There are no experimental research studies to report in the areas of musical ability, the plastic arts or in the dance medium since my (1962a) review of the literature. The prospects for generating programs of early musical education on some level from the earliest infancy, nevertheless, are very hopeful. The series of studies by Hissen (1933), Jersild and Bienstock (1931, 1934) and Updegraff, Heiliger, and Learned (1938) all produced significant gains in 2- to 4-year-olds in singing, pitch and interval and tonal discrimination, and reproduction performance, following a few weeks or months of fairly limited training. The intense early musical stimulation of many great musicians remains one of the most exciting forms of challenge with respect to the power of early stimulation (Fowler, 1962a). Recently, the play-oriented methods of the Japanese musician, Shinichi Suzuki (*New York Times*, February 28, 1964) for teaching preschoolers to play the violin have met with widespread success. The virtually built-in motivational arrangements intrinsic to tonal systems enmeshed in many cultural fabrics further suggest that musical learning may be easy to harness to the earliest phases of development.

Related to the dimensions of the motor sphere as well as to

musical structure is the dance idiom. Although early training is found in occasional programs for 2- to 4-year-olds, no studies in the professional literature have been uncovered. This author observed a number of 3- and 4-year-olds learn with little difficulty, in the period of a few months, a variety of contemporary dance movements, with varying degrees of competence and precision.

The areas of drawing and painting and other plastic arts are limited in evidence to the single research study of Dubin (1946). She brought about significant advances in developmental progress in drawing ability of 2- to 4-year-old nursery school children over their undirected controls during a six-month period of instruction.

Language Learning

The question of the role of language in the development of thought has come in for increasing consideration in the current era. Vygotskii (1962) and Luriia (1961) have accorded it a highly central role, which through its symbolizing properties permits the child to come to represent the world and its activities in shorthand, abstract form, and plays an essential part in enabling the child to regulate and direct his own activities. Based on these assumptions, and spurred by widespread and repeated findings of social-class differences in language complexity between advantaged and disadvantaged children at nearly all ages by Bernstein (1961), Deutsch and his associates (1965a), Hess and Shipman and their group (1965), and in a myriad of verbal IQ studies over many years (Anastasi, 1958), today's pre-school programs feature elaborate schemes and varieties of activities for fostering language development.

In Luriia and his colleagues' (1961) extensive series of experiments, language mediation has been shown to be one basis for facilitating cognitive development. Through simplifying the form of verbal instructions and relating them to concrete interests of the child, younger children were able to respond to ground (weaker stimuli) instead of figures (stronger stimuli) in performing a motor discrimination task.

Learning stimulus names has been frequently found to facilitate discrimination learning between similar classes of stimuli which carries over to transfer tasks in 3- to 5-year-olds (Cantor, 1955). Carey and Goss (1957) found consistent differences between two groups of 4- and 5-year-olds, who had been trained in the use of verbal labels as against nonsense syllables, in their ability to classify blocks on a height-size basis. In an interesting test of the Vygotskii hypotheses on the critical role of language in cognitive development with 4-year-old advantaged and disadvantaged Negro children, Stodolsky (1965) found that *no* child performed at a high level cognitively (on Kohlberg's [1962] Sort Scale) who did not also attain a criterion level of adequate language functioning on the Peabody Picture Vocabulary Test.

A central problem inherent in the study of the role of language mediation is the difficulty of obtaining a measure of cognitive development independent of language mediation. The resultant confounding of language and cognition is apparent in many of Luriia's studies and is evident in Stodolsky's study, since Kohlberg's Sort Scale was administered through the vehicle of language instructions.

The significance of age in the development of language and the timing of the application of stimulation is central to many normative studies of language development. El'konin (1960) found no discrimination of vocal from other auditory stimuli in infants of 7 to 8 months, but in infants of 10 to 11 months, conditioning to words occurred four times faster than to other sound stimuli. Lyamina (1960) reports great difficulty in teaching language to children less than 16 months of age, corresponding to Luriia's observations on lack of motor inhibition. Through verbal instructions, though, Mallitskaya (1960; see also Slobin, 1965a) was successful in developing object word-label learning techniques to train infants from 9 to 16 months of age. Rheingold (1956), Weisberg (1963) and others have demonstrated the possibility of increasing the amount of vocalizing in 3-month-old infants as a function of both social and non-social conditioning stimuli.

These studies furnish no more than a good start in showing that early language development can be altered as a function of planned stimulation programs. There are only a few studies which do more than touch on the early and cumulative effects of language stimulation continuing from infancy. In a study by Irwin (1960), working-class children 13 to 30 months of age who had picture-story books read to them for fifteen minutes daily by their mothers were found, after the eighteenth month, to be significantly greater in phoneme frequency than controls. A far more complex language stimulation program and set of measures has been devised by Shvarchkin (Ervin and Miller, 1963). Infants between 11 and 22 months of age were taught Russian words, varying only one phoneme at a time. Phonemic features were thus presented in a carefully planned sequence, the vowels first. At age 2 years, children were able to recognize the entire gamut of Russian phonemes.

In this investigator's (1962b) study on teaching reading to his daughter Velia, there was also a background exploratory program of stimulation in language (as well as cognitive stimulation generally), which was carried out from birth. Much of the stimulation, consisting generally of engaging the infant's attention to the objects and dimensions of her physical and social world, was conducted during the caretaking operations of both parents. Her first clear words were recorded at 8 months. Her speech vocabulary was about 100 words at 14 months and more than 200 at 15 months, expanding exponentially in number from about 12 months on. Two- and three-word sentences were observed at 14 months and complete, simple sentences of four to eight words were typical by 18 months, with an occasional compound sentence of ten to fifteen words in evidence. Vocabulary was rich, laced with words like *hippopotamus, chrysanthemum, spaghetti,* and *theater,* and speech was exceptionally clear and complete. While admittedly an experimental case study, the child's progress may be compared with age norms for mean sentence length: 1.5 words for normal girls, and 3.9 words for "gifted" girls at 18 months (McCarthy, 1954).

There was a research project on second language learning at the University of Chicago Laboratory Nursery School, conducted by Mrs. Senkoff in collaboration with myself. Using a sequential, play-oriented approach and expansion of concepts from nuclear situations, 3- and 4-year-old children learn up to 50 words which can be constructed in simple sentences across varied contexts.

These studies, backed by informal and less detailed accounts in the literature on "gifted" children, indicate that we have hardly begun to tap the realm of language learning potential in early development.

It is important to distinguish between initial courses of language stimulation and remedial programs, such as the current research program of Bereiter's group (1965) on fifteen socially disadvantaged 4-year-olds. Using a high teacher-child ratio, they have organized a curriculum of language concept learning spelled out in terms of clearly defined operations for the child to perform. Bereiter has been able, over a period of two to three months of intensive, highly directed daily instruction, to extend many children's language ability in the production of object labels and class names, correct use of spatial prepositions, identity statements (same and different) and the like. Incomplete data (Bereiter *et al.,* 1965; Bereiter, 1965) shows that on the Illinois Test of Psycholinguistic Abilities, mean gains of many months in excess of gains expected on the basis of the children's chronological age were obtained on seven of the ten subtests.

Dawe (1942), conducted a language instruction program without the conceptual-operational analysis of language which Bereiter's group has made. Dawe's program embraced observations, discussions, story sessions, and excursions over a series of weekend sessions with deprived 3½- to 7-year-old orphanage children during a three-month span. Experimental children scored significantly greater than controls in several language and other cognitive measures at completion of training. Luriia and Yudovich (1959) succeeded in markedly improving the language and cognitive functioning of one of two severely language-retarded, identical 5-year-old twins through a ten-month program of analytic language and activity instruction. Using an operant conditioning framework, Bricker (1965) has produced dramatic improvements in the speech functioning of an autistic 4-year-old boy.

All of these studies support the currently strongly held belief in the value of pre-school compensatory language education with disadvantaged children. But such programs should probably be explored with somewhat different motivational systems, problems, and methods in mind than those employed in early, non-remedial programs to control and possibly accelerate language development from infancy on.

Problems of method have received little systematic consideration, which—in view of the primitive state of the art—should occasion no wonder. The emergence of extensive activity on the front of linguistic analysis and development, partially occasioned by Chomsky's (1957) generative model for studying syntactic structures, is beginning to modify various reinforcement and imitation theories of language learning. As Menyuk (1964) and others (Ervin, 1963; Slobin, 1965b) have shown, language learning requires some model which will account for the development of rule-governed language structures. But we need a model which is more complex than the simple, linear vocabulary-increase models which imitation-oriented theories of learning have tended to espouse.

Reading

There is no area of early stimulation which provokes more controversy than reading instruction, despite the almost total lack of evidence of deleterious consequences that can be traced to early stimulation. One of the latest and most authoritative of a long series of pronouncements, going back to Morphett and Washburne (1931) and before, on the hazards of early reading is that of Hymes (Barman, no date), a leading national figure in Nursery School Education. He states:

> I am thoroughly persuaded both that all the evidence in every area makes it very clear that it is hazardous to teach before a child is ready and that, when a child is ready, teaching him to read need not mean sitting him down at a desk with a workbook or primer.

It is difficult to disagree with either of these propositions, but it is not difficult to show that neither has been characteristic of either research or educational programs on early reading. It is equally easy to understand, however, how some of the florid claims appearing in commercial magazines (Doman, Stevens, and Ormen, 1963) on the Puritan duty of mothers to teach their tiny babies to read and how they love it, might occasion or justify some of these counterreactions.

Much of the apprehension appears to have evolved historically in revolt against harsh methods of the past, and may reflect concern and confusion over learning problems apparently associated with learning to read under mass instructional methods prevailing in elementary schools.

There are a plethora of programs currently in progress around the country and perhaps the world, with varying degrees of control. These range from the crawling, creeping accompaniments of Delacato's (1959, 1963) program on young retardates to those employing more refined methodologies like the typewriter technology of Moore (1963). Reading for 4-year-olds has been for many years, primarily a by-product of Montessori pre-schools in Europe and occasional private schools. Apparently many 3- and 4-year-olds make steady progress in such programs, under quite varying methods. The range of methods employed extends from straight "look and say" word memorization methods (Terman, 1918), through my own play-oriented, but linguistically sequenced method, to simple operant conditioning (Staats, Minke, Finley, Wolf, and Brooks, 1964).

Of all the information collected on early learning by the "gifted," documentation on early reading is the most complete. Biographical accounts and retrospective surveys (for example, Dolbear, 1912; Root, 1921) abound with notations of children mastering alphabets as early as their second year and reading texts as early as their third year. It would seem that reading has long been considered a pivotal process for opening the gateways to the mind. A child's learning is occasionally described as self-initiated and self-sustained. But the character of the intellectual atmosphere in the home, coupled with the quality of parent responsiveness, make clear that early reading was a valued achievement and that self-instruction, in short, might be more accurately described as highly effective parent manipulation of reinforcement conditions. In this manner, these families deviated from the heavy-handed didacticism which has plagued earlier eras.

The generally superior sociopersonal adjustment and achievement we have reported for the early stimulated children applies with equal force to those early instructed in reading. In the one controlled investigation, Durkin (1964b) found that a group of children who learned to read early at home maintained their mean relative advantage significantly over controls as far as the sixth-grade level. It would not be fatal if they had not, however, since the further removed from the early period, the more intervening experiences might be expected to neutralize differences between the two groups. It is useful to note that the children constitute a group who learned at home, largely from untrained parents employing a variety of methods.

In the realm of completed and well-documented research studies, there are two instances of individualized programs with 2-year-olds, one cited by Terman (1918) and one conducted by myself (1962b). Both children acquired a stable reading vocabulary of several hundred words and some facility in reading sentences and texts well before the age of 3. Later development of competence and interest of both children in reading, literature, writing, and learning generally remained persistently high.

If early reading programs are to be established with any degree of currency, they must meet several criteria, especially, feasibility of instruction with groups of children in a school situation. As I have indicated, a number of such programs are in operation, but details and follow-through are available only in the classic study by Davidson (1931) and my own projects (1964, 1965a). Davidson demonstrated that 3-, 4-, and 5-year-olds, each age level participating in a separate group of four or five children, could all make some progress in reading, through participating in ten to fifteen minutes of daily instruction.

Success in beginning reading is consistently marked by a lower limit mental age criterion of about 4 years. There have been several efforts to teach average or even socially and cognitively deprived children to read, including Davidson's (1931) and mine with twins (1965a); Bereiter (*et al.*, 1965), has carried out some work on beginning reading with disadvantaged 4-year-olds. There are no clear instances of fluent reading reported for any children below the index cited. In my educational project with 3-year-old disadvantaged twins, the mental age of two low IQ children was below 3 years. They were instructed individually in a carefully paced reading program but learned to identify no more than a few words and letter-graphemes over a period of several months.

Reading, often defined as a largely perceptual learning process, requires mastery of several key conceptual operations before any real progress can be made. Among these are sequencing from left-to-right and unit-for-unit correlating of aural and visual stimuli, as well as synthesizing meaning from successions of visual stimulus sequence units. It was precisely in these primary concepts which the low IQ, disadvantaged 3-year-olds failed completely. They could learn to identify individual units with considerable reliability, but they could not learn to read a single sentence.

Bereiter's (1965) 4-year-olds are placed around a 4-year-mental level, enabling "about two-thirds of them . . . [to] blend simple three-letter words (p. 4)." This is an encouraging sign of generalizing behavior which may facilitate subsequent progress in learning to read, although no text reading is yet reported.

In our studies to date, we have made substantial headway in teaching well over eighty 4-year-olds and fifteen 3-year-olds to read fluently. Over three- to five-month spans, for a few minutes each day, all of these children have covered from two to seven or more short, graded primers I have composed, and acquired reading vocabularies of from 20 to 70 or more words. One of the more promising aspects of the process is the degree to which we find that nearly all children, utilizing my phonemically graded approach, can come to generalize principles of word organization which enable them to read new words without help.

Since my (1962a) review, the series of projects in which I have been engaged appear to be the only additions to the literature on the effect of early reading or any other form of stimulation upon the fate of personality development. In my controlled project with identical twins and triplets (1965a), as well as in our subsequent work, stimulated children do at least as well as controls and usually appear to thrive on the experience. In the realm of visual functioning, long an area of concern, there was no evidence that early reading had any differential effect upon the visual development of the experimental children compared to the controls. The fate of the intellectually stimulated, for the short run as well as the long, apparently remains, as reported earlier, a predominantly happy one.

Mathematics

We have only lately begun to explore with any seriousness the possibilities of learning mathematics structures, whether defined entirely as language systems as Bereiter (*et al.*, 1965) does or as linguacognitive systems. Historical accounts again disclose that early learning has been the rule for children of high mathematics ability, "exceptional ability usually being identified at about 5 to 5.5 years in 75 per cent of the cases," according to Mitchell (1907) and Révész (1940). Until recently, there have been no formal studies on the stimulation of mathematics abilities and little documentation in survey reports of the early conditions of learning.

Many of the current pre-school programs for disadvantaged children incorporate minimum types of counting and grouping activities which can be identified with arithmetic and mathematical concept learning (Bereiter, *et al.*, 1965; Deutsch, 1965; Gray and Klaus, 1965; Weikart, 1964). These are introduced in a more integral and systematic manner than the incidental focus on like tasks and books which has characterized traditional nursery schools of the century. Bereiter's (*et al.*, 1965) project appears to be one of the most elaborately conceptualized and worked out mathematics programs for disadvantaged children. Nearly all of his fifteen 4-years-olds, following six months of intensive but brief daily sessions, have demonstrated astonishing mastery of a variety of counting, symbol identification, and grouping and reversibility operations.

Sigel, Roeper, and Hooper (1965), and myself, independently, are engaged in a series of projects on mathematics learning with advantaged children in nursery school settings. Sigel and his group, working with gifted 4- and 5-year-old-olds, have concentrated on the problem of developing conservation of quantity following Piaget (1952a), utilizing techniques which emphasize the prerequisite abilities of multiple classification, multiplicative relations, and reversibility.

At the Laboratory Nursery School, we have incorporated something of a Piaget-type orientation toward multiple grouping and relations, but are additionally focused on analytic and synthesizing operations sequentially in three different but particular spheres of measurement: number, length, and liquid quantity. One of the salient differences in emphasis is a concern for building general concepts, operations, and principles through focus on *specific* subject areas and dimensions of structure.

Preliminary data on these two programs discloses that seven of eight children in Sigel's groups made some progress in acquiring conservation of quantity in a variety of dimensions, substance, liquid substance, weight, and volume, on the basis of a five-week training program, compared with no change for controls.

Our program is currently uncompleted, but a preliminary course of instruction in number concepts the first year with 3- to 5-year-olds appeared to move children toward conservation of number in four or five of our nine 4-year-olds, in both 5-year-olds, with signs of progress in our one 3-year-old. All children made substantial progress in counting, discrimination, and identification operations with number sets up to ten units, and in identifying graphic number symbols.

Related Issues

What do we know of early development as a foundation and critical period with respect to the establishment of cognitive learning sets and styles? What do we know of the relations between systematic stimulation, structured learning, teaching methods on one side and curiosity, creativity, and inquiry on the other? All too little. But we are on the edge of a new epoch. The single IQ indices and diffuse socially oriented programs that prevailed until the Sixties are giving way to complex analyses of dimensions and variables involved in and between the forms of stimulation and personality-cognitive development.

Much of what we know on learning sets comes from the work of Harlow and his group (1960, 1962) and others (Zimmerman and Torrey, 1965) on animals, although discrimination learning sets have been well established in children (Reese, 1963). The ease of establishing learning sets generally progresses with age. Account must be taken, however, of the far more complex cortical development of humans, even over primates, which may require quite different conditions for the establishment of more complex cognitive sets based on different principles of organization.

We have marshaled evidence from a variety of sources—from deprivation to acceleration studies—which indicates the possibility and value of early learning experiences in general. But few investigators have attempted to define or study the development of cognitive sets more complex than those involved in simple discrimination learning tasks (Reese, 1963). We find ourselves with much descriptive data, little of which is experimentally derived, on the early formation and long-term development of complex learning sets. In the broadest form, there is evidence of an orientation toward "learning to learn" emerging in many children who are early and intensively stimulated. We can also note the obvious high levels of competence and dispositions to persevere which get established in specific language or other subject areas of cognition.

The few controlled studies we have touched on permit us to say something with respect to general orientations and subject area sets; for example, early reading or language stimulation may lead to continuing high performance and motivation over long spans of development in these areas in later life. But not only do we need many more studies, tracing the specific conditions under which sets do and do not get established and persist, we also need more precise and complex definitions of cognitive sets.

We know even less of cognitive styles, the particular organizational forms, modes, and strategies for processing information. The concept itself is of a comparatively recent vintage, hardly ripened conceptually or tested empirically. Only lately with the national surge of interest in problems of early deprivation have investigators begun to focus on learning styles at the early childhood level (for example, Hess and Shipman, 1965; see Chapter VIII, this volume).

Despite the potential significance of problem-solving styles with respect to the early generation of effective and creative forms of learning, I have encountered no investigations on the origin of styles, aside from our projects on analytic, synthesizing, contextual, and classificatory styles in the Laboratory Nursery School (Fowler, 1965b).

Methods

With respect to method, the state of affairs is equally bare—other than the general point that there is a determining and direct relationship between early stimulation and the development of cognitive complexity both generally and in particular spheres of knowledge. It also seems clear that adult-guided stimulation, as opposed to unguided and self-guided exploratory learning, produces higher levels of learning and adjustment (Carr, 1938; Fowler, 1961, 1965a; McCandless, 1940; Peters and McElwee, 1944; Strodtbeck, 1964; Thompson, 1944).

One of the few controlled studies on method was performed in the 1930's by Luriia's group (Levit, 1935) on five pairs of (apparently) 4-year-old identical twins. In this study, Luriia found that a more open-ended method of teaching the dimensions of block construction resulted in more complex performance levels—after an initial disadvantage—at the end of a four-month training period. The task for both methods required the child to copy a model block construction. In the open-ended method, only the total configuration of the model was exposed, the child having to experiment with unit combinations to achieve a final model. In the alternate method, defined as that of "elements," the unit blocks of the model were exposed to the child's view. Differences between the twins remained ten months after training was terminated.

In all of our projects, children participating in conditions of guided stimulation (including many of the more conflicted or immature children) fare consistently better than children attending school under conditions of free play alone. The ingredients which typically contribute to developments in this direction must be attributed to a complex of variables operating in the social situation, perhaps including a stress on warmth, positive reinforcement, dramatic play orientations, and provision for active, exploratory, and problem-solving roles for children in all situations of free play or guided learning. We can report no evidence that guided stimulation is a detracting agent. If anything, the opposite is evident, since competence or achievement motivation and a sense of efficacy in R. White's (1959) terms appear to evolve with participation over time. Moreover, interest transfers to creative play activities and the home situation.

Knowledge and Creativity

Guilford's model of the structure of the intellect (1956, 1959) defines creativity in terms of divergent as against convergent types of thinking. Getzels (1964) has recently formulated creativity as an orientation which involves the generation of new systems of problem-solving.

The literature on curiosity—which appears to be somehow closely related to creativity in its implications of openness, dealing with the new, and so on—rather consistently supports the importance of complexity, novelty, and incongruity as stimulus conditions favoring curiosity behavior, both in children and in animals (Fiske and Maddi, 1961; Lucco, 1965).

The theories and findings of Earl (1961) and Dember (1965) and the studies of Fantz (1958) and Thomas (1965) in infants on preferred levels of stimulus complexity, which increase generally with age, furnish pertinent evidence with respect to the value of programming learning sequences. They also indicate that programs should be sequenced and presented in some direct relation to a pacing operation. In our projects, stimulus structures are analyzed, sequenced, and presented following cues from the child on his comfortable levels and rates of assimilation of stimulus sequences along a continuum of complexity.

A high value is currently placed on discovery and inquiry orientations in learning, together with an emphasis upon creative problem-solving. Bruner (1961) nevertheless suggests that discoveries are most likely to be made by those with the best prepared minds and places equal emphasis upon furnishing a child with foundation information and key principles which characterize the structures of knowledge in any field. Unfortunately, studies which compare open-ended vs. highly structured, detailed methods of stimulation on a longitudinal basis, are rare. Considering the fact that many highly creative persons (see Norbert Wiener, 1953) appear to have been instructed in a rather rigid fashion, the question is still very much open.

This is, of course, a burning issue in the field of nursery school education. Dominant professional groups affirm strongly in favor of open-system, creative play orientations, which are the heart of most nursery school programs. The only groups which avowedly aim for structured programs are Bereiter (*et al.*, 1965), Montessori, and the operant conditioners (Staats *et al.*, 1964), or social learning theorists (Vance, 1965). Yet analysis of their methods (Bereiter *et al.*, 1965; Montessori, 1912; Rambusch, 1962) suggests that the picture is not quite so simple. These latter groups construct their programs by complex dimensional analysis, both concrete and linguistic in form. Moreover, the operations in which children engage involve rather basic sensori-motor rooted concept learning. There is, nevertheless, close programming and reinforcement and, particularly in the Montessori schools, a frequent concern with ritualized handling of materials and exclusion of art, social role and creative play construction activities. All of these orientations would appear to generate closed-system styles of thinking and problem-solving, as well as impede the development of exploratory and active, decision-making styles of intellectual functioning. Yet most research schools in practice also provide some free-choice construction and sociodramatic play with a rich variety of relatively open-ended and malleable toys and art and craft materials.

Lucco (1965) found a consistent correlation between early cognitive stimulation and curiosity in 4-year-olds, although the correlations were less high at the higher IQ levels. Hess and Shipman (1965) also found a relationship between open-ended communication methods of instructing children and cognitive levels of functioning in 4-year-olds. Bishop (1960) reports positive correlations in 9- to 10-month-old infants between the amount of babbling and—not only the amount of verbalizing and physical handling by the mother—but also the amount of opportunity she gave the infant to explore. On the other hand, it will be recalled that Klatskin (1952) found higher Catell scores in infants reared flexibly, *except* on *verbal* and fine-motor items.

It is clear that we have reached a core problem in early childhood education: to what degree is it important to stress information as against open-ended system engagements with reality dimensions? Can we do both, as the Luriia twin experiment would suggest? Our projects at the Laboratory Nursery School are explicitly constructed on a model that attempts to include both an analysis and sequencing of conceptual structure, while building in synthesizing construction task operations. The search-type tasks, the active role provided the child, the encouragement of manipulation of concrete material, and the provision of roles for both peer interactive and autonomous learning are additionally intended to develop active, exploratory orientations toward cognitive functioning.

It remains a difficult task to test fully in humans the long-range consequences of different methods or, in fact, of any other form of experiences confined to the early periods of life. The first years are unquestionably important as the foundation for subsequent development and the epoch when cognitive sets and personality-cognitive styles may get launched. But how many experiences for any individual are critical enough to establish forms and modes so unalterable or fixed in direction as to remain untouched by the myriad of ensuing experiences every individual encounters? Our ultimate course might better be defined as, not only to discover the techniques which can establish rational and creative orientations in the early years, but to relate these efforts to a study of how we can foster the continuance of such courses throughout the span of development and adulthood. To do this, can we define what kind of adult human beings we ultimately hope to realize? In a rather eloquent but forlorn statement, Schachtel (1949) decried the institutional forms which slowly but ever so pervasively crystallize the lively world of the young child into the sterilized conventionalities of contemporary adult life. I would like to believe it possible for us to plant the seeds of logic in early childhood in ways which foster the interplay of creative imagination and logical reasoning throughout the course of life; to develop social beings with logico-creative styles strong enough to destroy the stultifying powers of our educational institutions.

HALBERT B. ROBINSON

and

NANCY M. ROBINSON

THE PROBLEM OF TIMING IN PRE-SCHOOL EDUCATION

Halbert B. Robinson (A.B. 1951, M.A. 1953, Ph.D. 1957, Stanford University) is Professor of Psychology and Director of the Child Development Institute, University of North Carolina; Nancy M. Robinson (A.B. 1951, MA. 1953, Ph.D. 1958, Stanford University) is Assistant Professor of Education and Research Associate, Child Development Institute, University of North Carolina.

NEVER before in the history of psychological investigation has there been such an opportunity to translate theory into social action as there is today with respect to the pre-school child. The current national preoccupation with early childhood education is thrusting developmental psychologists and educators into a realm where previously few have dared to tread, the sanctity of early childhood. There have been innumerable programs to further the welfare of children in public schools, to help them acquire knowledge and skill, and to give them new and broader horizons; where the pre-school child is concerned, however, we have attempted only short-term and tentative approaches to education.

Our caution is understandable and probably commendable. Certainly we are loathe to endanger the intellectual or emotional well-being of young children. We really know very little about this group, and most of our knowledge has been gleaned from observations of select groups, composed mainly of children in university nursery schools. Only sporadically have there been attempts, even in these facilities, to teach the children in any formal fashion or to record what they have been able to learn.

Despite this state of affairs, developmental psychologists and educators are currently being asked to plan and to guide extensive and expensive programs for young children, particularly for disadvantaged children such as those in the Head Start projects. Such responsibility immediately forces our attention to the available evidence for fruitful intervention in cognitive and emotional development,

Studies of Early Cognitive Development

Learning begins at birth and so does education, if by education we mean the influence of planned experience on the growing organism, Most early theorists who considered the problem of cognitive development during childhood concluded that learning tends to follow relatively predictable patterns, and that the rate of development is determined by the more or less permanent intellectual level of the child (for example, Dennis, 1935; Dennis and Dennis, 1940; Gesell, 1929; Gesell and Thompson, 1941). This view is still widely held.

During the past few years, however, many child-development specialists have paid increasing attention to the role of experience as an important factor in intellectual development. The time of earliest learning is thought, conjecturally at least, to occur in the prenatal period (Ourth and Brown, 1961). Neonates have been demonstrated to exhibit considerable learning potential (Lipsitt, 1963; Papousek, 1961; Wenger, 1943). Toddlers have been successfully taught to read (Fowler, 1962, and in Chapter II; Moore and Anderson, 1960). Despite the existence of some negative evidence, reviews of the effects of a variety of environmental conditions upon intellectual development (Fowler, 1962; Hunt, 1964; Skeels, 1940; Swift, 1964; Wellman, 1943) have tended to show that enrichment of the environment is propitious for intellectual growth. Investigators have found dramatic retardation in infants who have been institutionalized under impersonal and non-stimulating conditions (Dennis, 1960; Goldfarb, 1947; Skeels and Dye, 1939; Spitz, 1945, 1947), but measurable retardation has not been found in well-staffed institutions (Dennis, 1960; Rheingold, 1960, 1961). Though the essential elements producing retardation or acceleration of development have not been clearly identified (Casler, 1961; Yarrow, 1961), the conclusion is unmistakable: very small infants and young children are highly reactive to both enhancing and depriving conditions in their surroundings, as well as to highly specific teaching programs.

Enthusiasm for the significance of experience as a determinant of intellectual development may be based somewhat more upon personal equalitarian convictions than upon conclusive demonstration, for there is also impressive evidence that hereditary variables are important (Bayley and Schaefer, 1964; Burt, 1958; Gottesman, 1963; Newman, Freeman, and Holzinger, 1937; Shields, 1958). It seems very likely that when we better understand the development of functions of the central nervous system, nature and nurture will be viewed as interacting determinants at every stage of development.

Problems Concerned with Early Childhood Education

Prompted by the conviction that young children can learn much more than they are commonly being taught today, many workers have proposed early childhood education as a potent force to enhance intellectual behavior. Bright children, it is felt, can be made brighter; of even greater popularity has been the notion that concerted pre-school programs can save many children from the cycles of poverty, despair and ignorance in which their families have been caught for generations. In other words, the notion that the young child *can* be taught has been translated into the notion that he *should* be taught.

This equating of *can* and *should*, however, has been accomplished with little focus on a variety of intervening questions. Among these are the following:

1) What are the long-range goals of early education?
2) What is the long-range stability of early learning?
3) Are there special hazards in beginning too early?
4) Are there hazards in beginning too late?
5) Are some essential elements best learned early, while others are optimally acquired at a later age?

LONG-RANGE GOALS OF EARLY EDUCATION

It seems obvious that we should look to the end product of the educative process, the adolescent and the mature adult, in order adequately to formulate the goals of education; these distant goals must be kept in mind as we devise aims and methods for the pre-school years.

Teaching methods which bring about early mastery, for example, might not be best suited for long-range excellence. A major goal of reading instruction—reading silently at the fastest rate consistent with a high level of comprehension—is probably not achieved by teaching methods which emphasize reading aloud. The majority of today's college students read at an average speed of 250 to 300 words per minute (Committee on Diagnostic Reading Tests, 1963; Nelson and

Denny, 1960); by conservative estimate, they should be reading two to three times faster (Poulton, 1961). Many poor readers have been trapped with an inadequate system in which comprehension is accomplished by "listening" to what is silently said. That the standard teaching techniques have not been more often criticized is, at least in part, because goals for the lower grades are formulated in terms of achievement during each year of instruction rather than as progress toward the attainment of the final goals of the reading program. Techniques which seem quite natural during the early stages of instruction may interfere with effective mastery at a later stage of learning. The significance of this point is that unless constant attention is given to the ultimate goal of each teaching program, identical problems will develop with pre-school programs.

If we wish to relate teaching practices at every level to distant goals, research strategies must be longitudinal. The earlier the initial teaching, the longer the period required for follow-up. Moreover, we probably need a variety of ways of teaching, each relating to our best estimate of the eventual capabilities of the individual child and the general goals toward which he is likely to strive as an adult.

STABILITY OF EARLY LEARNING

There is little data pertaining to the long-range stability of early educational experiences. It is surprising that so many investigators who have spent so much time and energy in research efforts should fail to follow their young subjects to discover the outcome of their work. Those few who have traced subjects longitudinally have sometimes found positive, sometimes negative, and often ambiguous results.

Undoubtedly one of the most dramatic follow-up studies has been reported by Harold Skeels (1965). Skeels and Dye (1939) followed thirteen infants who were moved from the minimally stimulating environment of an orphanage nursery to a residential center for the mentally retarded, where they were given a great deal of stimulation, attention, and affection. The children were compared with twelve control children who stayed in the orphanage. The experimental children showed a net gain averaging 27.5 IQ points after 19 months, while the controls showed a net loss, after 21 months, averaging 27.2 IQ points. The recent follow-up (Skeels, 1965) has revealed striking differences between the two groups. All of the experimental children were eventually placed with families and now, as young adults, "All thirteen . . . are self-supporting. . . . Eleven of the thirteen . . . are married, and nine of these have children." In contrast, of the twelve children in the control group, "One died in adolescence following continued residence in a state institution for the mentally retarded; four are still wards of institutions . . . only two have married, and one of these is divorced," (p. 33). The disparity between the two groups in educational and occupational attainment is substantial: "In the experimental group, the median grade completed is the twelfth; in the contrast group, the third (p. 33). . . . The experimental group ranges from professional and semi-professional positions to semi-skilled labor or domestic work. In the contrast group, 50 per cent of the subjects are unemployed, and those that are employed are, with the exception of one person, unskilled laborers" (p. 34.) (It should be pointed out that the contrasting early experiences of these two groups were supported and extended by differences in their subsequent environments. In this sense, the study does not offer "pure" evidence about the stability of the effects of early experience.)

Other observations cast doubt on the permanence or irreversibility of the effects of infant deprivation. Dennis and Najarian (1957) studied children ages 0 to 6 in a markedly deprived institution in Iran. They found that the infants scored very low on the Cattell infant test, but that children from 4½ to 6 years old scored only slightly below normal on several performance tests. Dennis (1960), found dramatic motor retardation among very young children in two minimally stimulating institutions in Iran but not in a third which was able to maintain a quite stimulating environment. During this study, Dennis noted children 6 to 15 years old playing and working in the two unstimulating institutions, without any signs of retardation. The older children in both of these studies had apparently undergone the same early deprivation which the manifestly retarded very young children were experiencing.

Over a much shorter period, Rheingold (1956; Rheingold and Bayley, 1959) followed a group of toddlers who had been infant residents of a relatively stimulating institutional nursery. She gave half of these sixteen infants extensive "mothering" from the sixth to the eighth month and they became more socially responsive than the controls but did not show acceleration of development. Upon follow-up one year later, these children neither recognized her nor were they perceptibly different from the controls, except that more experimental subjects vocalized during social tests.

Kirk (1958) studied children living in the community and in institutions, some given special pre-school experience for one to three years before entering first grade, others not. The overall effects of the pre-school experience were positive: 70 per cent of the experimental children improved an average of about 10 points on various measures of intelligence and social maturity, and they maintained these gains during a follow-up period, which for some was as long as five years. After a year of school, the control children who were living in the community tended to catch up with the experimental group, but this was not true of the community children from very deprived homes or of the institutional group. For them, the pre-school experience provided a special advantage which was maintained in contrast with the controls.

A follow-up study (Durkin, 1964) of children who were reading when they entered first grade suggested that children whose parents deliberately set out to tutor them read more effectively upon entry into first grade than did those who had spontaneously involved their parents in helping them. The deliberately tutored children, however, read less well than the spontaneous readers at the end of third grade, though they were still some two years ahead of grade level. A small but consistent advantage was demonstrated for children who began reading at age 3, versus equally bright children who began at age 5.

There are several recent and current attempts to assess the effects of pre-school intervention with culturally deprived children (Bereiter *et al.*, 1965; Brottman, 1965; Deutsch, 1965b; Gray and Klaus, 1965; Long, 1966; Weikart *et al.*, 1964). Although long-range data are not available as yet, several tentative conclusions may be offered from the results which have been reported. First, relatively large gains in scores on intelligence tests are usually obtained during the first year; average gains have ranged from 5 to over 20 IQ points. Second, this spurt in development is not always maintained in the second year; the one study which presents the best documented data on this point shows an average decrease of about 2 IQ points during the second year, both in a group which stayed in the pre-school and in a group who left the pre-school to enter public schools (Weikart *et al.*, 1964). Third, the control groups tend to gain in IQ points once they are exposed to stimulating school experiences, so that the differences between the experimental and control subjects are further reduced after the first few years of public school experience (Weikart *et al.*, 1964).

Almost all programs in pre-school education have defined gains and losses in terms of scores from tests of general intelligence. These may not, however, be the most sensitive measures. Long (1966) for several years maintained two standard kindergartens for Negro and white children in a rural Southern community. One-half of the children in each kindergarten received enrichment programmed instruction about three times a week, and the remaining half served as controls. The average Stanford-Binet gains for all of the white children in both experimental and control groups ranged from 8 to 10 IQ points; there were virtually no gains for the Negro children in either group. On the Thurstone Tests of Primary Mental Abilities, however, both the Negro and white children showed significant increases in scores. Furthermore, there is some evidence on the PMA that the programmed instruction resulted in greater gains for the Negro children. These data suggest that the short-term gains and losses in intellectual level might be significantly influenced by the nature of the instruments used to assess intelligence. It would seem important that a variety of assessment procedures be used in all projects.

There are a few other longitudinal studies (for example, Burtt, 1941; Hilgard, 1932; McGraw, 1935, 1939) which point to the possibility that, particularly for the very young child given extensive training, there can be considerable stability and perhaps a generalization of a high degree of mastery.

What can be made of studies of the effects of early experience, with reference to the question of the stability of various types of learning? The only point on which we can be relatively confident is that prolonged deprivation of stimulation during the early years results in extensive and perhaps irreparable damage to the developing cognitive apparatus. This conclusion is strengthened by evidence such as that presented by Skeels (1965), although the intervening experience between 1939 and 1965 was not the same for Skeels's two groups. Dennis' (1960) observation also lends caution to the interpretation of the significance of early deprivation. Even that which we seem to know about the effects of early, severe deprivation may not be altogether certain.

There has been a tendency to use evidence concerning the dramatically deleterious consequences of gross deprivation to substantiate the argument that increasing stimulation will be beneficial to cognitive development. But it is quite possible that successive increments of stimulation, past the necessary minimum, are unimportant, and excesses in certain kinds of stimulation may even be harmful.

We can say little about the long-term stability of early education programs. There is evidence that individuals who have had the benefit of special education programs, started when they were very young and continued during the formative years, have proven to be clearly superior in achievement (for example, McCurdy, 1957). The most conservative interpretation of these findings is, however, that when superior endowment is nurtured in a superior fashion, superior ability results. There is no evidence which conclusively demonstrates that the child with average or below average endowment will profit greatly from pre-school interventions.

HAZARDS IN BEGINNING TOO EARLY

If we are to attempt educational interventions at an early period in a child's life, we must gear these programs to his capacities and interests at that point. Failure to do so will surely result in frustration and discouragement for child and teacher alike (Welch, 1940a).

Many workers who object to early education maintain that the young child is too fragile a creature to tamper with. They have suggested that the warmth of mother-love is the essential ingredient and that our concern should be with emotional security rather than with intellectual growth. Other critics feel that the early childhood years are crucial in establishing the child's orientation to his own subculture, and that the establishment of pre-school programs for the culturally different will impose middle-class values on the children. They point out that there are many positive aspects of the less affluent subcultures (Riessman, 1962) and that early intervention programs which emphasize intellectual skills and an achievement orientation run the risks of destroying these. They fear that this process will further deprive the children of a subculture and even of a family with whom they can completely identify. Still other critics, following maturational hypotheses, maintain that the very young child lacks the basic perceptual-cognitive equipment needed to learn more complex responses than those that are made spontaneously, or that such new responses are acquired at enormous cost. This concept of "readiness" maintains that until the time is right, the attempt to teach advanced skills is futile at best and damaging at worst.

Are there hazards in beginning to educate children too early? It is difficult to see how pleasant experiences, stimulating within reasonable limits, can be harmful either to mental health or to cognitive development. One need not deny that sound emotional development is important to contend that optimum intellectual growth is also important. The two are apparently intertwined, with development in the emotional sphere in part a function of development in the intellectual realm, and vice versa.

As concerns the "readiness" problem, the notion that a child cannot effectively learn higher-order skills before he masters fundamental lower-order skills should not be interpreted to mean that the lower-order skills cannot be effectively taught. The problem of the proper sequencing of learning steps must be faced in any educational program.

The problem of cultural discontinuity, and the possible alienation of children from their families because of the inculcation of different values, is a difficult one. For ultimate success, children must be prepared to make their way in a culture which values and rewards intellectual competence and achievement, and early exposure to these values could be beneficial. Yet some subcultural differences will be present in the best of societies, and it is possible and desirable that schools foster such differences. Many children who experience early educational endeavors will adopt values somewhat different from those of their parents, and their families will experience some problems because of this. Such has been the case in every acculturation process. Close work with the families should help to resolve some of the problems, and perhaps in the process some of the healthier aspects of the families can be strengthened. If acculturation does not take place, then we must envisage revolutionary changes in our public schools in order to deal more effectively with the millions of children who do not fit. Indeed, there are now concerted efforts to establish curricula and teaching materials which are more understandable and appealing to children of the working and welfare classes.

In large segments of our society, early childhood is neither pleasant nor secure. Surveys which we have conducted within our own relatively affluent community, find large numbers of children of working mothers cared for by very inadequate substitutes, under less than minimal conditions of hygiene or security, and often with the highest degree of restrictiveness and boredom. Siblings of these children are known to be borderline mentally retarded and apathetic to their surroundings. Rational, carefully planned programs of stimulation and social interaction should aid the health and growth of these children with little risk.

HAZARDS OF BEGINNING TOO LATE

Historically, the effects of very early experiences on the development of cognitive functions have been considered rather minimal. Psychoanalytically oriented theorists have emphasized the importance of very early experience, but their concern has been more with emotional factors in development than with the epigenesis of intelligent behavior. Recent investigators have, however, suggested that the very early years are crucial to the development of intellectual functions, and they have suggested that opportunities for development missed during these early formative years cannot easily be made up later.

The most impressive evidence in this area has been derived from studies with non-human organisms, which have demonstrated that important cognitive functions are crucially affected by very early experiences (see Scott, 1962). A reasonable conclusion from these data is that the period of greatest plasticity in the development of intelligence is the time of initial socialization.

While recognizing the difficulties inherent in generalizing from studies on subhuman animals, some workers have been convinced that the developing child similarly becomes less and less malleable as he grows older (see Ausubel, 1963). Bloom (1964), following a thorough review of the existing literature, suggested that the long-term effect of living in a deprived environment versus an abundant one is about 20 IQ points. He hypothesized that the cost of deprivation during the first four years is about 10 IQ points; from 4 to 8 years, 6 IQ points; and from 8 to 17 years, only 4 additional IQ points. Some workers have felt that the typically crowded, noisy condition of a "culturally deprived" home constitutes an adequately stimulating environment for the young infant; infants from culturally deprived segments of our society tend not to show retardation during the first year (Hunt, 1964). The handicap referred to by Bloom during the first four years, therefore, might really refer to ages 2 to 4, and it might be greater for children reared in very monotonous environments such as institutions.

There are a few studies which support the notion that in human beings, as well as in lower animals, the very early years are most important in the development of intelligent behavior. Mayer (1964) has pointed out that, "Except for singers and occasional composers . . . *every* major musical figure started as a child prodigy" (p. 106). Likewise, McCurdy (1957) has surveyed biographical information on twenty men of great genius. Their earliest years were particularly stimulating; the typical pattern included "a high degree of attention focused upon the child by parents and other adults, expressed in intensive educational measures and, usually, abundant love (and) . . . isolation from other children, especially outside the family" (p. 461).

In the Skeels and Dye (1939) study already mentioned, seven children who were taken out of the minimally stimulating environment of the orphanage nursery before they were 18 months old achieved an average IQ rating of 99.4 after an average of only 14.2 months in a more stimulating environment. Six children who were taken out after they were 18 months old received, in contrast, an average IQ rating of 82.8 after an average of 24.4 months in the more stimulating environment. The unreliability of very early test results must not, however, be ignored.

Several studies have suggested that children raised in inadequate environments during their early years do not readily respond to more adequate circumstances later on. Goldfarb (1943, 1945, 1947, 1955) studied several matched groups of children, half of whom had spent most of their first three years in an institutional setting before being placed in foster homes, and half of whom had been placed during infancy. He found marked differences between the two groups. The children who had spent their first years in the institution displayed severe personality difficulties and intellectual deficiencies. In a group tested at a median age of almost 12 years, the median IQ was only 74.

Speer (1940) studied children raised for varying amounts of time in families in which the mothers were mentally retarded (median IQ, 49). Those children placed in a foster home before they were 3 years old achieved a median IQ of 100.5 one or two years after placement; the median for children who were placed after 3 but before 6 was 83.7 at about the time of placement; the median for children placed between 6 and 9 was 74.6; for children placed between 9 and 12 it was 71.5; and for those placed between 12 and 16 it was 53.1. Both of these studies are open to major criticisms: Pasamanick and Knobloch (1961, p. 87) have proposed that Goldfarb's institutionalized group may have contained a large number of children who were brain-injured and who for that reason were not placed in foster homes earlier. There was inadequate follow-up of the Speer children; all of the children were tested at the time, or relatively soon after they were placed in foster homes, and we have no idea how they compared later in life.

Bayley and Schaefer (1964) recently presented a thorough re-analysis of data from the Berkeley Growth Study, revealing that the effects of the mother-son interactions during the first three years were of considerable magnitude and quite long lasting. For girls, however, there was apparently no such relationship between early patterns of interaction with the mother and later intelligence. Girls' IQ's after age 2 did show a much closer relationship than did the boys' IQ's with the mother's estimated IQ's and with the educational level of both parents, a finding supported by a number of other studies (Honzik, Macfarlane, and Allen, 1948; Kagan and Moss, 1959; Skodak and Skeels, 1949). Bayley and Schaefer suggest that males are permanently affected by the social and emotional climate during infancy in both emotional adjustment and intellectual development, but that girls are less permanently affected, possibly because their mental development may be more a function of genetic factors (1964, p. 69). In this study, IQ scores over the 18-year period showed "inconsistent rates of growth in the first two or three years, but by five or six years . . . they . . . settled into fairly predictable IQ's, or stable rates of growth in mental ability" (1964, p. 17).

Other data suggest that motivational systems which are closely related to intellectual development are strongly affected by experiences early in life. Observations of children from the more deprived segments of our society suggest that patterns of passivity, apathy, and discouragement are characteristic at very early ages, while children from more stimulating environments are active, inquisitive, optimistic, and continually engaged in mastery patterns.

Recent studies of achievement drive begin to show the importance of this impetus to successful productive activity. The achievement drive differs among children, and it has striking effects on their intellectual development. For example, children with a high degree of achievement motivation tend to become brighter as they grow older; those with a more passive outlook tend to fall behind their developmental potential (Bayley and Schaefer, 1964; Sontag, Baker, and Nelson, 1958). The degree of achievement motivation is related to the sociocultural background of the child; middle-class children are more strongly motivated toward achievement than are lower-class children (Douvan, 1956; Lott and Lott, 1963; Mussen, Urbano, and Boutourline-Young, 1961). There are also differences among children of different racial groups (Lott and Lott, 1963; Merbaum, 1961; Mussen, 1953; Rosen, 1959), of different religious backgrounds (McClelland, Rindlisbacher, and de-Charms, 1955), and of different geographic-ethnic origins (Rosen, 1959). In each instance, the group of more favorable social status has the higher motivation to achieve excellence.

The results of recent research suggest that the achievement drive ha; its origins in infancy, and that these origins lie in the unverbalized emotional relationships which children have with the adults around them (Bayley and Schaefer, 1964; Kagan and Moss, 1959, 1962; Moss and Kagan, 1958; Schaefer and Bayley, 1963). Like other motivational systems, the achievement drive is affected by subsequent experience. It seems to be bolstered by a verbalized value system taught when the child is able to grasp more abstract concepts, such as the notion that with hard work, foresight, and sacrifice, success can come to anyone (Rosen, 1958). But the effects of later childhood training will probably not be great unless the motivational system resulting from earlier experiences is already functioning.

Are there hazards in beginning the educational process too late? An accumulating body of data hints at the crucial significance of experiences during the first three years. Patterns of responding learned during this early period apparently provide important foundations for all later learning.

The long-range effects of pre-school programs initiated at age 3 or later do not now seem too promising. The initial results from several extensive projects have not been what many of us hoped and felt sure they would be. It is possible that programs should begin at even earlier ages or that different methods would be more effective. But we should not give up hope for these programs, for most of them are very new, and many of the investigators feel that they are just beginning to discover techniques which will lead to greater and more permanent gains.

OPTIMAL TIMING OF SPECIFIC EDUCATIONAL PROGRAMS

Concluding that the very early years of childhood constitute the optimum time for initiating educational intervention does not help determine the specific kinds of intervention. Early childhood has been viewed as crucial for the development of quite different sorts of capacities. The prevailing notion during the past half-century has been that early experiences are important for the establishment of emotional and personality patterns, but not for the development of intelligence.

Recently, a number of investigators have, in contrast, viewed the first few years of life as a period during which essential cognitive structures are formed. Hebb (1949) has emphasized the crucial role of early perceptual development in establishing the foundations for increasingly complex cognitive structures. R. W. White (1960) has stressed the importance of early mastery experiences. Piaget (for ex-

ample, 1950, 1952, 1954) has emphasized the importance of the early
sensori-motor structures and the emergence of primitive representational modes of thought.

There is as great diversity of notions about what is basically important during the later pre-school years as there is concerning the period
of the first two or three years. While infants and young children can
probably profit from a variety of experiences, it is probable that some
areas do and should take precedence in the early years, either because
these are crucial periods for their emergence or because they form
foundations essential to the development of other structures. Con-
versely, some areas may play no basic role until a later time. Perhaps
teaching a toddler to read is simply a gimmick, with no generalized
significance; on the other hand, this process may hasten discriminative
and conceptual functions in important ways.

SPECIFIC FACTORS IN EARLY EXPERIENCE

Some recent investigations provide us with hints as to kinds of early
experience which may serve as determinants of later intellectual behavior. The situation turns out to be more complex than we would like
it to be. One of the best documented conclusions is that there are
strong sex differences. Kagan and Moss (1962), in their re-analysis of
the data of the Fels longitudinal study, report that, "It appears that
the pattern most likely to lead to involvement in intellectual achievement in the boys is early maternal protection, followed by encouragement and acceleration of mastery behaviors (pp. 221-222)." The correlation between maternal protection of boys during the first three
years and their intellectual achievement during adolescence was .76.
"For girls . . . the pattern was quite the reverse. Maternal hostility
toward the daughter during the first three years, together with acceleration during ages [0 to 3 and] 6 to 10, were associated with adult intellectual mastery in the woman" (p. 222). Furthermore, hostile behavior towards boys in the first three years was negatively associated
with adult achievement behavior ($r = -.56$), while protective behavior toward girls during the first three years was negatively related
to adult achievement behavior ($r = -.50$).

Data from Bayley and Schaefer's (1964) analysis of the Berkeley
Growth Study are strikingly similar. The hostile, punitive, irritable
mother produced a son who scored high on developmental indices during his 1st year of life. There was, however, a strong negative relationship between such early behavior on the part of the mother and intel-

ligence scores during the age span 5 to 18 years. Early maternal behaviors which were negatively correlated with boys' test scores during infancy, but positively correlated with later intelligence, included such variables as equalitarianism, cooperativeness, and positive evaluation of the boy. In girls there were no long-term relationships such as these; intelligence was more closely related to the mothers' current behavior patterns.

What patterns should be encouraged in parents and caretakers of young children? Kagan and Moss interpreted their data as revealing an identification of the girls with their acceleratory mothers, who tended to be aggressive and competitive women, critical of their daughters and valuing mastery behavior. They suggested that these same kinds of women protected their sons during the first three years. The inclusion of other crucial variables, might have made the results more easily understood; for example, the father's behavior may be much more important for boys, and calm, "motherly" mothers may have brighter sons because they are married to more dominant, "fatherly" fathers with whom the sons identify.

Following our best judgment in estimating the most desirable patterns to follow with young children, our educated guess remains that high intelligence is fostered by warmth, support, and plentiful opportunity and reward for achievement and autonomy. Moreover, it is probably important to provide active, warm, achievement-oriented parental figures of both sexes after whom appropriate role patterns can be established.

The only really safe conclusion one can make of the available data, is that there is a vast amount we need to know about the role of experience in early childhood, and that the only effective way to go about investigating it is through longitudinal studies of rather large proportions. In view of the current pressure to engage in active intervention during the pre-school years, the urgency of initiating this long-term research must not be ignored.

IV

CONDITIONS THAT FACILITATE OR IMPEDE COGNITIVE FUNCTIONING:
Implications for Developmental Theory and for Education

Eugene S. Gollin (B.S.S. 1947, M.A. 1948, City College of New York; Ph.D. 1951, Clark University) is Chairman of the Department of Psychology, Fels Research Institute, and Professor of Psychology, Antioch College. The preparation of this paper was supported, in part, by Grant HD 01570 from NICHHD, in part by Contract No. PH 43 65-1011 sponsored by NICHHD, and in part by Grant FR-05537 from NIH.

PSYCHOLOGISTS who view behavior from a developmental vantage point are particularly well situated to provide information for the guidance of educational practice. I shall discuss examples of research findings which are likely to be useful to the *creative* educator. The word *creative* is stressed because the discoveries of the laboratory are not directly translatable into practice. The controls of the experimental chamber are inappropriate for the schoolroom. The artifices introduced by the experimenter are frequently remote from the world of things and of people. Furthermore, the curves of function reported by researchers are abstractions. They do not characterize individuals.

Attempts to convert either the methods or findings of the laboratory into classroom practice without regard for the changing context will lead to chaotic and frustrating outcomes for children and for teachers. Thoughtless attempts to convert research findings into educational procedure must lead to fetishism, cant, and methodological zealotry.

Psychologists, whether they intend to or not, frequently communicate with the educational community, with parents, and with the general public in a manner which fosters devotion to practice rather than alertness to children. There are those in our profession who do not hesitate to offer their half-baked wares to the consumer—and half-baked means that the loaf has not been left in the oven long enough, and may prove to be indigestible.

Lest these remarks seem excessive, let me point out that the ultimate target of these ministerial efforts are children, who in our society are essentially defenseless. Certainly, you are all aware of the nostrums that are offered. They range from personological manipulations to that apex of civilized man, the teaching machine.

The suggestions of psychologists, appropriately employed, may prove to be useful. However, before a generation of children is committed to a new or refurbished educational assembly line—whether its orientation be clinical or mechanical or even electronic—some thought ought to be given to the implications of current research for the course of development.

Educators and psychologists are interested in those factors, both organismic and environmental, which play a role in the modification of behavior. When research on behavior is conducted in a comparative-developmental context it is likely to be useful in special ways. Comparative-developmental analyses attempt to vary organismic and task properties within the same research design (Gollin, 1965). This manner of doing research provides a more extensive check of the alleged universality of observed functional relations than is usually forthcoming, and also serves to alert investigators to individual differences.

The investigations to be discussed are of comparative-developmental quality either by themselves or in conjunction with other studies.

Transfer

Transfer of training has traditionally been an area of interest to both educators and psychologists. As Hebb has indicated (1949), most investigations of learning are really investigations of transfer effects. The researcher who conducts transfer experiments attempts to make explicit the relations between successive learning experiences.

FAILURE SET

Zeaman and House (1963) have directed attention to a kind of interproblem transfer which is likely to have relevance for education at all levels. They report that trainable retardates who had been able to solve simple "junk" discrimination problems were unable to solve such problems after they experienced prolonged failure on a more difficult (conditional reaction) task. Zeaman and House name this phenomenon *failure set*.

Failure set was also observed by Hill (1965), who reported that performances of 4-year-old children on a simple object discrimination task were easily shaken by previous adverse conditions. The 4-year-olds were capable of final performance levels comparable to those of 6-year-old children when conditions were optimal. Hill also reported that the effects of adverse experience upon subsequent learning varied with age, producing greater disruption in younger subjects.

OVERTRAINING

Furth and Youniss (1964) trained children in the early elementary grades to make a form or a color discrimination. Half their S's were trained to criterion, and half were given postcriterion training. When training was complete, children were shifted to a second task. Some S's learned a reversal task wherein the same stimuli and responses were used but matched differently; some S's were given an intradimensional shift problem wherein different stimuli within the same dimension (color or form) were used and the earlier response had to be associated with the new cues; the remaining S's were required to make an extradimensional shift, that is, responses which had previously been made to color cues were now made to form cues, and vice versa. It was found that the intradimensional shift was easiest under both criterion and overtraining conditions. Overtraining facilitated performance only on the reversal shift condition, where it also led to a significant reduction in perseverative errors.

In a subsequent study Youniss and Furth (1965), using first-grade children as S's, investigated the effects of overtraining upon a reversal and a non-reversal shift. They found no shift difference after criterion training; however, overtraining facilitated reversal shift but not non-reversal shift.

In another investigation of the effects of overtraining on reversal, using children aged 3½–4 years and 4½–5 years, it was found that overtraining facilitated reversal for the older children but was disruptive for the younger children. The two age groups did not differ on original learning.

The overtraining variable intensified the tendency of children in the older group to perform in a qualitatively distinct manner from those in the younger group. Increased numbers of 4½–5-year-old children tended to shift to the new positive cue without further error after the first reversal trial as a function of overtraining. In contrast, overtraining the younger children increased their cue perseveration tendencies to respond to the positive cue of the original learning task (Gollin, 1964).

These studies represent but a small sample of current research in which transfer effects are analyzed. It is apparent from even this brief survey that the effects of prior experience upon later performance is related to content, training conditions, and status of the child. Curriculum planners, obviously, must consider this complex of interactions.

Strategies

It is becoming increasingly apparent that children approach laboratory tasks and, it may be assumed, learning situations in general with different cognitive strategies. While the state of research art does not as yet permit unambiguous specification of the cognitive dispositional systems which govern approach to a problem-solving or learning situation, research techniques are sufficiently advanced to alert us in a general way to developmental trends. Investigations directed at uncovering cognitive strategies make it quite clear that performance measures of success and failure reflect both organismic response tendencies and experimenter arrangements of the training environment.

Whether a particular subject's approach will lead to success or failure is dependent upon the experimenter's criterion and the demands of the task. Success or failure, then, is not a characteristic of subjects per se. It is, at least in part, determined by task demand or, in a broader sense, by societal demand. The attention of both researcher and educator ought to be directed at *how* the child succeeds and *how* he fails rather than at performance outcomes.

Illustrative of the relationship between subjective strategy and performance is a study by Weir (1964), who observed the behavior of subjects from the 3rd through the 18th year in a probability-learning task. Subjects were confronted by a panel containing three buttons. Only one of the buttons, when pressed, led to reward on a proportional basis. The other buttons never produced a reward. S's were scored in terms of maximizing, that is, how often they responded to the pay-off button. Three- to 5-year-old children tended to respond to the pay-off button from the outset. Subjects in the age range 15–18 years tried a variety of strategies before maximizing response to the pay-off button. Intermediate-aged children (7–10 years) tended to respond to the buttons in a sequential manner; for example, left-middle-right. Their pay-off rate was relatively low. The terminal performances of the youngest and oldest subjects were very much the same. The youngest S's "play the game" by following a very simple rule: stay with the response that gave the reward. The oldest S's entered the game with a strong expectancy that there was a solution that would yield 100 per cent reward and employed complex strategies in an attempt to discover the appropriate solution. Eventually they settled on what may be called the pre-school strategem. Intermediate-aged children have a system, and like the storied victims of gambling palaces the world over, they did not abandon it, even though their rewards were minimal.

In an investigation directed explicitly at response tendencies, Jeffrey and Cohen (1965) presented children with a two-choice task using undiscriminable stimuli. They found strong age-related tendencies to respond in stereotyped fashion. Three-year-old children showed strong perseverative position tendencies, while 4½-year-old children tended to alternate their responses.

Schusterman (1964) compared response strategies of mentally retarded children (MA approximately 5 years), normal 5-year-old children, and normal 10-year-old children. He used a two-choice task with undiscriminable stimuli and uncertain outcome. An initial training phase was introduced during which there was continuous reinforcement of one position. During this phase of the experiment, both the mentally retarded and normal 5-year-old children learned the discrimination more rapidly than the normal older children. During later phases of the experiment, it was found that the normal 10-year-old children used strategies which were sensitive to outcome contingencies, while the younger children and the retarded children tended to employ strategies based on factors other than outcome contingencies.

Schusterman's experiment provides an excellent example of comparative-developmental analysis. It demonstrates that the very response dispositions which produce preferred outcomes under one set of contingencies prevent preferred outcomes when reward contingencies are changed. Such results also point out the fallacy of using a simple learning task to differentiate groups (and individuals as well, it may be added) and then concluding that the group with the superior performance is the group with the superior intellect. Schusterman's point, which has been stated in other contexts (for example, Hebb, 1949, 1958; Gollin, 1965), bears further illustration since it is one that is frequently overlooked.

Interaction between Complexity and Developmental Level

Klugh and Roehl (1965) recently investigated concept learning in 5-6-year- and 9-10-year-old children using two levels of task complexity. Their apparatus was a modification of the Yerkes problem box. It housed twelve evenly spaced levers. Any one or more of the levers could be pushed forward toward the subject. The correct choice in both the simple and complex task was the second lever from the right. When it was pressed a buzzer sounded, signifying correct choice. In the simple problem, four adjacent levers were always presented, the particular four varying from trial to trial. In the complex problem, a varied pattern of four to nine bars was presented. S was told that there was a rule he could discover which would allow him to be correct on every trial. It was found that there were no age-related differences in trials to criterion on the simple task, but on the complex task the younger children required more than three times as many trials to reach criterion than did the older children.

Gollin investigated tactual form discrimination with children of various ages and with adult subjects. In one condition (simple) the discrimination of forms was between figures built up with rounded tacks; in the second condition (complex) the same forms were used but discriminably larger tacks were scattered through the field (Gollin, 1960, 1961). It was found that the presence of these interfering or "noisy" stimuli was more disruptive for the younger than for older children. Further, while both younger and older children benefited from training under the simple discrimination condition, only the older children, within the limits of the experiment, were able to benefit from training under the complex condition.

Discussion

Perhaps the most important lesson we have to learn from comparative-developmental analysis is to be wary of performance. It is understandable, in terms of the stress of behaviorism, that epiphenomena should play the role they do in much current psychological thinking. An anecdote related by Hebb (1968) is relevant:

Several years ago an investigator working with a non-mammalian species asked me at a public meeting to account for the apparent similarity of the learning he had observed with what had been found in mammals, despite differences in brain structure . . . he had taught the subject to avoid a white square. He described the animal's neural structures and asked, "What pathways are involved in the learning?" . . . I asked what transfer tests (test of stimulus equivalence) had been made. But all this was a new idea to the investigator in question, and as I started to outline the necessary experimental steps, he interrupted and said, "Never mind the alibis, stop evading the question, what paths are involved?" (pp. 454–455).

In this regard, it might be useful for us to accept instruction from the clinician who is faced with the problem of interpreting symptoms. We would do well to pay some attention to the methodological postulates, for example, which guided Kurt Goldstein's assessment of brain-damaged patients (1939). He asserted that symptoms of disease and the results of experimental observations belong to the same class of phenomena, and that the appearance of a particular symptom is dependent on the method of examination. And so may we regard the appearance of a particular performance as being dependent upon experimental procedures. Writing about brain-damaged individuals, Goldstein cautioned that one may be led astray if one evaluates the individual's capabilities only in terms of solution of a task. The final performance may be achieved in a variety of ways. Experimenters must acquire "clinical" ingenuity in evaluating performances obtained under restricted circumstances, and must recognize that performances observed in isolated contexts are not sufficient indicators of intellectual functioning.

In addition to methodological considerations, there are a number of heuristic principles which ought to be useful to investigators of development. These derive in part from Piaget (1950, 1952a) and in part from Werner (1937, 1948). Piaget and Werner have taken the position that there is a developmental shift in cognition from dependence upon sensory-perceptual properties of tasks or stimuli toward a reliance upon inferential or conceptual manipulations. Wohlwill (1962) has recently introduced three dimensions along which perception and conception may be specified. They are:

1) *Redundancy:* As one proceeds from perception to conception, the amount of redundant information required decreases.

2) *Selectivity:* As one proceeds from perception to conception, the

amount of irrelevant information that can be tolerated without affecting response increases.

3) *Contiguity:* As one proceeds from perception to conception, the spatial and temporal separation over which the total information contained in the stimulus field can be integrated increases.

I should like to add two further dimensions, or really one-and-a-half (the half is an amendment to Wohlwill's contiguity dimension):

3b) *Contiguity:* As one proceeds from perception to conception, the spatial and temporal crowding over which the total information contained in the stimulus field can be integrated increases.

4) *Complexity:* As one proceeds from perception to conception, the number of diverse stimulus properties contained in the stimulus field that can be integrated increases.

Although there are many investigations, including some of those referred to earlier in this paper, which indicate ontogenetic changes consistent with these dimensions, neither Wohlwill nor I regard them as having exclusive ontogenetic reference. Wohlwill notes that the dimensions are stated in such a way as to be applicable to intertask as well as to intersubject differences. Paradoxically, we may achieve enlightenment concerning individual development by distinguishing between developmental change and chronology. An excellent discussion of these issues may be found in a recent paper by Kaplan (1966). He writes, "It would not be grossly unfair or inaccurate to state that most psychologists . . . have taken 'development' to designate *a subject-matter to be studied* rather than *a manner of studying any subject-matter.*"

The perceptual-conceptual dimensions described above provide a framework for selecting observational techniques and for ordering observations. They suggest, as both Werner and Kaplan have indicated, that development entails, "not merely change or numerical increase in complexity, but the emergence of new forms of organization, novel structures and modes of operation of a kind eventuating in increased differentiation, increased subordination of parts to wholes and means to ends, increased stability and flexibility of . . . functioning" (Kaplan, 1966, p. 38).

If we are to talk sensibly to educators about the "timeliness" of training, the substance of training, and the methods of training, we ought to do so in the context of comparative-developmental analysis. If we do this, we provide educators at once with a way of viewing behavior and a guide for modifying behavior.

The principles and directions suggested by this approach apply to all levels of education. They would seem particularly relevant to pre-school groups since this is apparently a period in which fundamental bases for future behavior are established.

Witkin (1965) has recently characterized Heinz Werner's main contribution to psychology as

> an approach to problems and a mode of inquiry suggested by this approach. . . . He proposed . . . a set of categories, or general principles, intended to serve the heuristic function of guiding the observation and description of psychological phenomena. These principles were also meant to serve a second function of generating hypotheses about the developmental relations assumed by these principles. It is from the specific results gained in testing these hypotheses . . . that the laws of development and a theory of development are derived. The formulation of developmental theory was for Werner an ever evolving affair . . . an "indefinite project."

And so must it be with the educational process.

Postscript

In problem-solving and learning situations, subjects—particularly young subjects—are likely to attend to perceptually salient properties of the stimulus array. If the subject is asked to solve a problem or accomplish some goal with the stimulus materials, his initial manipulatory efforts are likely to be dominated by the perceptual properties of the materials. The following questions are of research and education interest:

1) What factors will induce subjects to shift from one set of perceptual properties to another—for example, from form to color or color to form?

2) What factors will induce a subject to shift from perceptual to conceptual operations—for example, from an absolute to a relational judgment?

3) What effects will initial success with perceptual modes of approach have upon subsequent demands for conceptual manipulations?

4) To what extent are conceptual operations dependent upon prior perceptually based operations?

5) Does a shift in cognitive operations in one area generalize to other areas—how situation-specific are shifts?

6) What is the nature of the relations between various organismic

dimensions and shift behavior—for example, what roles do factors such as intelligence, organic conditions, prior experience history, etc., play?

In a broad sense, these are questions about the adaptability of organisms, about conditions which promote or impede adaptation to changing environmental demands.

During this Conference, a number of people have indicated that one of the chief objectives of intervention programs is the fostering of creativity. If creative behavior is defined, at least in part, as an increase in the individual's discernment of alternative modes of behavior, an increase in awareness of alternative goals, and an increased mastery of multiple behavioral skills, then creativity and adaptability become partly synonymous. It is the thesis of this paper that comparative-developmental analyses of behavior will provide the kind of information required for optimal influence on the development of creative functioning.

SUSAN W. GRAY

and

RUPERT A. KLAUS

V THE EARLY TRAINING PROJECT AND ITS GENERAL RATIONALE

Susan W. Gray (A.B., Randolph-Macon Women's College; M.A., Ph.D., George Peabody College) is Professor of Psychology, Associate Director of the Institute on Mental Retardation and Intellectual Development, and Director of the Demonstration and Research Center for Early Education, George Peabody College. Rupert A. Klaus (B.S. 1949, Southeast Missouri State College; M.A. 1953, Ph.D., 1959, George Peabody College) is Associate Professor of Psychology, George Peabody College, and Director of the Early Training Project for Culturally Deprived Children, Murfreesboro City Schools, Murfreesboro, Tennessee.

THE Early Training Project is an intervention research study which attempts to test the possibility of offsetting, with specially planned techniques, the progressive retardation in school achievement and general cognitive development that is the usual fate of the culturally deprived child as he passes through the elementary school.

Our general research strategy grows out of the fact that research in the field has not yet demonstrated whether it is possible to offset substantially this progressive retardation. It is true that—at the time we began—several studies had demonstrated 5 to 15 points IQ gain in young children with special interventions no longer than three months. These gains, however, tended to be temporary, and are probably explicable in part by the changes in motivation from pre- to post-test that may be associated with experiences in which children learn to respond to a range of adults, particularly verbally, and to become somewhat task-oriented. A pilot study which our group completed in 1959 illustrates this kind of finding very nicely—one in which we had a significantly greater gain in intelligence test scores for an experimental than a control group of 6-year-olds, but in which differences were not found after the first year in school.

Our effort in the Early Training Project was to design an "experimental package of best bets" for intervention. From available research on social class, cognitive development, and motivation we attempted to derive those characteristics which appeared to be related to the differences in school performance of middle-class and culturally deprived children and which also appeared to be subject to possible manipulation. Since we were concerned with school applications, as well, we attempted to do this within a framework it would be possible to duplicate on a wide scale, should the project prove to be successful.

Because of the transitory nature of the gains made in our pilot study, our attempt in the Early Training Project was to begin with younger children (we started three summers prior to first-grade entrance), and to extend the study over a longer period of time. Our intent was to make our intervention *developmental* rather than *remedial*. We thus set up four groups of children. Three of these groups were randomized from a group of 65 deprived children born in 1958 in a small southern city. One of these groups had three summers of a specially planned pre-school, plus weekly visits during the remainder of the year by a specially trained home visitor. The visitor's task was to involve the mother and child in activities similar to those of the summer experience. In addition, she attempted to give the mother some help in learning the instrumental steps involved in enabling her child to realize her aspirations for him, educationally and vocationally.

A second group had a similar intervention schedule, except that it began one year later and thus involved only two summer schools. Both of these groups had the services of the home visitor during the first grade. The third group served as the local control group. A fourth group, in a town similar in economic structure, but sixty miles distant, served as an additional control group. This last group was added to the design since we anticipated the possibility of diffusion in the small city in which we worked, and hoped by the additional group to arrive at some estimate of such diffusion effects.

The group with which we worked are deprived urban Negro children. We selected Negro children primarily for two reasons: at the time we began the study, the schools of the city were segregated and it seemed wise not to initiate an integrated group at that time since our study, longitudinal in nature, did require continued community cooperation. In addition, we had reason to believe that in this particular setting our chances of success with the Negro children were somewhat greater than with the whites. These children were selected on the basis of housing conditions, father's or mother's occupation, education, and income. At the beginning these incomes were well below the present cutting point of $3,000 for poverty. The parents' occupations were unskilled or semi-skilled, their education was eighth grade or below; housing conditions were poor. In most of the homes there were television sets but no books or magazines, and little in the way of toys. The median number of children in the family at the time we began the study was five; in about one-third of the homes there was no father present. This group is stable geographically: of our 87 families, we have lost only four over the five years.

The pre-school summer experiences were arranged so that each group of approximately twenty had a head teacher, who was an experienced primary teacher with special training for the project, and three or four assistant teachers, the assistants being largely trainees in our school psychology program or undergraduates especially recruited for the program. This made possible a high ratio of adults to children, which was of particular importance for the form of intervention we planned. The staff was about equally balanced as to race and sex. We made special efforts to have men teachers in the group to serve as appropriate role models for the little boys, particularly those from father-absent homes.

The summer experience we planned around two main categories of variables. These were:

1) *Attitudes relating to achievement*. These included achievement motivation, delay of gratification, persistence, interest in school-type activities, and identification with achieving role models.

2) *Aptitudes relating to achievement*. Under this heading we grouped perceptual development, the development of concepts, and language.

These variables represent the original rationale in our study; they grew out of our attempts to distill the relevant literature as to the particular deficits of the deprived child as he attempts to cope with the usual expectancies of the elementary school. Our problem as we saw it in the beginning was to build upon the motivations which the child already had and, by a gradual process of appropriate reinforcement, to move him closer to the patterns of motivation and performance of more privileged children.

Because of these children's backgrounds and general immaturity, we expected to find that the most effective positive reinforcements for them would be immediate concrete reward and physically expressed approval from an adult—hugging, patting, carrying around, and the like. Our task was to reinforce the child selectively so that he could find that he received reinforcement, in terms of our aptitude variables, when he could tell the difference between the picture of a pig and of a little girl (a task with which one of our little boys had considerable difficulty), or when he could count five blocks correctly. As one would expect, we proceeded by a rough-and-ready method of successive approximations. In the beginning we reinforced every attempt to achieve, to persist, to defer immediate gratification, and the like. As time went on, we became more selective in reinforcement. In language, for example, the child who could say "milk" at the lunch table got a second glass. Later on, he had to say, "Milk, please," or some variation thereof; even later he had to make a complete sentence. I might add parenthetically that we were not concerned at this point with correct grammar; all we wanted was to get the children to talk.

Over the period of the three summers, our efforts were directed toward bringing the child's behavior more under the verbal control of adults, of encouraging the child to internalize standards of performance, and of helping him move from the highly concrete way in which most of the children were operating to a more abstract level in his ways of processing the information in his environment.

Once the children were in public school, we no longer worked with them directly. The one exception was that during the first grade the home visitor visited each home every other week in an effort to interpret the school program to the mother, and to enable the mother to help her child cope with the demands of the first grade.

With pre-and post-test batteries each summer, first-grade tests, and various miscellaneous experimental measures, we have collected an enormous amount of data upon the children, and a certain amount upon their families. Our crucial comparisons are still in the future, however, since not until they have been in school for several years can we see whether the effects we appear to have created have any degree of permanence.

Briefly, what we have found so far is as follows: On tests of intelligence and language (the Binet, the WISC, the Peabody Picture Vocabulary Test, and the Illinois Test of Psycholinguistic Ability), until the point of school entrance our two experimental groups were clearly superior to the two control groups. Over this 27-month period, the first treatment group showed a gain of 9 IQ points on the Binet; the distal group lost 6 points, despite repeated testing. During the first year in public school, our three groups in the main city have moved closer together. Differences are still significant on the Binet and the WISC; they are no longer significant on the other two measures, although the relative positions are the same. The local control group is not significantly different on first-grade measures of achievement. The distal control group has not shown comparable progress. We think that what we are observing is a diffusion effect, and we have some evidence to document this. This evidence at present is not complete enough, however, that we can be sure that diffusion is indeed what we are observing. We hope at a somewhat later date to report upon this and also upon diffusion downward to younger siblings of the experimental children.

As we have worked with the children over the years, observed their homes, and speculated with each other and with our colleagues, we have begun to conceptualize what is happening in the deprived family setting a little more clearly than we did at first. Thus we have developed a more specific rationale for our reinforcement procedures.

This conceptual scheme is built around viewing the home situation in terms of three stimulus-potential and five reinforcement dimensions which seem applicable to observing young children in the home. These same dimensions also seem relevant to viewing social class and other differences in the home as they relate to the development of young children.

The possible stimulus dimensions [1] we listed as these:

1) *Gross amount of stimulus input.* Our guess here is that the culturally deprived child receives as much or more stimulation than his more favored counterparts in the middle class. For our children, four or more noisy siblings in a small household seems to provide a built-in guarantee of this.

2) *Number of different kinds of stimulus input.* On this dimension it is probable that the culturally deprived child does receive less variety in stimulation, particularly as he moves beyond infancy.

3) *Figure and ground relationships.* The noisy, active home of the culturally deprived child is probably so full of conflicting and un-ordered stimuli that the child cannot attend to those stimuli most relevant in terms of increased intellectual development. The home lacks organization both spatially and temporally. The television set is flipped on in the morning and booms all day. Everybody's possessions are hig-gledy-piggledy, and the day is not organized around such standing patterns as regular mealtimes.

These stimulus dimensions are derived from the work of such writers as Caldwell (1964) and Hunt (1961). In fact, these dimensions

1. This discussion of stimulus-potential and reinforcement dimensions has appeared in a slightly modified form in *Child Development*, 1965, *36*, 887–898.

could be ordered in terms of their implications fairly neatly with Hunt's three stages of intrinsic motivation in his Nebraska Symposium paper (Hunt, 1965).

Although the last of these three stimulus potential dimensions may be of considerable importance in the kinds of deficits the deprived child shows, our best guess is that such deficits are even more the result of the particular patterns of interactions between the child and others, especially the child and adults. These we have called reinforcement dimensions. There are five such dimensions we would suggest:

1) *Total amount of reinforcement.* Adults, specifically mothers and mother surrogates, are the chief reinforcing agents for small children. In deprived homes, the time and energy of the child-caring agent must be directed toward subsistence activities. Thus, less actual time is spent with the child, and the child is often shooed out of the way of the mother at work.

2) *The source of reinforcement.* If the child receives less reinforcement from the adult, it is probable that he seeks reinforcement, and perhaps receives it, from other sources. Older siblings and peers may serve as reinforcement agents. With peers and siblings, reinforcement is probably less verbal than with adults. Also much of the child's reinforcement in these circumstances may come from his own sensations—the pleasure of gross motor activity, for example, in racing around—or from the immediate meaning of objects to him—a chair is to sit on, for instance. This suggests that the reinforcement he receives will tend to keep him on a more concrete and non-verbal level than would the reinforcement the middle-class child receives.

3) *The nature of the reinforcement.* From his position on the first two dimensions, it is clear that the culturally deprived child will receive a relatively small amount of verbal reinforcement. Even when the parent is the reinforcer, there are probably fewer verbal responses than in the middle class, particularly those involving more complex language, or, in Bernstein's (1961) terms, those that involve an elaborated code rather than a restricted one.

4) *The direction of the reinforcement.* Where the child caretaker's energy must go into subsistence activities, where it is all she can do to cope with the immediate situation, little time and affect can be directed to shaping the child's behavior toward desired goals. Rewards will be given for those behaviors that make such coping easier. Thus, the parent rewards inhibitory rather than exploratory behavior. The deprived child probably learns very early that the best way to stay out

of trouble is to be quiet and keep out from under foot. The "natural" curiosity of the child may die for lack of encouragement. You will recall the emphasis that Piaget (1952b) places upon the stage at which the child learns that things have names, the "What's that?" stage. But the rapid strides in language that Piaget assumes follow this stage are based upon the assumption that there is someone there to tell the child what the name of each thing is, and to take joy in the child's discovery.

5) *The focus of the reinforcement.* It is possible for reinforcement to be diffuse—a generalized approval or disapproval of an individual— or it may be precisely focused on the adequacy of the child's performance. Zigler and Kanzer's (1962) research would suggest that the deprived child is more often the recipient of the diffuse type—"Nice, girl, good boy," and the like, while the middle-class child more often has reinforcement focused on the adequacy of his performance. Bernstein's (1961) work on language codes would also suggest that the diffuse, or restricted, response is more characteristic of the lower class. Where reinforcement is diffuse, the child's attention is not directed toward the quality of his performance; he cannot become self-reinforcing in terms of learning to evaluate and to improve his own performances.

On the three stimulus variables, we speculate that deprived children may come to an intervention project such as ours without having had contact with the range and variety of objects and experiences that the middle class takes for granted. In addition, we surmise that because of the spatial and temporal disorganization of the home, the child has not been able to learn to process what information does exist in his home. One important goal of the Early Training Project was to construct an environment that would be relatively rich in learning potential but at the same time structured in such a way that figure-ground relationships and predictable sequences might emerge. (Parenthetically, I would like to add here that we have not been happy with the term *enrichment* as applied to such a study as ours. Throwing new information at the child is not only valueless but even harmful if it is not accompanied by carefully devised plans to enable him to process that information and by pacing it with his ability to do so.)

On the five reinforcement variables, we believe that children such as those with whom we worked will come to pre-school projects with their behavior not too well under adult verbal control. They will probably be most responsive to social reinforcement of a non-verbal kind—hugs, pats, facial expressions; they will tend to approach new situations with inhibiting rather than exploring behavior. When they do not inhibit behavior, they are apt to be explosive rather than expressive.

The task in intervention projects with young deprived children, as we see it, is one of taking advantage of the motivational patterns that appear to be already built up, and—starting with these patterns—to gradually move the child toward motivational patterns that appear to be more adaptive to success in school. How this may be done is something else again. We believe it is possible to do so, however, by planning a setting with a high ratio of adults to children, so that there is an opportunity to reinforce when and where needed, and in the appropriate manner. Starting with M&M's or sugared cereal, and with cuddling a child in one's lap, one may move on to more abstract and more delayed rewards. One can help the child with the rude beginnings of a process of internalization of reinforcement. One can serve as a role model—a model oriented toward those qualities that make for adequate achievement in school.

Rather than quick and dirty, ours has been long and dirty research. One must make many extrapolations, many compromises, many quick decisions when one attempts to take any theoretical position in field research. As to whether our rationale is a fruitful one, we do not yet have a definite answer. The fact that our gains in intelligence have held up for a period of 39 months, and that we have evidence of diffusion effects is encouraging. We believe the approach looks promising. More time is needed with our children, more attention to subsequent schooling, and more exploration with other groups before we can be sure.

BETTYE M. CALDWELL

VI THE FOURTH DIMENSION IN EARLY CHILDHOOD EDUCATION

Bettye M. Caldwell (A.B. 1945, Baylor University; A.M. 1946, State University of Iowa; Ph.D. 1951, Washington University) is Professor of Child Development and Education, College of Home Economics, Syracuse University, and Director of the Children's Center, Upstate Medical Center, State University of New York. The work described in this report repesents the joint thought and efforts of the author and Dr. Julius B. Richmond. The work has been supported by Grant No. D-156 (R) from the Children's Bureau, Department of Welfare, Social Security Administration, and by Grant No. MH-07649 from the National Institutes of Health, Department of Health, Education, and Welfare.

IT is not often that I am asked to discuss the theoretical position that underlies our work in early infant learning and environmental enrichment. I like to think that one possible reason for that is that what we are doing is so interesting that the research itself draws all the available attention that people have to send our way. However, I suspect that the major reason that no one asks me about it is that I have never done or said anything that would lead anyone to conclude that I have an identifiable theoretical position. And I am not sure that I do. Although a graduate student at the University of Iowa, I did not become a Hullian. I did, however, find more interesting than most of my fellow students Beth Wellman's meticulous recital of data from what I later learned were disparagingly called "The Iowa Studies." I must confess that I was fascinated with the prospect of changing IQ's (though that was not very popular at the time)—the technological aspects of cognitive research intrigued me even then. Later I had some clinical training, but I certainly did not become psychoanalytically-oriented, to use the jargon; in fact, I did not even become a good clinician. One reason was that I did not seem comfortable with the empirics of the clinical situation, and it was becoming obvious even to me that I was an empiricist—right or wrong.

In subsequent periods there have been flirtations with many theo-

71

retical positions. With Skinner (1950), for example—and that could have been a serious one except for the fact that he always insisted that his intentions be considered atheoretical; with Piaget (1952a), only here it was necessary for me to use Hunt (1961) and Flavell (1963) as matchmakers, and that somehow weakens the emotional reaction; with Bowlby (1958), who almost persuaded me that the only important learning task for the human infant was the discovery of its mother; with Montessori (1912), who, I discovered, was really a Skinnerian in disguise (or perhaps vice versa, if I may appear to blaspheme); with Dewey (1902), who should not have been dismissed by modern educators and psychologists any more than he should have so summarily dismissed Montessori; with Hebb (1949) and other neurologizers; and certainly with Bruner (1966), whose vital concern with educational technology strikes in many ways the most responsive chord of all.

But through all of these brief encounters I have remained always a bridesmaid and never a bride, always an eclectic and never a convert; always an empiricist interested in testing specific hypotheses, and never willing to work on problems if the forthcoming answers would supply only another fact to fill in a theoretical mosaic. At my age, I suppose that means that I am destined to be an old maid, for I am now structured so that perhaps no theory would ever want me. But I prefer to switch my metaphor at this point and suggest rather that, like Ulysses, I am part of all theories that I have met. And I am glad. My only regret is that I have not had meaningful encounters with still other theoretical systems.

Through this developmental period, the debates of the theorists have interested and amused me, but I have always remained a little bit aloof from their struggles and their polemics. Those are exercises for the bigger minds, I thought. While paying lip service with students to the need for integrating theories, I always felt that our big need was for *data*—for facts, for answers to specific questions. And, as a consequence, I have been content to remain an hypothesis-tester. But now my colleague, Julius B. Richmond, and I, and the many people working in one or another capacity on our project, find ourselves testing a big hypothesis. And big hypotheses have a way of looking and sounding like small theories. So it is with our current efforts.

And what is that hypothesis? I like to call it, for the general field of human development, *the Inevitable Hypothesis*. It is one that would fit comfortably in any one of the above-mentioned theoretical systems. It deals with four major variables: the developing child's learning ability, the environment in which this learning occurs, the input that the child receives, and time. The fourth variable—time—is obviously the "fourth dimension" of my title. As now being tested, our hypothesis looks at all these major variables in a context of deprivation of environmental experience, but this restriction is not crucial to the hypothesis in its broadest form. Specifically it states that the first three years of a child's life represent the most important period for priming a child's cognitive, social, and emotional development—a critical period, if you will —and that it is during this period that the environment will exert maximum effect for either facilitation or inhibition of the child's genetic potential for development.

Ah, you might demur, that is not your hypothesis; that is Bloom's hypothesis (1964). And, to be sure, it is, and we are grateful to Bloom for such a concise and articulate inductive statement of the hypothesis, together with the painstaking summarization of the research literature of the past thirty years or so that relates to its tenability. To quote from the preface of Bloom's book, which was published shortly after we began our project: "Variations in the environment have greatest quantitative effect on a characteristic at its most rapid period of change and least effect on the characteristic during the least rapid period of change." He then goes on to document the fact that for many human characteristics, and certainly for such variables as physical growth and intelligence, that period of most rapid change is during the first three or four years of life.

But then still others might rebut—That is neither your hypothesis nor Bloom's hypothesis. J. McV. Hunt (1961) has been suggesting for five years now that we need to pay more attention to the importance of the very early years, and particularly so when there is evidence that a child has been deprived of "standard" environmental supports. Likewise the exciting work of the last decade or so in the fields of developmental neurology forces acceptance of the necessity for optimal amounts of early stimulation appropriate for a particular sensory channel if the neural systems which monitor that pattern of stimulation are to develop properly. So is it their hypothesis? Then, again, there is the rich and abundant data from the animal behaviorists (Hebb, 1947; Thompson and Heron, 1954), suggesting that early experience is crucial for proper development of problem-solving and interest in the environment. Many workers have come to the conclusion that the development of intelligent behavior in animals is profoundly influenced by the variety and extent of experiences which the animals have in earlier developmental periods.

A previous wave of interest in pre-school education could also have comfortably accommodated our hypothesis. I know of no more exciting study in the psychological literature than the report by Skeels and Dye (1939) on the fantastic spurts in development shown by a group of retarded infants who were transferred from a standard institution (orphanage) to a ward for mentally retarded adolescent girls, in contrast to a pattern of decline in a control group remaining in the institution. The study seemed too improbable at the time for people to realize its implications. And the fact that these changes were not evanescent is attested to by recent follow-up data indicating that the gains shown by the children were largely sustained into adulthood. Whatever the methodological limitations of the original study (the possibility that the transferred and retained infants were not perfectly matched), this is a remarkable social experiment.

There is at least one other area which should have led to our hypothesis but which, paradoxically, probably provided the main inertial force that prevented an effector system from being started. This is the research and clinical concern with the consequences of maternal deprivation. In the early studies which investigated the cognitive consequences of the separation (Goldfarb, 1945; Spitz, 1945), a striking finding was the loss in cognitive efficiency which seemed to be associated with the deprivation. It was so easy and so logical to assume that the major missing ingredient was the consistent emotional rapport with the mother figure. I remember experiencing, a few years ago, a reaction of annoyance upon reading Casler's review (1961) of the literature on maternal deprivation, which he subtitled "a critical review." He concluded that we should not refer at all to "maternal deprivation" but should instead call the phenomenon by its true name—sensory deprivation. What difference does it make, I recall asking myself, whether we call it sensory deprivation if we are still forced to conclude that the mother is the best available "package" of sensory stimulation? Any deprivation would still be "maternal." But since that paper, the reviews of Siegel and Haas (1963), and Stolz (1960), and the studies of Siegel, Stolz, Hitchcock, and Adamson (1959), Gardner, Hawkes, and Burchinal (1961), Hoffman (1961), Yarrow (1961), and Caldwell, Herscher, Lipton, Richmond, Stern, Eddy, and Drachman (1963), have shown that young children can sustain with no clear loss in functional efficiency an emotional tie with a mother figure even under conditions of intermittency of contact.

Such data force a reconsideration of the semantics of deprivation. The term we use may not only make a difference in the inferences we make about etiology; it may also make a profound difference in the area of social technology and innovation. As long as we use the label *maternal deprivation,* we are implying that the mother is an essential source of stimulation for all children during the infancy period. (I stress the time factor here, as all the literature on maternal deprivation stressed the importance of keeping this relationship inviolate during the infancy period. Society has already given formal approval to a disruption of the relationship at age five or six, or perhaps three or four. But in some states it is actually against the law to do anything that would disrupt or weaken this relationship prior to age three.) This implication may turn out to be one of the most misleading deductions of all time. Please understand that I have nothing against mothers. I happen to be very favorably disposed to them and to think that, next to children, they are nature's noblest creatures. I just happen not to have complete faith in them as teachers during the period I happen to think is the most important in the child's entire life.

So with all this as background—all of it basically a disclaimer of our right to any credit for the idea—I should like to repeat the designation we have given—not our theory—our hypothesis: the Inevitable Hypothesis. And it is an hypothesis which can be deduced from many theories. So, as well as being atheoretical, I think it is not having delusions of grandeur to claim that it is also to some extent pantheoretical.

Description of Children's Center Program

Since October of 1964 we have been operating in Syracuse, New York, an educationally oriented day-care center for children between the ages of 6 months and 3 years. This program represents our attempt to test the hypothesis that the optimal time for beginning an enrichment program is during the first three years of life. The unit is small, with 25 children, divided into three age groups, in attendance. In all three groups the educational philosophy is similar, although obviously the specific activities programmed for the subgroups varies according to age. Controls for the project are drawn from a longitudinal study of early learning patterns in which the children are observed and assessed at different points in the life cycle, but not provided any specific intervention other than the amount automatically involved in participation in the longitudinal study.

Almost all the children enrolled in the program are from families whose economic and cultural resources are limited. Occasional exceptions have been made, but in general this selection principle has prevailed. Although the daily attendance pattern is individualized, most children are in attendance six to nine hours daily, five days a week. A sliding fee schedule is worked out by the project social worker, with most families paying token fees ranging from nothing at all to twelve dollars per week. These fees include not only the specialized care provided by the teaching, nursing, and research staff, but also lunches and snacks, plus transportation to and from the Center. Thus, subsidization by research funds is essential to the conduct of the program. The Center is housed in a very inelegant building on the periphery of the campus of the Upstate Medical Center. After about six months of operation, the amount of available space was enlarged slightly by the addition of a trailer, which now houses the infant group (see Fig. 1).

Perhaps the most concise statement of the general philosophy that guided the development of the program can be found in a quote from an earlier paper by Caldwell and Richmond (1964):

> The basic goal of the Center is simple but global: to provide what is regarded as the highest quality care for young children. . . . Every event arranged for a given child will be directed toward the task of helping him to become maximally aware of the world around him, eager to participate in it, and confident that what he does will have some impact on it. That is, the programmed environment will attempt to develop powers of sensory and perceptual discrimination, an orientation toward activity, and the feeling of mastery and personal accomplishment which appear so essential for the development of a favorable self-concept (pp. 485–486).

In trying to translate this philosophy into a program, we have found helpful a model which specifies three areas of influence in which we have an opportunity to facilitate the development of the child and to program specific learning activities. These are as follows:

1) *Personal-social attributes.* Much of the literature on deprived children has been devoted to an almost monotonous enumeration of personal characteristics of the children which set them descriptively apart from middle-class children and which may explain the learning difficulties which often begin to plague the children soon after their introduction to formal education. Accepting for the moment the descriptive validity of these deficits (although they are undoubtedly over-generalized in the literature), one could turn them around into program goals. These goals include: increasing the child's sense of trust

FIGURE 1. EXTERIOR OF CHILDREN'S CENTER.

in adults (and in events), fostering a positive self-concept, increasing achievement motivation, improving social skills (such as the ability to take turns, "veneer" behavior such as manners, etc.), encouraging the feeling of a sense of mastery, increasing curiosity and exploratory behavior, helping the child learn to tolerate delayed gratification, and encouraging independent intellectual endeavor. These are conceptualized as representing broad personal-social attributes, and influencing them will involve programming teachers' responses and the creation of a supportive learning atmosphere, more than programming any type of specific learning activities.

2) *Sensory, perceptual, and cognitive functions.* This category refers simply to any kind of sensori-motor or conceptual procedure necessary for the task of information-processing. Included under this rubric are: listening, watching (attending), classifying, evaluating (counting, ordering), coordinating and relating, remembering, conceptualizing, solving problems, and forming learning sets. Also included are more complex patterns of receptor-effector integration such as duplicating and producing from memory both sounds (talking) and visual patterns

(drawing and writing). It will be noted that these functions can be classified as ranging from simple to complex, as requiring intra- or intersensory organization (see Birch and Lefford, 1963). It is hypothesized that these operations can be influenced by programming the learning activities arranged for the children.

3) *Culturally Relevant Knowledge.* The third way in which the enrichment program will influence the learning careers of the children is by broadening their experiences and facilitating their acquisition of culturally relevant knowledge. This will involve the constant exposure to new words, experiences, and events leading to images "placed in storage," thence to be called forth in carrying out subsequent cognitive operations. In terms of the curriculum, this involves programming the content of what is presented to the children. Experience in the current Children's Center program has suggested that this type of topical or content organization helps to keep the interest of children (even toddlers and babies) and teachers at a high level as well as to highlight certain relatively more valuable bits of information from the child's point of view. Also, by planning activities that relate to the various cognitive functions within many content areas, one can hopefully help to establish the generalization that the functions or processes themselves are content-free.

A schematic summary of these three interdependent areas of influence, together with the type of programming appropriate to each of the areas is shown in Table I.

At this point in time it is difficult to present any definitive data about the effectiveness of our program. The main deterrent is that, logistically, it was not possible to start collecting data on the controls at exactly the same time as on the enrichment subjects. Furthermore, even though the program officially began approximately a year and a half ago, it took some time before a full quota of subjects was enrolled in the Center. Accordingly, it will be some time before we can present data demonstrating the precise effects of the program.

However, in order to reassure ourselves that such a program was at least not harming our subjects—a possibility which was considered by representatives of the point of view that the only appropriate day care arrangement for a child younger than 3 is with his own mother in his own home—we recently evaluated the progress of all the children who had participated in the program for more than three months. At the time of the first examination, the children represented in the analysis ranged in age from 6.7 to 43 months. (During the first few months of the program, at a time when families needing such a service

TABLE 1

SCHEMATIC MODEL FOR STRUCTURING THE EDUCATIONAL ACTIVITIES

FOR A DEVELOPMENT-FOSTERING ENVIRONMENT

Area of Influence:	Including:	Involves programming:
1) Socioemotional attributes conducive to a positive orientation toward self, others, and events.	Sense of trust Positive self concept Achievement motivation Persistence Social skills Sense of mastery Curiosity about environment Delay of gratification Independent behavior Joy of living	The interpersonal environment The experiential environment The physical-spatial environment
2) Motor, perceptual and cognitive functions that facilitate adaptive behavior	Motor agility and balance Fine muscle coordination Ability to attend and discriminate Classification and evaluation Formation of learning sets Problem solution Memory Attention span Communication ability Artistic expression	The experiential environment The physical-spatial environment The interpersonal environment
3) Culturally relevant knowledge	Words, phrases, sentences Storehouse of experiences	The experiential environment The physical-spatial environment The interpersonal environment

had not yet begun to beat a path to our door, we accepted a few children beyond the anticipated 3-year age ceiling.) The initial mean IQ (Stanford-Binet for children over 2, Cattell Infant Intelligence Scale for children under 2) for the total group was 104.5. The subsequent mean IQ for the group, after a mean enrichment interval of 7.5 months, was 110.1. Since for this analysis we had no appropriate control group, we examined the distribution of differences to determine whether they differed significantly from zero. The mean difference of 5.6 quotient points was significant at the .01 level of probability. It is particularly noteworthy that, on the average, the children in the project showed relative gains during a period when quotients—particularly those for children from disadvantaged backgrounds—tend to drop. Thus we felt reassured that, whatever the eventual outcome, we certainly did not seem to be in any way damaging the overall cognitive development of the children and that, furthermore, there was every reason for optimism that we were significantly benefiting them. In the data there were suggestions that the children from the most disadvantaged and disorganized homes showed the greatest rate of gain, and that those who had attended longer gained more than those who had been exposed to the enrichment experience for less than the median period. However, longer attendance for a larger group of subjects will be necessary before this can be determined conclusively.

In addition to changes in intelligence test scores, the children also made many gains in the area of social competence and showed no unusual number of emotional symptoms during their participation in the project. During this first year of operation we were even reassured that such a group program did not necessarily have to mean an increase in the number of physical illnesses, a possibility which had been of concern to us. All in all, we are quite reassured after these first few months and look forward to subsequent years of functioning during which time the growth pains of this first year will have subsided and the growth gains of the children hopefully demonstrated.

Summary

Implicit in this presentation is a plea to pay closer attention to the fourth dimension—time—in current research concerned with the inauguration of enriching enducational programs. The project briefly described here represents an attempt to put to empirical test the general hypothesis that the timing of enrichment experiences may be as important as the nature of the experiences themselves. The specific hypothesis that the first three years represent the period when enrichment will have the greatest generalized impact has been labeled the Inevitable Hypothesis, in that evidence from both physiological and psychological investigations point to the logic of this point of view.

I arrogantly referred to our work as a test of the Inevitable Hypothesis. For the basic hypothesis, we can claim no original credit; however, we are pleased that we have been able to activate a program designed to provide a formal test of it. Other such tests will soon also be in motion. However, there is one further aspect to this inevitability that is just a little bit frightening, and which I am reluctant to articulate. That is the inevitability that comes from failure to produce effects when enrichment efforts are presented to older children, adolescents, and adults. Most of us engaged in such efforts—no matter how much lip service we pay to the genetic potential of the child—are passionate believers in the plasticity of the human organism. We need desperately to believe that we are all born equalizable. With any failure to demonstrate the effectiveness of compensatory experiences offered to children of any given age, one is entitled to conclude parsimoniously that perhaps the enrichment was not offered at the proper time. Due to our massive intervention efforts with older children (that is, public school) —albeit some of them may be ill-conceived and poorly executed (as may be the case with our own project)—there is essentially only one way that we can go along the fourth dimension of age-time. That, of course, is downward. And one hears mention of the possibility that, if our pre-school programs do not accomplish what we would hope, we should begin at an earlier age. That is an aspect of the Inevitable Hypothesis that I do not like, for it is incumbent upon us to continue to search for effective ways of achieving maximal impact at every age. And, finally, may I suggest that in such attempts at designing and carrying out effective educational programs, we have an incomparable opportunity to understand the process of development. For undoubtedly the best way to understand any social process is to try to influence it.

CYNTHIA P. DEUTSCH

and

MARTIN DEUTSCH

VII BRIEF REFLECTIONS ON THE THEORY OF EARLY CHILDHOOD ENRICHMENT PROGRAMS

Cynthia P. Deutsch (A.B. 1948, University of Missouri; Ph.D. 1953, University of Chicago) is Senior Research Scientist, Institute for Developmental Studies, and Professor of Education, School of Education, New York University. Martin Deutsch (B.A. 1943, M.A. 1947, Ph.D. 1951, Columbia University) is Director of the Institute for Developmental Studies and Professor of Early Childhood Education, School of Education, New York University.

TO present a theoretical point of view and some program description in so brief a paper is a difficult task. In the interest of brevity, references have been largely omitted, and no attempt has been made to list experimental evidence for many of the assumptions explicitly discussed, nor to indicate the particular historical development of, or collateral references for, the ideas presented. Also, no attempt has been made to compare or contrast one point of view with another, or one programmatic application with another. Instead, what follows is a brief—at times almost telegrammatic—statement of our theoretical point of view, the assumptions which underlie our programming, and some description of the program involved.

There are several basic theoretical assumptions which are at the foundation of our thinking and programming. The first assumption is that environment plays a major role in the development of cognitive skills and of the functional use of intellectual capabilities, such as learning how to learn. The environmental role is probably greatest in the large central area of the continuum of intellectual skill, with biological factors making their greatest contribution at the lowest and the highest ends. Environment influences the development of cognitive processes as well as the content of thought and ideas. The assumption is that processes develop either as a result of the *interaction* between the neural substrate and the environmental stimuli, or as a result of the *impact* of the external stimuli on the neural substrate.

83

The second assumption is that the impact of different aspects of the environment is different for different functions at different times. A corollary to this is that environmental influences on the development of particular functions are greatest at particular times. One hypothesis is that this influence is greatest at those times when the functions being influenced are having their period of most rapid growth; presumably this is correlated with the period of most rapid growth and consolidation of the neural substrate which subsumes the particular function. Since the neural substrate remains functional even in a more consolidated form—after its period of fastest development—this amounts to an *optimal* time, rather than a critical time, hypothesis: a much more optimistic position with respect to influencing fuctional growth.

A second corollary to this assumption is that the various psychological functions have different "adequate stimuli"; not only are certain functions more open to influence at certain times, but also the kinds of stimuli which influence development in one area may not do so—or may do so to a lesser degree—in another area.

A third assumption is that some types of environments are consistently more stimulating to cognitive development than others. In general, the social class rubric yields consistent categories in this respect, with lower-class and slum environments contributing fewer or less well-timed or less adequate stimuli to cognitive development than middle- and upper-class environments.

A fourth assumption is that cognitive development proceeds by stages, and these probably follow a consistent order. This would be especially so within particular areas; perhaps it would be less true for the timing or progression of different, relatively independent abilities. There is a variety of somewhat conflicting views of stages in cognitive development. While Piaget's seems to offer the most logical basis for formulating enrichment programs, we do not espouse or follow one to the exclusion of others from consideration. (This assumption relates only to the *existence* of stages, not to their specific definition. The correct identification of the stages will still involve a massive empirical effort.)

A fifth assumption, related to the fourth, is that some kinds of skills or abilities are basic to others, and that, in general, there are fewer basic skills than there are more specific ones. This relationship would be diagrammed as an inverted pyramid, with each basic skill contributing to a number of adjacent specific ones, and those specific ones, in turn, being basic to some which are narrower and more specific. This basic-specific progression pertains both to temporal relationships and to generality of functions. For example, visual discrimination must develop before reading can be acquired, but visual discrimination ability underlies artistic skill, driving ability, and various other functions as well as reading.

These theoretical assumptions about environment and development underlie our programmatic formulations and provide the source of many of the hypotheses investigated in our basic research projects. Other assumptions, or hypotheses, rest on these and directly underlie the action research and demonstration programs which we conduct.

One such major assumption is that the proper tasks for early childhood education for disadvantaged children include identification of the stimulation "lacks" in the environment; diagnosis of the areas of retardation in cognitive development of the children; prescription of particular stimuli, and strategies, and techniques for their presentation in order to accelerate the development of the retarded functions; and evaluation of the efficiency of the techniques used. We will discuss each of these activities in turn, recognizing that this creates the impression of a rather artificial separation of each from the others, but doing so in the interests of clarity of exposition; in practice, of course, most of the activities should be strongly interrelated, and a recycling and feedback process is constantly in operation.

The identification of the stimulation "lacks" in the environment involves some knowledge about slum environments, family structure in various disadvantaged groups, child-rearing practices, and the atmosphere in different homes. Since stimulation lacks are in part inferred from functional retardations and poor performance in various skills, some of this diagnosis must go on simultaneously. Relevant to the analysis of the environment is the fact that social-class groups are far from homogeneous on most parameters, and they are undoubtedly heterogeneous in the provision of cognitive stimuli for their children. This heterogeneity can be put to good use in the process of determining stimulus-behavior relationships. An instrument currently being developed and analyzed at the Institute for Developmental Studies is the "Deprivation Index." Its purpose is to subdivide large social-class groupings into smaller, deprivation-level ones in a way which will be meaningful for predicting children's performance on verbal and intellective measures. (The most complete description of the "Deprivation Index" so far is in a paper by Whiteman, Brown, and Deutsch, "Some effects of social class and race on children's language and intellectual abili-

ties," 1966.) The goal is the development of instruments which will subdivide groups into smaller and smaller units in order to define specific
background stimulation-behavioral development relationships.

The diagnosis of the areas of retardation in particular children and
in groups of children involves application of a number of techniques,
more and less well suited to the purpose, and broad-scale normative
studies of cognitive abilities of children at various ages. Standardized
tests have been used largely for holistic measures such as IQ, though
use has also been made of subtest patterning on such tests as the Illinois Test of Psycholinguistic Abilities. Specific measures of particular
functions have also been employed, many of them still in experimental
stages. With these measures, large groups of children from different
background categories must be tested in order to obtain some picture
of the relative strengths and weaknesses to be found in different populations. Among the measures in this category are modifications of
some of Piaget's techniques, the Kendler and Osler concept formation
paradigms, the Continuous Performance Test (to measure vigilance or
attention), the Wepman Test of Auditory Discrimination, some specially constructed auditory discrimination measures, and the like. (An
Institute for Developmental Studies Index of Tests [1965] gives pertinent data about each one used, including the samples to which it was
administered.)

An important question raised by the decision to seek out the areas
of retardation in development is: On what level does one seek deficits?
If only the most complex areas, such as reading, are analyzed, then
the factors which may contribute to deficits might be missed. On the
other hand, if only the smallest definable components, such as visual
perception of the diagonal, are measured, then a great deal of time
might be spent in seeking procedures to train a skill that may not be
too important to overall functioning and that, perhaps, would develop
as a by-product of some other training procedure anyway. This is one
situation in which the middle-ground truly seems the best answer—at
least until it can be tested. The middle-ground between perception of
the diagonal and reading, for example, might be visual discrimination.

With the necessity to prescribe particular techniques for the stimulation of the functions found to be retarded, we arrive at one of the
most difficult points of procedure, the one about which probably the
least is known. Essentially, this is a problem in curriculum formulation,
and a certain amount of trial and error is inevitable. However, certain

further assumptions, prescriptions, caveats, and requirements underlie our development of training techniques.

It is easy to assume that the kinds of experiences which should be provided are those which the child has lacked; it is this assumption which lies behind taking children on various trips—to the zoo, to museums, and the like—and expecting that development will be stimulated in response to the trips. The assumption is not a true one, however: experiences missed at one age or developmental level cannot be retrieved at another. In order to conduct a special enrichment program, one must assume that functions which would have developed, or developed more fully, in response to the missed stimulation can later be retrieved. But that development at a later time must be stimulated by experiences which are consistent with the child's level of development, cognitive organization, and knowledge at the later, rather than at the earlier, time. Here, the theoretical assumption, stated earlier, that cognitive development proceeds in stages, is relevant. The formulation of curriculum procedures must be consistent with the cognitive level, or stage, achieved by the child at that time. This will be recognized as a variant of Hunt's concept of the "match."

The concept is also a clinical truism: If an adult is suffering poor interpersonal relationships because his childhood deprivation of parental love and attention prevented his working out initial identifications and relationships with his parents, it would not be therapeutic, even if it were possible, to treat the adult as a child and recreate the primary family—that is, to supply at 25 the exact experiences which he lacked at 5 or 10. Instead, the aim must be to help him develop, by a method appropriate to his adult level, the same skills he would have learned years before by a method appropriate to the childhood years.

The same principle holds true for the formulation of compensatory educational procedures. There is no logic to assuming that a simple supplying *now* of what was missing *then* will have a beneficial effect on the current deficit areas. The experiences and stimuli to be presented in order to ameliorate retardation in function must be appropriate both to the child's developmental level and to his background of experience and knowledge. They must also be appropriate to the level of generality of the skill to be stimulated and developed. Here the whole body of theory and evidence on generalization of response and transfer of training is relevant, though some caution must be exercised in translating procedures into those appropriate for disadvantaged children. Often, tasks which are apparently simple ones, composed of single units, are in reality much more complex and must be carefully analyzed and adapted before they can be applied.

Another principle of curriculum development is that the simple provision of a particular experience is typically not sufficient: it must be structured, labeled, and the aspects relevant for the knowledge it is to convey, or the function it is to stimulate, pointed out. And this structure and emphasis must be meaningful for the child in terms of his previous experience and understanding. This point was illustrated particularly strongly for us when we had the opportunity to speak to a number of children of migrant families. These children had traveled thousands of miles in cars and trucks, and at age 10 or 12 had made several round trips between Oregon and Texas. Yet they were not able to answer simple geographical questions, such as mileage or travel time between particular points. Their vast travel experience was cognitively meaningless in these terms because it had never been made meaningful to them: simply experiencing it was not enough. Some of our major reservations about the efficacy of brief and redundant programs stem from this point.

It seems appropriate to state briefly what we consider essential for the intervention environment and curriculum. The environment would demand development and stimulate it along certain parameters. It would include sensori-motor stimulation, opportunities for making perceptual discriminations, interacting with a verbally adequate adult, receiving some individual attention, linking words and objects and meaningfully relating them in stories or to varying experiential contexts, being assisted in experiencing positive self-identifications, being encouraged toward task perseverance, and being helped to receive both tangible and verbal rewards for relatively competent performance. Such an environment includes stimulation which would be demanding of responses consistent with achieved developmental capabilities, and which would have sufficient and continual feedback from adults.

In evaluating the effects of curriculum techniques, the testing problems are similar to those discussed under diagnosis, except that the measures used must also be capable of registering the particular changes which are sought. Achievement measures can be used, as well as retesting on particular experimental procedures. Perhaps the most important point about evaluation is the necessity for analyzing performance both in as small units as possible and in their interactions. Often a particular component skill can be the only apparent one to be affected by a particular training procedure, and yet analysis of skill-interaction patterns will reveal changes in the more complex ones as well. This information could be invaluable, not only for its feedback into curriculum planning, but also for the insight it yields into the relationships among particular functions and skills.

Another element to be considered in evaluating the effects of special programs is time. There is no reason to suppose, ipso facto, that all effects will be immediately visible, nor that immediate gains will be maintained. It is possible that continuing enrichment programs in the elementary years will be necessary if these gains are not to be lost. It is highly likely that certain functions need a long time to mature once they are stimulated, while others develop at a fairly rapid rate. It is also likely that some curricula will stimulate development in areas which seem far removed from the content. Further, it is eminently plausible to assume that stimulation of a basic function at a time later than that at which it would ordinarily develop might not automatically yield that consequent development of the more specific skills which it underlies. Many similar questions can be formulated, all pointing to the necessity of an evaluation over time in order to ascertain the effects of an intervention program. To yield the information of which it is capable, evaluation must go on over a period of years.

The use of evaluation techniques constructed for particular populations and now used for disadvantaged children in and outside of enrichment programs raises the further question of whether artificial ceilings are not being imposed on the children's measurement. More experimentation needs to be done with restandardizing old tests on this population.

Following from these statements and assumptions, our enrichment program is under constant evaluation and is constantly in evolution. This year we have special classes for nursery-school-age children, for kindergarteners, and to a limited extent for first- and second-graders. The plan is to carry special enrichment through the third grade for as many children as possible in several successive groups, and then to continue follow-up evaluations through the sixth grade. When we began the program, we believed that such a time trajectory was necessary; today, more than six years later, we know that it is essential.

Our initial results indicate that IQ as well as achievement levels and various verbal functions can be significantly increased as a result of special enrichment programs. But so far they indicate, too, that simple increases in content, such as vocabulary, do not necessarily imply or beget improvement in the more abstract and conceptual functions.

We are now preparing for what we call the "second generation" of research on early childhood education. We believe that the first level of research and demonstration has shown the possibility of arresting or retarding the accumulation of deficit (Deutsch and Brown [1964] have characterized it as a "cumulative deficit") to which these children are almost certainly subject in the absence of special programs. The task now is to refine both the diagnostic instruments and the curriculum techniques so that the disadvantaged children can produce performances which substantially overlap with middle-class norms.

The final goal would demand a further, or "third generation" of research; that is, to develop methods and curricula to enhance the cognitive functioning of all children, and to come closer to ensuring that each individual's intellectual potential will have opportunity to reach its maximum growth and usefulness.

These defined goals are consistent with a step-like approach to enrichment programming, which is, in turn, related to the definition of stages in cognitive development. Through the formulation of stages in enrichment, and their evaluation, the application of programs to children can contribute to theoretical understanding of cognitive stages. It is this kind of process that provides the feedback which enables the continuing evolution of both practice and research.

Contrary to some statements appearing from time to time in the popular press—and to views held on occasion by some government agencies—work in early childhood stimulation is far from done: it is in fact just beginning to develop the necessary prototypical models.

ROBERT D. HESS

and

VIRGINIA C. SHIPMAN

MATERNAL INFLUENCES UPON EARLY LEARNING:
The Cognitive Environments of Urban Pre-School Children

Robert D. Hess (B.A. 1947, University of California; Ph.D. 1950, University of Chicago) is Lee Jacks Professor of Child Education, School of Education, Stanford University. Virginia C. Shipman (B.A. 1952, University of Rochester; M.S. 1954, Pennsylvania State University; Ph.D. 1960, University of Pittsburgh) is Research Associate (Associate Professor) and Lecturer, Committee on Human Development, and Director, Head Start Evaluation and Research Center, University of Chicago. *The research described in this paper was supported by Research Grant No. R34 from the Children's Bureau, Social Security Administration, by the Ford Foundation Fund for the Advancement of Learning, and by grants-in-aid from the Social Science Research Committee of the Division of Social Sciences, University of Chicago.*

Conceptual Orientation

SEVERAL studies now under way at the Urban Child Center of the University of Chicago are designed to describe the maternal influences that shape, or socialize, the cognitive behavior of children. The major study, now nearing completion, is an examination of the effect of maternal behavior upon the growth and structure of the child's thinking and upon his orientation (including achievement motivation) toward the school and formal classroom learning. While we do not discount the significance of genetically or congenitally determined mental resources which the individual child has at his disposal or the developmental sequences through which he may, or perhaps must, proceed, our concern is with the input processes—the features of the external world and the child's interactions with them which are particularly relevant in determining the form his ability will take and the patterns of interaction with adults which will elicit various responses and response sequences.

In line with this orientation, we are studying groups of mothers and children from different social-class levels in an attempt to understand the variations in cognitive experience that children from privileged and underprivileged homes encounter. From this perspective, this is a study of the specific cognitive components of mother-child interaction in different social classes. An examination of the details of cognitive exchange makes it possible to exploit two lines of analysis— the cognitive features of maternal behavior (which have received little research attention in the past) and the description of social-class experience and impact in terms of specific points of exchange between the young child and his environment. Social class is a useful but gross variable—a statement of probability that the child will encounter certain types of experiences. More precise and detailed information is needed in order to understand the effect of social class and of cultural or educational deprivation upon cognitive behavior.

Our project, which began in 1962, is based on the notion that the mother can be viewed as a teacher, as a programmer of input, during the pre-school years and that mothers from different social-class levels will program or socialize the cognitive behavior of their children in different ways. This is not primarily an inquiry about differences in *level* of mental performance by child and mother from different social classes but an investigation of the different *styles* or *strategies* of information processing that the young child develops in interaction with his mother.

The feature of this interactive system which we regard as particularly important is the extent to which the mother and other instruments of the environment provide an array of alternatives for thought and action which permit the development of the child's ability to discriminate and select the relevant stimuli in the environment and to make rational choices among the possibilities that the environment makes available to him. The significance of the mediating functions of maternal and other important figures in the young child's experience, so far as early education and cultural disadvantage are concerned, derives from the fact that the mother-child dyad is part of a larger social system: the nature of the interaction between mother and child reflects the position and circumstances of the family in the community. In short, we argue that the development of thought—that is, strategies for dealing with information and with one's own inclination to act—is most usefully considered in terms of its relationship to the social and cultural structures in which it occurs.

These considerations lead to four related arguments which constitute the conceptual context of the study: first, that strategies for processing information and for dealing with the environment, whether they lead to cultural deprivation or poverty or to affluence, are learned;

second, that a significant part of this learning (and teaching) typically takes place in the early (pre-school) interaction between mother and child; third, that the growth of cognitive processes conducive to success in formal educational settings is fostered in family control systems which offer a wide range of alternatives of action and thought, and it is constricted by systems of control which offer predetermined solutions and few alternatives for consideration and choice; and fourth, that the nature of the dyadic exchange between mother and child is related to the social structure in which the exchange takes place.

Research Plan and Variables

In attempting to delineate the input features of the socializing process, the research focused on three characteristics of the mother-child interaction. The first is the nature of the control or regulatory system employed by the mother in her interaction with the child. We define three types of maternal control.[1] The first of these, *imperative-normative*, is based on appeals to social norms, to what is generally regarded as right and proper, and to the power and authority of the participants; for example: "Girls don't act like that," or, "You'll do that because I told you to," or other arguments based on norms or on the arbitrarily vested power or authority of the rule-enforcing figure. This approach asks the child for a minimum of thought; indeed, it often cuts off thought, giving regulations without rationale or with a rationale based only on tradition or status. The information provided the child is limited. The child is offered no alternative to consider, to compare, to evaluate, to select. It is a system of control based on non-rational appeals, and it does not require complex linguistic communication. (Bernstein, 1961)

In the second type of regulatory maneuvers, *personal-subjective*, authoritarian demands and norms are modified by personal considerations, feelings, and preferences. Where the imperative-normative system imposes the rules of the group, the personal-subjective attends to the motivations, the intent, the inner states of the individual. Control statements such as, "You shouldn't say things like that—they hurt your sister's feelings," or, "How do you think you will feel if the other kids

---

1. This formulation of family control is related to the research and conceptualization of several other researchers, particularly unpublished papers and personal communication with Basil Bernstein, but also of Baldwin (1949), Kohn (1959), and Hess and Handel (1959), as well as our current work.

get better grades than you do?" or, "Do your homework now, you'll feel better when it's done," are examples. The basis of appeal is inter-personal or intrapersonal comfort. This type of regulatory procedure encourages a more specific and complex mode of communication with which to describe the motives and other inner states of the participants. It obviously orients the child to be aware of a somewhat different type of stimulus or cue in his environment than does an appeal to norms.

In the third control maneuver, *cognitive-rational,* appeal is to the results of a sequence of events, a long-term payoff, or a principle which states the rationale behind a rule or demand. Examples are: "If you eat cookies now, you won't want your dinner," or, "You should keep quiet in school because the teacher can't teach when kids talk, and then you won't learn your lessons," or, "Wear your rubbers today so you won't get your feet wet and catch cold and have to stay in bed." These explanations are obviously much more complicated than the imperative appeals. They call for a more complex response on the part of the child, for he must attend to a sequence of ideas and observe the relationships of events which, though separated in time, are brought together in anticipation of alternative consequences which may be ex-pected to follow different immediate actions. They offer more informa-tion, they call for more cognitive activity, language, and attention, and they give the child a means of applying a logic of long-range conse-quences as a basis for behavior. Unlike the normative appeal, this technique orients the child to the future and toward symbolic manipulation of his world.

The relevance of complex language in contrast to simple restricted codes in the process of cognitive development and educability we take as given, although there is still a great deal to be learned about the nature of the relationship between language and the development of thought. Thus the second important concept of the study is that the communication modes of the mother may usefully be described as *elaborated* or *restricted.* This view of communication is taken from the work of Bernstein of the University of London (1961). In his definition, *restricted* codes are stereotyped, limited, and condensed, lacking in specificity and the exactness needed for precise conceptualization and differentiation. Sentences are short, simple, often unfinished; there is little use of subordinate clauses for elaborating the content of the sentence; it is a language of implicit meaning, easily understood and commonly shared. The basic quality of this mode is to limit the range and detail of concept and information involved.

Elaborated codes are those in which communication is individualized and the message is specific to a particular situation, topic, and person. They are more particular, more differentiated, and more precise. They permit expression of a wider and more complex range of thought, tending toward discrimination among cognitive and affective content.

The third cluster of variables and ideas we have used is related to the development of educability in the child, particularly the mother's influence upon the child's understanding of what it means to be a pupil in the public (or private) school. Educability is defined for our purposes as a composite of three attributes: cognitive skills specific to the classroom, motivation to achieve within a formal learning situation, and learning the role of pupil in relation to the class, the teacher, and the authority system of the school. The transition between the methods of control and cognitive exchange in the home and those in the school is especially difficult and important for the child from an underprivileged background. The teacher has less to build on that is familiar and consistent with her own background and frequently, perhaps typically, she has little accurate conception of the experiences with school-type tasks and images of school that the child brings to the classroom. In this connection, we are especially concerned with the images and beliefs the mothers hold about the school and about the role of a parent in relation to the efforts of teachers and the task of the school. This early maternal orientation has consequences for the emergence of the motivation to succeed which the child develops in his initial experiences in the classroom.

This general set of ideas attempts to relate the linguistic and regulatory behavior of the mother to the information-processing strategies and styles induced in her child. By this we mean such things as the child's tendency to adopt an *initiatory, assertive* approach to the world of information around him or a *passive, compliant* stance to new experience, including the teacher and the stimuli of the classroom. Other strategies or styles are expressed in problem-solving behavior, which may be *reflective* or *impulsive,* borrowing the concepts of Kagan and his associates (1963, 1964). Our hypothesis is that the mothers who exercise control through appeals to norms or to status tend to induce styles in their children which are passive, that is, waiting to be told, and impulsive, that is, moving to a solution without reflective thought and comparison of a range of possibilities.

These teaching styles also have implications for the child's *self* concept and for the motivational components of his learning style. This can be clarified by describing briefly some results of the project in which we and our colleagues, Dr. Ellis Olim, Mrs. Roberta Meyer Bear, and Mr. Jere Brophy have been engaged for the past three years. This project includes four groups of Negro mothers and their 4-year-old children—Group A from upper middle-class, professional, and managerial family backgrounds; Group B from skilled-work occupational levels, Group C from unskilled occupational origins. Each group had approximately forty mother-child pairs; all subjects came from intact homes, were economically self-supporting, with equal numbers of boys and girls within each subgroup. A fourth group (D) of similar size was composed of mothers on public assistance who were not living with their husbands or other adult males. The three working-class groups were evenly divided between those from public and those from private housing.

We have studied various aspects of the mothers' behavior—language, concept formation, resources of the home and community, aspirations, and other variables relevant to the cognitive stimulation of the child. Mothers were interviewed in their homes, then brought with their children to the University of Chicago for testing and additional interviewing. This was necessary in order to obtain sessions between mothers and children uninterrupted by noise and by other members of the household, telephone, neighbors, etc. The interview included a number of semi-structured techniques designed to elicit attitudes toward methods of family control and the mothers' orientation toward the school and the teacher. The most useful technique on this point was the question: "Let's just imagine that *(child)* is old enough to go to school for the first time. How do you think you would prepare him? What would you do or tell him?" Two typical responses of the mothers were these:

1) "First of all, I would take him to see his new school, we would talk about the building, and after seeing the school I would tell him that he would meet new children who would be his friends; he would work and play with them. I would explain to him that the teacher would be his friend, would help him and guide him in school, and that he should do as she tells him to. That she will be his mother while he is away from home."

2) "Well, I would tell him he going to school and he have to sit down and mind the teacher and be a good boy, and I show him how when they give him milk, you know, how he's supposed to take his straw and do, and not put nothing on the floor when he get through."

These replies were grouped along the general lines described above; using categories such as *imperatives*—an unqualified injunction or command, such as, "Mind the teacher and do what she tells you to do," or, "Be nice and do not fight," and *instructives*—information or commands which carry a rationale or justification for the rule to be observed, such as, "I would tell him that it is important to mind the teacher. If he doesn't obey the teacher won't be able to teach the lesson." Other data were coded and grouped in various ways in keeping with the orientation of the study.

The conclusion of the testing and interview sessions for each mother-child pair was an observation of the mother's teaching behavior in a semi-structured situation. We brought mother and child to the nursery school, taught the mother three simple tasks involving cognitive and motor performance (sorting objects and copying designs) and asked her to teach these tasks to her child. Her verbal behavior and that of the child were recorded on tape; the non-verbal interaction was described by an observer and recorded on a parallel tape. Here is an illustration from one interaction session in which the mother is attempting to teach the child to sort objects by color:

MOTHER. Do you want a cracker? Now . . . do you want one? . . . You want to sit there? . . . Okay. . . . Mommy will show you something, sit down, here, now you watch, okay? You see these three different sections on the board, hmm? . . . I'm going to put these things together, in three sections, and I'm going to tell you why I'm doing it that way, and then I want you you to be able, you have to listen to Mommy and then you tell me why I did it, okay? . . . (extended pause) Okay.

CHILD. What is that for, Mom?

MOTHER. Wait, you're going to tell me. Now what are these?

CHILD. Trucks.

MOTHER. Trucks, yes. Why did Mommy put these things here? In this section, what is there . . . why did I put all those together? . . . First, I'll tell you, see I'm putting them off, I, I'm . . . making groups, here, and we have three different things to work on, and I put all these in groups because they're all trucks . . . All right? And I put all these together, because they're chairs . . . and I put these things, articles, together because they're all spoons, right? . . . And—okay, now. You see the color of this truck? It's red. . . . And this color is yellow . . . right? And this color is green, just like your. . . . Okay. . . . Now I'm going to group all the red things together, I've got a red truck, a red chair, and a red spoon. I've got a

green truck, a green chair, a green spoon. Have a yellow, no,
I've got a yellow truck—wait, let me do it first—a yellow chair,
and the yellow spoon. Now I put this group together 'cause
it's all red. . . . I put this group together because they're all
green . . . and I put this group together because they're all
yellow, right? Okay. Mommy going to do all this over again
and you tell me why I put these things together. . . .

CHILD. Mommy, can I have a turn?

MOTHER. Wait you can have a turn, if you tell me this time, then
you can have a turn, okay now wait . . . then you supposed to
do what I do, you supposed to learn this now. . . . Now why
did Mommy put these things in this section? . . .

CHILD. [?] right there.

MOTHER. Why? . . . You weren't listening were you?

In line with the theoretical context of the study we have concentrated upon these aspects of maternal behavior:

1) the mother's use of various control techniques in dealing with her child;
2) the mother's teaching style in the laboratory teaching situations;
3) orientation toward the school, particularly the mother's feelings of efficacy in relation to the power of the teacher or principal;
4) language from protocols of the interview session;
5) measures of preference in sorting tasks.

The age of the children limited the amount and complexity of information we could obtain, but these measures indicate the cognitive performance of the children:

1) scores on Stanford-Binet IQ test (Form LM);
2) performance in the maternal teaching sessions;
3) concept attainment on the Sigel Sorting Task, which requires the child to group objects and verbalize the basis for his grouping;
4) behavior in the test-taking situation as rated on the face sheet of the Binet.

Additional measures of the children's scholastic and cognitive performance are being obtained in a follow-up study. The association between maternal behavior and these subsequent behavioral data will be reported when the analysis is complete. Evidence that these relationships exist is available in the research of Stodolsky (1965) who did a short-term follow-up on a part of the research group.

Results and Conclusions

Consistent with the familiar social class differences in mental performance, there are marked discrepancies between the upper middle-class and the three working-class groups on all cognitive tasks. Mean intelligence test scores for the mothers (WAIS Verbal IQs) ranged from 109.4 for high-status mothers to 82.4 for mothers from Group D. The range for children was not great—109.4 to 94.5 (Stanford-Binet, Form LM).

One of the most striking differences among the social-status groups was in their verbal behavior. This is reported in detail in papers by Olim (1965) and Olim, Hess, and Shipman (1965). However, Table 1 gives a very gross picture of differences in *verbal output* on open-ended responses to a number of questions asked of all the mothers. (Table 1 shows the total number of lines of type used to transcribe these verbatim protocols.)

TABLE 1

MEAN NUMBER OF TYPED LINES IN THREE DATA-GATHERING

SITUATIONS

	Upper Middle N = 40	Upper Lower N = 40	Lower Lower N = 36	ADC N = 36
School Situations	34.68	22.80	18.86	18.64
Mastery Situations	28.45	18.70	15.94	17.75
CAT card	18.72	9.62	12.39	12.24
Total	81.85	51.12	47.19	48.63

Similar differences existed in the *control strategies* of the mothers as indicated in the content of the responses to open-ended questions. Figure 1 shows the proportion of comments made in response to the first-day question which were categorized as *imperative*. In passing,

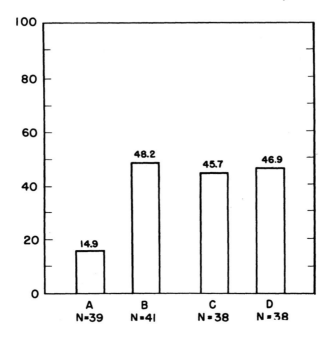

FIGURE 1. PERCENTAGE USE OF IMPERATIVE RESPONSES ON FIRST DAY
PROTOCOLS (MEANS).

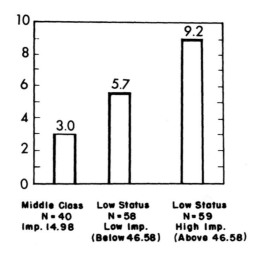

FIGURE 2. NUMBER OF NON-VERBAL RESPONSES ON SIGEL SORTING
TEST BY CHILDREN WHOSE MOTHERS ARE HIGH AND LOW ON IMPERATIVE
RESPONSES (MEAN SCORES).

it should be mentioned that the tendency to use imperative statements is negatively related to the child's cognitive performance for both the total group and within the three working-class groups (see Fig. 2).

There were also differences among the social-status groups in their behavior in the teaching sessions that appear to be related to style rather than to intelligence. In the third teaching session, we use an Etch-a-Sketch, a commercially available toy. This is a flat, small box with a screen on which lines can be drawn by a device inside the box controlled by two knobs: one for horizontal movement, one for vertical. The mother is assigned one knob, the child the other, and the mother is given five designs which are to be copied, or reproduced, on the screen of the Etch-a-Sketch through cooperative effort. It is the mother's task to instruct and guide the child through the necessary maneuvers. One helpful technique is to show the child the design which is to be copied. Usually this was placed on the table where the mother and child were working, but a considerable number of mothers did not utilize the design in working with the child on this task. Figure 3 shows the percentage of mothers in each status group who

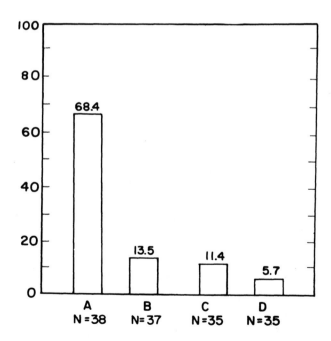

FIGURE 3. PERCENTAGE OF MOTHERS USING MODEL FOR AT LEAST FOUR DESIGNS DURING ETCH-A-SKETCH TEACHING SESSION.

showed their children at least four of the five designs they were asked to help reproduce. It is in the use of simple, orienting techniques such as these, as well as in the more difficult problems, that social-class differences appear.

The performance of the children showed similar social-class differences, as indicated in Table 2 which shows the relative success of children in each social-status group in attaining the two concepts involved in the first maternal teaching session. Similar differences appear on other measures, although there is considerable variability in the magnitude of these social-class discrepancies from one task to another.

TABLE 2

DIFFERENCES AMONG STATUS GROUPS IN CHILDREN'S

PERFORMANCE IN TEACHING SITUATIONS (8-BLOCK TASK)

Social Status	Percentage Distribution					N
	Placed Correctly	One-Dimension Verbalized		Both Verbalized		
A. Short O:						
Upper-middle	75.0	52.5	70.0 °	25.0	33.3 °	40
Upper-lower	51.2	29.3	57.1	2.4	4.8	41
Lower-lower	50.0	27.5	55.0	15.0	30.0	40
ADC	41.5	19.5	47.1	2.4	5.9	41
B. Tall X:						
Upper-middle	60.0	47.5	79.2 °	27.5	45.8 °	40
Upper-lower	48.8	31.7	65.0	17.1	35.0	41
Lower-lower	35.0	17.5	50.0	7.5	21.4	40
ADC	26.8	9.8	36.4	0.0	0.0	41

° Percentage of those who placed object correctly.

The study was designed to examine these social-class differences in specific terms of maternal behavior and mother-child interaction. Reporting an obtained correlation of —.41 between social-status level and Binet IQ, or .49 between mother's WAIS Verbal IQ and her child's Binet IQ, does not sufficiently explain such differences. We wish to determine the predictive power of certain maternal behaviors, and to be more specific about the behaviors encompassed in a global measure like IQ. To do this, we computed multiple *r*'s and found that maternal behaviors are as useful or better than IQ or social class in predicting the child's cognitive behavior. The performance of children in our teaching situations can similarly be predicted with considerable efficiency; for example, using three such teaching variables, the multiple *r* with performance was .64; the multiple *r* using the mother's IQ, the child's IQ, and social-class level as predictors was .47. When all measures were combined, the multiple *r* was .67, or only slightly higher than that obtained by using maternal teaching variables alone.

This general pattern is repeated in other sectors of the data. The child's performance on cognitive tasks is associated with specific maternal behavioral variables at a level comparable to or higher than that obtained by the more traditional measures of maternal IQ and social class. We regard this finding as progress toward identifying the specific maternal behavior in the mother-child interactional system which codes and translates social class and maternal intelligence into modes of interaction that affect the child's cognitive processes.

It appears that the learning styles and information-processing strategies that the child obtains in these early encounters with his cognitive and regulatory environment may set limits upon the potential mental growth of the child unless an intervention program is instituted which *resocializes* or *reeducates* the child toward more effective cognitive strategies.

The cognitive environment of the culturally disadvantaged child is one in which behavior is controlled by imperatives rather than by attention to the individual characteristics of a specific situation, and one in which behavior is neither mediated by verbal cues which offer opportunities for using language as a tool for labeling, ordering, and manipulating stimuli in the environment, nor mediated by teaching that relates events to one another and the present to the future. The meaning of deprivation would thus seem to be a deprivation of meaning in the early cognitive relationships between mother and child. This environment produces a child who relates to authority rather than to rationale, who may often be compliant but is not reflective in his behavior, and for whom the consequences of an act are largely considered in terms of immediate punishment or reward rather than future effects and long-range goals. If this general picture is valid, it would seem that the goal of early education is to promote the development of strategies or structures for dealing with information, rather than merely transmitting a supply of concepts, information, and mental skills.

LAWRENCE KOHLBERG

MONTESSORI WITH THE CULTURALLY DISADVANTAGED: A *Cognitive-Developmental Interpretation and Some Research Findings*

Lawrence Kohlberg (A.B. 1949, Ph.D. 1958, University of Chicago) is Associate Professor, Department of Psychology and Committee on Human Development, and Director of the Child Psychology Training Program, University of Chicago. The research discussed here was funded by Office of Economic Opportunity Grants O.E.O. 1284 and ILL. CAP-66-9255. A complete report of the project is obtainable at cost from the author.

I HAVE recently been conducting a small research project evaluating the effects of a Montessori pre-school program upon the cognitive development of a group of Negro children from families in the Aid to Dependent Children category. The program has involved bringing a group of these children into classrooms for middle-class children in a parent-organized Montessori school in Hyde Park. In addition to the usual concern of a Montessori program, some special efforts are being directed at encouraging verbalization and representational play in these children. The mothers of the children also meet in a group with two social workers.

Let me quickly summarize our current sketchy research results and then move to some of the conceptual issues involved in the Montessori approach. During the summer, three Head Start classrooms were held in the Ancona Montessori school in the context of a general summer school program. Two of the classrooms were integrated: they were composed of half Head Start children, half middle-class children. The third classroom was entirely Head Start. One integrated classroom was a Montessori classroom, the other was run by an elementary schoolteacher stressing readiness for public school, while the non-integrated classroom was run by a teacher who had previously worked in, and believed in, a permissive child-development oriented pre-school.

Alternate forms of the Stanford-Binet were given at the beginning and the end of the program. There was little overall change in IQ, but there was some patterning by classroom. The two integrated classrooms remained unchanged, with only a 2 or 3 point increase in mean IQ's. There was, however, a small but significant *decrease* of 5 points in the IQ's of the children in the non-integrated permissive classroom. A careful set of behavior ratings made by the testers suggests the basic reason for this IQ decrease. For the permissive classroom, there was a 3-point mean increase in ratings of distractability in the test situation on a 9-point scale.[1] There was a slight decrease in distractability in the other classrooms. Furthermore, drop in IQ was correlated with increased distractability; the rank order correlation between the two change measures was .63. Behavior observations in the classroom support this rating data. Glen Nimnicht reports that the New Nursery School project at Colorado State College has also found some decreases in IQ in permissive non-integrated classroom programs for culturally disadvantaged children.

In light of this absence of IQ change in the summer Head Start program, the IQ changes found in our year-long Montessori program seem astonishing to us at the moment. Our ten ADC Negro children showed a mean IQ increase of 17 points between October and January.[2] A comparison group of middle-class children in the same classroom showed a mean increase of 10 IQ points in this time. The increase of our ADC children was matched by an increase in attention as reflected by a mean 2-point decrease in the distractability ratings. A correlation of .65 was found between IQ increase and attention increase.[3]

1. The distractability scale was as follows:
1) Completely absorbed by task. Maintains interest throughout, remains oriented to E between items.
3) Interested and attentive, with little attention to things external to the test.
5) Normal attentiveness. Tasks elicit sufficient attention, though attention may occasionally wander between items.
7) Attracted by things external to the test, but can return to task. If child tries to maintain attention, it is with some effort.
9) Difficult to get and hold attention.
The tester's ratings correlated significantly with the teacher's classroom-behavior ratings on the same scale, as well as with an experimental measure of stability of attention. This measure is one of stability of reaction time in response to a light signal with varying preparatory intervals. Intercorrelations between rating and experimental measures of attention are reported in Krebs (1967).
2. This IQ increase was apparently not due to artifacts in IQ retesting. Different forms of the test and different examiners were employed in retesting. The children of average IQ on first testing increased as much as did the children of low IQ on first testing.
3. It should be noted that these IQ attention changes occurred in four months in the winter program when no substantial change occurred in the two-month summer program, even in the summer classroom taught by the same teacher. In part, this difference is probably due to the short duration of the summer program; in part, to the general first summer Head Start confusion, with the

Let us, for the moment, take our findings with the Binet as suggesting that there is something about a Montessori program which can facilitate cognitive functioning. What might it be which is truly effective in the Montessori approach? Unfortunately, it is very difficult to discuss this problem, because Montessori represents three distinct things: a set of general ideas, a set of specific materials, and finally an ideology and a social movement with a strong insistence on orthodoxy. For purposes of intellectual discussion, I will ignore the contemporary Montessori movement as an ideological group and consider only the ideas of Montessori and the particular materials used to implement them.

Discussion of the Montessori movement as an ideology has often focused on the polarities of structure vs. permissiveness, of work vs. play, and of the cognitive vs. the social-emotional. I wish to go over these dichotomies briefly to indicate that they are false polarities, both in terms of the thought of Montessori and in terms of the findings of psychological research. With regard to the opposition between structure and permissiveness, it is important to distinguish between providing the child with a structured environment and the imposition of discipline upon the child in the sense of the imposition of a large number of rules of behavior upon the child by the teacher's authority. Montessori was clearly a believer in permissiveness if permissiveness is to be opposed to discipline, since she said her method "has for its basis the liberty of the child" (Montessori, 1964). In contrast to discipline, Montessori did believe in ordering the environment to the end of stimulating the development of cognitive order in the child's mind. Montessori would hardly be surprised by recent research findings indicating that moral behavior in school children is more facilitated by cognitive structure variables than it is by punishment, reward, and discipline (Kohlberg, 1966c). As an example, unpublished research by Kounin indicates that variations in effectiveness of teacher structuring of the learning and attentional processes of the classroom are clearly related to amount of classroom misconduct, but that variations in amount and type of punishment and reward are not related to amount of classroom misconduct.

---

head teacher being out of the classroom a good deal in the summer on various advisory and administrative chores. The findings are generally consistent with findings of Weikart, of Gray, of Bereiter and Engelmann of IQ increases of about 15 points in the first six months of quality year long pre-school stimulation programs as opposed to much smaller changes in summer Head Start programs.

With regard to the work-play polarity, Montessori insists that play is not opposed to "work" but to "labor." The child enjoys work, that is, he enjoys performing and solving self-chosen cognitive and practical tasks. Montessori attempted to design intrinsically motivating "work" for the child while firmly prohibiting labor in the sense of teacher-demanded performance of given tasks and teacher-dispensed reward or punishment for such task-performance. Again, Montessori would hardly be surprised by the spate of recent theories and findings supporting her assumption that cognitive and achievement activities are self-rewarding and that their performance need not be based on adult demands and reinforcement (Hunt, 1965; White, 1959).

While Montessori did not oppose pre-school play in the sense of not-work, she did oppose play in the sense of fantasy or the deliberate disregard of "reality."

I have tried to elaborate elsewhere (Kohlberg, 1966b, 1967) my objection both to Montessori's "reality orientation" and to the traditional permissive emphasis on "creativity" and "self-expression" with regard to the issue of symbolic and dramatic play. These objections spring from the Piaget findings on the young child's difficulties in distinguishing reality and appearance, and on the natural developmental appearance of this differentiation without specific adult teaching of "reality orientation." The young child's involvement in symbolic play is neither an unhealthy preoccupation with fantasy, nor—in the adult sense—a manifestation of creativity. Its modulation and decline with age is not the stifling of the child by adult repression but the result of cognitive growth. Recent unpublished research in Israel by Smilansky and Feidelson suggests that the characteristic restriction of stimulation and opportunities for dramatic and symbolic play in culturally deprived homes has some retarding effect on *general* cognitive advance, not only on "creativity" as such. The opportunity to openly engage in make-believe is a facilitating condition for the differentiation of reality and appearance rather than a force leading to fixation in the realm of fantasy. On the other hand, a whole pre-school world devoted to make-believe cannot help stimulate the child's development toward the differentiation of reality and appearance which the elementary school presupposes. To put off "reality" until elementary school, is only to divorce the pre-school world of the subjective from the school world of the objective. What is required is rather a non-repressive modulation which would stimulate the gradual transformation of pre-school cognitive and play energies into more mature reality-oriented forms. While the Ancona program has not moved especially far in this direction, it does balance the usual Montessori emphases with some dramatic, representative and expressive play experiences.

Finally, with regard to the social vs. the cognitive, there appears to be a dual conflict between Montessori and other approaches. In contrast to Montessori, the conventional public school approach and its application to pre-school readiness programs stresses attention to, and social interaction with, the teacher as a central focus of learning. On the other hand, "progressive" pre-school programs stress teacher satisfaction of the child's deeper needs and stress peer group interaction as vehicles for social development. I would argue that this dichotomy in either form is also a false one and that the individual cognitive activity stressed by Montessori may be both more effective from a cognitive view, and more conducive of social development, than are purely group-centered programs. With regard to the cognitive values of individual activities, it is evident that some of the most striking and obvious cognitive defects of culturally disadvantaged children are defects in attention. This obvious fact was shown in our research project by the lower scores of the culturally disadvantaged compared to their middle-class classmates on both rating and experimental measures of attention. It is equally obvious that one of the major reasons for these defects in attention in the disadvantaged is due an environment of constant distraction by siblings and peers. Culturally disadvantaged children in large families and crowded surroundings are never alone with any engrossing task or toy. Our research suggests that a conventional permissive peer-oriented pre-school classroom for the disadvantaged exacerbates these tendencies; when one observes pre-school programs of cognitive stimulation carried on in groups, one is struck by the extent to which such group programs are engaged in an uphill struggle against the distraction of one child by another. There is little doubt that either sustained teacher-pupil dyads or solitary or parallel task-activities much more easily sustain prolonged and stable attentional behavior than do group programs. While the child must learn to attend to cognitive activities in a group, it may be easiest to promote such learning first in a less group-like context.

The Perry Pre-School Project (Radin and Weikart, 1966) report some preliminary data in line with these considerations. This project combined an experimental morning pre-school program with almost daily afternoon home visits by teachers who engaged the child in learning activities. In one year, this program produced Stanford-Binet IQ increases of 12 to 20 points in various groups, as compared to control group increases of 3 to 7 points.

In Weikart's research analysis, children participating in the program were divided into groups of high and low gainers (above and below the median of 17 points in IQ increase). Only two factors were found to distinguish the two groups. The first factor was that low gainers came more often from a public housing project. The second factor was that the siblings of the low gainers entered into the home visit teaching activities much more often than did the siblings of the high gainers. The correlation between IQ gain and percent of visits in which other children participated was —.46. It is likely that this rather striking relationship is not only due to the fact that the participation of the other children interfered with learning in the home visits, but that it produced "poor attenders" who were less likely to learn in the small group pre-school setting.[4]

Montessori believed that her individual self-guided tasks not only led to concrete learnings but stimulated the development of the child's attention. Stable attention, she claimed, developed not from the teacher forcing a passive attention upon some object through authority, but rather from the child's natural interest in objects with which he could interact in an organized way. Observation of both our middle-class and culturally disadvantaged children points to the correctness of Montessori's claim that the young child is capable of very lengthy absorption in a task, if the task is at the right developmental level for the child and if the child is not distracted by adults or other children. While empirical research has not established the existence of a cross-situational "faculty" of attention, it does suggest that there is a consistency to attentional behaviors which is related to, but distinguishable from intelligence (Grim, Kohlberg, and White, 1967; Krebs, 1967), and it is plausible to expect that this "faculty" would be enhanced by the type of opportunity stressed by Montessori.

Given the enhancement of intellectual performance and of attention which the Ancona Montessori program seems to have effected, what is its implication for social development? Perhaps the feature of social development most focused upon by the permissive pre-school approach has been the child's participation and cooperation in the peer group. While this is commonly thought to be a function of the child's deep needs and their satisfaction, research studies suggest that it is closely related to intellectual maturity. Parten and Newhall (1943)

---

4. In this regard, the poorer prognosis for "poor attenders" may be only one of many poorer prognoses for remedial efforts for children. A study of many possible predictors for child psychotherapy indicated that the best predictor of improvement in therapy was a rating of attentiveness (Mayers, 1965).

found maturity or cooperativeness of social peer play was correlated .61 with age and .38 with IQ, so that mental age or cognitive maturity appears to be the prime personality determinant of peer cooperation.

Turning to the aspects of social development focused upon by upholders of conventional school programs, it would appear that moral character or conformity is the most identifiable component of these aspects. Here again the development of intellect and attention appear to be important contributors to this social goal of education. Both teacher's ratings of morality and experimental measures of resistance to cheating correlate moderately with IQ (*r* around .40), and very well (*r* around .60) with experimental measures of attention (Krebs, 1967; Grim, Kohlberg, and White, 1967). It seems likely, then, that the stimulation of cognitive development by the school may be both easier to accomplish and more important in serving the long-range social development of the child than either direct efforts to change the child's deeper emotional needs or the imposition of adult social authority upon him.[5]

Turning from beclouding issues of ideology to Montessori's more unique ideas concerning cognitive stimulation, it must be realized that these ideas were a synthesis of two separate streams of thought in education. The first and, I believe, most basic stream was that of developmentalism, a stream commencing with Rousseau and continuing through John Dewey and Piaget.[6] The second stream of ideas contributing to Montessori's thought was that of the sensationalistic and associationistic psychology of the eighteenth and nineteenth centuries, which saw ideas as based on simple sensations, and which lay behind the methods of Itard and Seguin from which Montessori started.

In common with the general developmentalist line of thought, Montessori has stressed that organism and the mind form a structured whole, that the child is not a little adult but a qualitatively or structurally different organism, that there is an invariant sequence or succession in the structural development of the child's mind, and that this

5. A general review of research suggesting the importance of cognitive stimulation and development for psychosexual development is contained in Kohlberg (1966a); a review indicating the importance of cognitive stimulation in moral development, in Kohlberg (1964, 1966c).
6. I have attempted to provide a general summary of this intellectual tradition in its implications for education: Kohlberg, 1967a. Montessori's own theories are presented in Montessori (1912 and 1965; the latter contains an introduction by J. McV. Hunt relating Montessori's ideas to the Piagetian viewpoint). Detailed description of Montessori methods and materials is found in Montessori (1964). A collection of recent writing on Montessori for the disadvantaged is found in Orem (1967).

sequence indicates that mental development is neither the direct product of maturation nor of environmental teaching, but of the interaction between the structure of the organism and the structure of the environment. These assumptions are most specifically set forth in the Piaget doctrine of stages—where stages refer to qualitative or structural changes in level of thought proceeding through an invariant sequence—a doctrine which has received much recent empirical support. Developmentalists such as Piaget have claimed that the existence of stages indicates that mental structure and development is the product of neither innate maturation nor the direct teaching of the environment, but of structural patterns of interaction between the two. If the child goes through qualitatively different stages of thought, his basic modes of organizing experience cannot be innate or they could not change. Neither can they be the direct result of adult teaching, or they would be copies of adult thought from the start. They must then be due to the reorganizing forces of general forms of social and physical experience upon the child's thoughts, rather than representing direct cultural and verbal learning.

This interactional notion of development is expressed in Montessori's statement that "the mental organism is a dynamic whole, which transforms its structure by active experience obtained from its surroundings."

The notion that experience causes development and transforms structure implies an active role for experience in the developmental view. Developmental experience is assimilation through activity, not simply stimulation undergone. Like Piaget and Dewey, Montessori stresses the notion that competence and epistemic motives exist from the start of life, and the mere presence of appropriate activities will arouse them without the need of extraneous reinforcers for learning.

Pedagogically, the first major implication of the developmentalist doctrine is the creation of *self-directed and self-selected cognitive activities.* According to Montessori (1912), her "method has for its base the liberty of the child; and *liberty* is *activity.*" The emphasis on free activity, is, of course, balanced with a notion of order and control, but the control is to come from the organization of the environment rather than from the direct control of the child's behavior by the teacher. In practice, this means the following:

1) Design of materials in which learning may occur through activity.
2) Free selection of materials or activities at the individual child's own pace.

3) The construction of materials or activities which can be used with minimal instructions (what can be done with materials appears in the doing).
4) Materials designed to be self-correcting, rather than to require judgment of success by the teacher.
5) Construction of a child-sized world in which as many activities of the adults' as possible can be carried on by the child.

The second major implication of the developmental doctrine is regard for *sequence* in the activities of the child. This—in turn—implies, first, the search for the *sensori-motor roots* of symbolic and conceptual activities, and the creation of a bridge of activities and stimulation between the sensori-motor and the conceptual. Second, it implies a careful *programming of sequence* within each activity. Third, it implies allowing each child to proceed *at his own pace* in moving from task to task. As Hunt (in Montessori, 1965) and I (Kohlberg, 1967) have stressed, in these general principles there is little to distinguish Montessori from John Dewey, from Piaget, or even perhaps from Omar Moore. It is from the other sensationalistic stream of ideas that the more controversial side of the Montessori approach arises. In considering this side of Montessori, it must be recognized that she was in an uneasy rebellion against the Herbartian faculty psychology which divided the mind up into powers of memory, judgment, abstraction, attention, etc., and then attempted to drill each of these separately. Like John Dewey, she insisted that these cognitive operations were not independent entities or faculties but mere manifestations of the organized activity of the child. But at the same time Montessori (1965) accepted the notion of cognitive faculties by identifying intelligence with a faculty of classification: "to be able to distinguish, classify and catalogue on the basis of a secure order established in the mind, this is at once intelligence and culture." Such classification, she says, rests upon "analyzing an object and extracting a determined attribute therefrom. If this capacity for the selecting of single attributes be not acquired, association by means of similarity, synthesis and all the higher work of intelligence becomes impossible." Thus, Montessori conceived of intellectual ability in terms of a faculty of classification and ordering, and held that this capacity developed as a direct result of experiences of discrimination, of sensory attributes, and of ordering of objects on these attributes. She believed that if the child would only become clearly aware of the pure sensation "red," for example, and clearly discriminate it from other color sensations, he would then have an abstract concept or dimension of "red" which would give him a basic system of classification.

Montessori's notions of intellectual development very directly determined her construction of her sensory tasks and materials, which all involve a set of operations basic to classification and quantitative ordering. These are usually presented to the child in the following sequence:

1) Making discriminations of same or different and matching in terms of sensory quality such as color or pitch or size.

2) Ordering qualities or quantities along some dimension; for example, pitch, light-dark, big-small.

3) Differentiation and integration of sensory dimensions or modalities; for example, systematic differentiation between an order of length from one of width, between an order of increasing loudness and an order of increasing pitch.

The most distinctive features of Montessori's conception of cognitive development, then, are her emphasis on classification and ordering, and her training of these operations through direct sensory experiences (with a corresponding minimizing of their training through verbal labeling and description). With regard to her emphasis on classification and ordering, Montessori is in close agreement with the recent thought and work of Piaget. Piaget identifies the major cognitive advance of the pre-school period (age 3 to 7) as being the formation of concrete operations and their organization into a logical grouping (see Flavell, 1963; Hunt, 1962; Piaget, 1950). These operations correspond to concepts of classes, concepts of serial or quantitative orderings, and concepts of number (which represents a synthesis of concepts of class and concepts of relation). According to Piaget, the operation of classification represents more than the ability to discriminate perceptual sameness or difference among pairs of objects. It implies forming groupings which are consistent, inclusive of all members, exhaustive of all objects to be sorted, and organized in terms of hierarchical inclusion of one class in another.

While infants and animals may be readily trained to respond to sameness, to the bigger of a number of stimuli, or the heavier, or the brighter, they do not classify in this sense; nor do they possess relational operations. Relational operations are indicated by ordering objects in a series, and by an understanding that this order is transitive (that is, that if A is greater than B and B is greater than C, then A is greater than C). Possession of both classification and relational operations is believed to be manifested by the existence of conservation or invariance of classes and relations under various perceptual conditions (for example, the relationship "bigger than" between two sticks stays the same regardless of their relative spatial positions).

Piaget, then, agrees with Montessori's view of classifications and relations as ordering activities of the child which are relatively independent of the acquisition of verbal labels.[7] Unlike Montessori, however, he does not view these ordering operations as inherent in, or resulting from, sensory discriminations. Rather, ordering operations are conceived by Piaget to be mental actions of the child which are distinct from particular perceptions, and which are generalized to a wide variety of particular objects. Recent correlational studies by Smedslund, by Zimiles, by myself, and others indicate that Piaget is correct in assuming that operations develop which are quite general or apply across a variety of objects and concepts—that is, that the child who develops an operational system with regard to one concept area is likely to display it in other concept areas as well (see Kohlberg, in press).

Because of the convergence of Piaget and Montessori upon systems of classification and ordering as the basic cognitive advance in the preschool/early-school period, it seemed appropriate to assess the effect of the Montessori program upon performance on Piaget concrete-operations tasks. Studies in progress (Kohlberg, 1963) indicate that performance on these tasks correlates well with Stanford-Binet or psychometric type intelligence measures. It might be, then, that the IQ increase we found resulting from pre-school experience could be partly explained as being due to the attainment of concrete operations through experience with the Montessori materials. (In part, we expected it to also be due to development of attention, which we and Montessori have stressed, as well as to verbal learnings of the expected sort.) To test this hypothesis, we had to create methods of assessing concrete operations useable at a younger age, and with less verbal children, than were available. Our methods consist of presenting the child with lengths of bubble gum, glasses of Coca-Cola, etc., and simply telling him he can pick the bigger one to keep or consume. The position of the gum or the Coca-Cola is then manipulated in such a way that the non-conserving child will pick the objectively smaller quantity for himself. In addition to these two conservation tasks (length and mass), the child is given a task involving ordering and measuring

7. The capacity of deaf children severely restricted in language for certain logical operations suggests the validity of Piaget's belief in their non-linguistic origin; see Furth (1966).

length which requires the understanding of the transitivity of length. The conservation tasks are solvable at a younger age (4–6 years) than is customary for Piaget tasks.

We found little change in any of the summer classes on performance of these Piaget tasks. In light of the absence of IQ increase as a result of the summer program, this is not surprising.[8] However, we also found little change on these tasks after four months of the year-long program. It seems, then, that the marked change in Stanford-Binet intelligence cannot be attributed to the effect of Montessori procedures upon Piaget-type logical operations. What are the implications of this unsurprising but disappointing finding? It may be that our Piaget-based focus upon testing conservation and transitivity was too narrow for tapping operations of classification and ordering. Evidence appears to be mounting that the development of conservation is not really dependent upon concrete logical operations as Piaget has defined them (see Kohlberg, 1963).

While our negative findings raise issues as to the adequacy of conservation tasks for indicating general advance in classification and ordering, they also raise an issue of greater significance for the theory behind the Montessori approach: that of the adequacy of Montessori's view of cognitive operations as resting directly on sensory experience. We said that Piaget agreed with Montessori in deriving cognitive operations from sensori-motor actions (rather than from verbal learning), but viewed these operations as distinct from sensory experience as such. Furthermore, the research evidence did suggest that use of concrete operations was general and not tied to particular sensory situations or experiences. In contrast, particular sensory discriminations do not have this general quality nor do they appear to correlate with intellectual abilities as usually conceived. The early efforts of Cattell and others to measure cognitive abilities started with various measures of sensory acuity. Measures of one type of sensory acuity were not found to be correlated with measures of another type, nor did any of the measures clearly relate to intellectual abilities as usually conceived. Neither does more recent work on discrimination learning give much support for Montessori's conceptions of sensory training (see White, 1963). Discrimination learning is essentially the modern definition of Montessori's "analyzing an object and extracting a determined sensory attribute

8. We did obtain an exciting tentative finding which will require replication to be trusted. All five of the initially low IQ (below 85) children who showed IQ gains of over 10 points during the summer, initially passed the Piaget tasks, whereas none of the fifteen other low IQ children did. It seems as if the Piaget tasks initially tapped non-verbal cognitive operations which were tapped only later by the Stanford-Binet—when retesting and school experience gave the child greater ease, verbal fluency, and attentional stability in the test situation.

therefrom." It does not appear that discrimination learning actually produces a generalized faculty of discrimination. Furthermore, to the extent to which there is transfer from one discrimination learning task to another, it does not appear to be the result of the child's generalized abstraction of a sensory dimension useable under various concept-attainment situations.

There seems to be no reason, then, to accept Montessori's restriction of classification and ordering activities to materials involving pure sensation or sensory dimensions. This emphasis was based on Montessori's view that classification and ordering rested on "abstraction," in the sense of isolation of pure general sensory attributes. Current theory and research, especially that in the Piaget tradition, give us no reason to think that the ordering of pure sensory objects provide the easy or royal road to conceptual ordering. Work by Zimiles (1967) and by myself (Kohlberg, in preparation), indicates that conservation of number or length is not attained more or less easily with meaningful and perceptually complex objects (for example, pictures of animals or people or lengths of candy) than it is with pure sensory objects (circles or squares or length of sticks). It would seem, then, that experience with meaningful or complex objects has neither a favored or disfavored status in facilitating attainment of operations of quantity and order. While studies of level of development on tasks of classification (as opposed to quantitative ordering) comparing meaningful and sensory objects have not been conducted, research findings suggests that classification systems first develop with meaningful objects (kinds of people, of animals, of utensils). A child's first categories (for example, boy and girl) are not based on a single sensory cue inductively abstracted from perception. Rather they represent a rule for using a variety of perceptual cues (hair, clothes, behavior) to indicate an underlying non-perceptual grouping of objects with a common functional meaning. The use of a variety of games of classification of meaningful objects (animals, tools), such as are being developed by William Fowler (see Chapter II), would seem to be more stimulating than the use of pure geometric or sensory forms for this aspect of cognitive development.[9]

9. While the Montessori emphasis on sensory materials may be an over-restriction from the point of view of conceptual development, it does have some other justifications. Montessori was probably correct in pointing to the natural interest of the pre-school child in basic sensory phenomena, and capitalizing upon it in the stimulation of sustained attention. Furthermore, this emphasis may have major value for aesthetic, if not for pure cognitive development. In line with this notion, an experimental program of musical education based largely on the Montessori approach is being carried on at the Ancona school by Jeanne Bamberger (1965) of the University of Chicago Music Department.

Our preliminary findings that Montessori experience does not greatly facilitate development on Piaget tasks of conservation and transitivity also points to a second difference between the Piaget and Montessori notions of classification and ordering. In addition to a different view of the primacy of sensation in thought operations, Piaget differs from Montessori in his definition of these operations in terms of logical systems rather than in terms of simple discrimination, comparison and generalization processes. There is considerable research evidence which suggests that sets to discriminate sameness and difference in objects, sets to compare objects along a quantitative dimension, and to differentiate one dimension (for example, height) from another dimension (size or area) are necessary prerequisites for Piaget-type concrete operations, logical groupings, or conservation. In themselves, however, these abilities, or training on them, does not directly lead to concrete operations (see Sigel and Hopper, 1967). Some current experiments on training conservation by Sigel, by Smedslund, and others suggest some additional ordering experiences which might be used to supplement the Montessori activities for the development of systems of ordering, number and conservation.

There has been considerable recent interest in the use of Montessori methods with culturally disadvantaged children. Our pilot research suggests promise for the method in stimulating cognitive advance, and suggests that the Montessori emphasis on attention and on operations of classification and ordering are at least partially in line with current theory and findings on children's cognitive functioning. As yet, however, we do not have any of the detailed research testing of each of the components of the Montessori approach which would be required for intelligent discussion and evaluation.

DONALD M. BAER

and

MONTROSE M. WOLF

X THE REINFORCEMENT CONTINGENCY IN PRE-SCHOOL AND REMEDIAL EDUCATION

Donald M. Baer (B.A. 1950, Ph.D. 1957, University of Chicago) is Professor of Human Development and of Psychology, Head of the Division of Child Development, and Research Associate, Bureau of Child Research, University of Kansas. Montrose M. Wolf (B.S. 1959, University of Houston; M.A. 1961, Ph.D. 1963, Arizona State University) is Associate Professor of Human Development and Research Associate, Bureau of Child Research, University of Kansas.

IN both pre-school and public schools, the reinforcement contingency plays an exceedingly important role. If the reinforcement contingency does not operate, education simply may not proceed. In the pre-schools, it will often prove impossible for the reinforcement contingency *not* to operate, and unless its role is recognized and deliberately planned, the preparation of the pre-school child for school—and life—correspondingly often may go astray.

Since 1963, the authors have been engaged in research programs aimed at demonstrating the potential for social reinforcement implicit in the ordinary behavior of the *pre-school* teacher directed toward her children. The outcome of this research has been so uniform that certain conclusions seem inevitable and compelling of future reaction.

The purpose of the experimental design used throughout these studies was to evaluate any reinforcing effect on child behavior that might inhere in the ordinary social responses of teachers to children. These responses may consist simply of a glance or a steady regard; they may be more complex and include nods, smiles, and other facial expressions; or they may be quite complex and embody forms of attention that could be called approving, amused, affectionate, or disapproving or angry. These responses are all essentially attentive. There are basic theoretical grounds for assuming that attention will be the most pervasive and primitive form of the social reinforcer operative in the social interactions of children (Bijou and Baer, 1965), although the

119

most effective form of the stimulus may well vary from child to child (Bijou and Baer, 1963). Thus, a reinforcement contingency may inhere in any of the forms of attention that teachers offer to children, even though the teacher has neither the intent nor the ambition to strengthen the particular response of the child which has captured her interest.

Ultimately, the teacher's intent is irrelevant: the behavior-changing function of her responsiveness lies in its stimulus function for the child, not for her. Thus, the experimental design of these studies embodies simply a deliberate manipulation of the teacher's pattern of attending to specific behaviors of her children. Five successive stages of the design exemplify the basic logic of laboratory studies of operant conditioning, but now in a pre-school setting.

The *first stage* consists of observation of some behavior of the child under study and of its social consequences from teachers. Typically, this behavior will be an undesirable one which needs reduction, or it will be a valuable but inadequately developed behavior.

This stage continues until a stable picture or *baseline* of the child's behavior and the teacher's response to it is gained. Often enough, the details of this baseline are that a strong undesirable behavior frequently evokes an attentive response from the teacher, or that a weak desirable behavior rarely does. In either of these cases, a hypothesis is generated: the teacher is reinforcing the undesirable behavior, or is extinguishing the desirable one through non-reinforcement. The testing of the hypothesis takes place in the second stage.

The *second stage* begins with the teacher changing her pattern of responsiveness to the child's behavior. If previously she has been attending at times to an undesirable behavior, now she ignores it—perfectly. If the baseline picture was one of a desirable but infrequent behavior rarely capturing the teacher's notice, then the teacher sets herself to detect and reinforce *every* instance of this behavior.

Sometimes the behavior desired is so infrequent that the teacher cannot find a sufficient number of examples of it to reinforce. In that case, approximations to the desired behavior are reinforced, causing the emergence of closer approximations; these are reinforced until still closer approximations are produced, and so on to the desired goal.

The most desirable form of the second stage may be a combination of reinforcement and extinction operating concurrently. In almost any case where an undesirable behavior is to be weakened, a desirable alternative can be found to be strengthened; and where a desirable behavior needs building, some undesirable incompatible behavior can be simultaneously extinguished.

If a behavior is to be ignored, all teachers should ignore it. And if another behavior is to be reinforced, then all teachers should reinforce it *when they can.* Yet, initially, every instance of the behavior should be reinforced for maximal effect. It is not difficult for every teacher in a group to ignore a certain response; it is much more difficult for every teacher to reinforce every example of a certain response. The logistical solution seems to be that one teacher be assigned the responsibility for reinforcing every response of the desired class, the other teachers covering for her in the group as a whole and also contributing to the reinforcement program when they can.

The second stage continues until it succeeds in accomplishing the desired change in the child's behavior, or until it is clear that it is not going to succeed.

Judgments of success or failure require a precise quantitative estimate of the child's behavior over the time period. The technique used in these studies was the hiring of observers to score the child's behavior through every nursery-school day during the term of the study. The best technique so far has proven to be continuous time sampling in ten-second blocks. The observers make a check for every ten-second block of the day during which the behavior in question occurred, and for every block during which the child was attended to by a teacher. (Observer reliabilities in the high 90's were obtained.) Thus the temporal distribution of the particular behaviors and the teachers' pattern of attending to them is apparent to the eye, and amenable to adding for a daily summary. If the proportion of blocks during which the behavior occurred is graphed in a daily progress chart, frequent judgments of developing success or failure can be made easily and objectively. (It is extremely important that a teacher not undertake projects such as these without an objective observer: the teacher's own estimates of daily improvement or worsening of the child's behavior have often proven inaccurate during early phases, not only in magnitude of change but even in direction.)

One of the striking results of these studies is the rarity with which the second stage fails to work as specified. Children in this age bracket typically are extremely sensitive to social reinforcement and the peer group usually has not yet developed into a powerful competitor for control of the child's behavior. Thus, during the daily pre-school session, the teachers are unrivaled in their *potential* for managing the child's environment and behavior.

When the changes produced in the second stage are of a stability and magnitude of practical value, a check on the nature of this success is mandatory.

The *third stage* involves a return to the conditions of the baseline period of observation. The teachers stop their experimental program of reinforcement and extinction; they resume the patterns of attending and ignoring they had shown previously. The entire purpose of this stage is to see whether the behavioral changes occurring during the second stage were caused by the changed patterns of social reinforcement and extinction which the teachers adopted during that stage. The third stage continues until the child's behavior has returned to (or at least approached) its previous undesirable state.

The *fourth stage* is basically a reinstating of the experimental procedures which had proved effective during the second stage. Typically, the desirable behavior changes are very quickly recovered in the fourth stage, whereupon the teacher sets about achieving an optimal form of these desirable behaviors. A teacher may decide that she does not wish to determine the final form or direction of the child's behavior too closely, and will deliberately refrain from further refinements, leaving these to the interplay of whatever other factors may operate. In any event, she will discover that she has a problem on her hands: a fairly large proportion of her time is still tied to a single child. He is much improved in his behavior, but her experience during the third stage has convinced her that if she suddenly discontinues her techniques, he may again lose those desirable behaviors. The solution, of course, is not to discontinue her techniques, but rather to use them more and more intermittently; and more importantly, to look for allies in reinforcement who may replace her as a source of reinforcers.

In the *fifth stage*, the transition from reinforcement of every instance of the desired behavior to only occasional reinforcement is accomplished—gradually. The initial phases proceed best if only an occasional response is not reinforced, perhaps one of every four. If the child shows no loss of the behavior, then the teacher may gradually retreat to reinforcing only one of every two or three, and so on until the daily records show that the behavior is being maintained and that the teacher is offering the child only a normal amount of reinforcement. Typically, the changes effected by the intensive reinforcement program will maintain under the gradually accomplished intermittent reinforcement program, because the child finds other reinforcers produced by his new behaviors: peer interactions, fun and games, and the like. The automatic reinforcement contingencies of the pre-school situation will take over the behavior.

The first study in which these techniques were developed into the experimental design just described centered about a 3-year-old girl who exhibited a very high rate of crawling about the pre-school (Harris, Johnston, Kelley, and Wolf, 1964). Her typical baseline rate exceeded 80 per cent of the daily morning session. Her teachers considered her behavior to be a form of regression, precipitated by the birth of a second child in her family. They had fallen into a pattern of attending to her very sympathetically, especially when she crawled. However, when the teachers began to ignore her crawling behavior and attend to her constantly whenever she was upright for any reason, a normal pattern and rate of upright behavior emerged within one week. Only two days of reversal of this experimental procedure reproduced the original 80 per cent rate of crawling, and four days of reinstated experimental procedures again produced a normal level of standing, walking, and running behaviors. Within a few weeks, the child was upright most of the session and became well-integrated into a number of the play groups of the pre-school.

In an almost identical application of this research design (Hart, Allen, Buell, Harris, and Wolf, 1964), a 4-year-old boy showed a high rate of crying in response to very mild frustrations: eight full-blown crying episodes each morning session. This rate was reduced to virtually zero by a ten-day period during which the teachers ignored crying episodes, but attended to verbal statements and questions and any examples of self-helping behavior in response to frustration. However, when the teachers resumed attention to crying episodes, the previous rate was recovered within three days and maintained for another seven. Thereupon the teachers once again took up their experimental procedures of extinguishing crying and reinforcing talking and self-helping responses, and recovered within three days the virtually zero rate of crying.

Similar applications have been made since to children displaying extremely low rates of interacting with other children in the pre-school, often coupled with strong responses toward the pre-school teachers. Since one of the prime functions of a pre-school environment is to develop social skills with peers, these cases were considered problems and were studied in the same way as the behaviors previously described. With one such child, a 4-year-old precocious girl who greatly impressed teachers with her knowledge of science and nature, only proximity to other children needed reinforcement to initiate widespread changes in her overall social repertoire (Allen, Hart, Buell, Harris, and Wolf, 1964). Six days of ignoring the child's sophisticated commentary when it was addressed to teachers only, in conjunction with attending to her or any other child or group of children she might be near or interacting with, produced a quick increase from a typical 15 per cent of her pre-school morning spent in peer interaction to an approximate 60 per cent. Reversals and re-reversals followed the familiar pattern. Many changes made up these all-inclusive "social interactions": the child's vocabulary quickly came to contain the simple words understandable by her peers, and her slow pace of speaking quickened into a pattern of delivery which other children would wait to hear finished, and respond to. Subsequently, many game-playing behaviors appeared, and the child's social integration into the group was consolidated. Postchecks showed that these changes were maintained without special planning of daily techniques by the teachers.

In a parallel study on a similarly adult-oriented girl (Foxwell, Thomson, Coats, Baer, and Wolf, 1966), the child was much more thoroughly withdrawn at the outset. One teacher set about making herself the child's special friend, producing a more intense adult orientation, but also increasing the teacher's reinforcing effectiveness to efficient levels. As in the previous study, the child was then reinforced for child-oriented responses. Progress was considerably slower, and all child-oriented behaviors, rather than mere proximity, were reinforced; at first, many of these interactions were set up, or "primed," by the teacher, who marshaled other children into the girl's play area. The outcome of this study offers a striking parallel to the prior study, despite differences in the details of procedure.

A more recent study of a similar case demonstrates the need to use social reinforcement in contingency with the response desired, rather than in an undiscriminating, non-contingent manner, if the results are to be predictable in advance (Hart, Reynolds, Brawley, Harris, and Baer, 1965). In this case, the child was a 5-year-old girl with a very unattractive social repertoire: she was balky, verbally insulting, occasionally foul-mouthed, and prone to tell disjointed stories about violent accidents. Her approaches to others, while frequent, tended to be quite brief. Although she was in near proximity to children about 50 per cent of her typical pre-school session during the baseline observations, her rate of *cooperative* interaction with them was consistently less than 5 per cent of the time available. The teachers averaged slightly more than 10 per cent of their mornings interacting with the girl. As an experimental prelude to the usual procedure of reinforcing social behavior, the teachers spent seven successive sessions offering the child a great amount of non-contingent attention. A teacher now stood near the girl 35 per cent of each session, talking to her and often touching her, watching activities, supplying her with materials and toys, laughing, and generally being quite appreciative of the child. As a consequence, other children were attracted to the scene, and the girl underwent increased proximity to her peers. Despite these changes, her rate of cooperative play with them remained unchanged. When the teacher switched to contingent reinforcement, offering the girl approval only for approximations to cooperative interactions with the other children, the girl's cooperative behavior began to grow, achieving an unprecedented 40 per cent of session after twelve days. When the teacher resumed non-contingent reinforcement, the child's cooperative behavior declined immediately to its usual low value. Reinstatement of reinforcement for cooperative play quickly reproduced a high rate of cooperation; after four days of this, other behaviors considered conducive to cooperation were reinforced as well, in order to generalize the child's play skills. The generalization, while variable, was consistently well above baseline levels of cooperative play.

These studies have emphasized reinforcing proximity to other children, staging or "priming" the initial social interactions, and then reinforcing them powerfully. With some children, the route may be simpler. In one case, a boy showed little social interaction with his peers; the other boys of the pre-school typically were engaged in vigorous play which this boy rarely displayed. He seemed lazy rather than asocial, and the teachers decided to shape merely some form of vigorous activity and see what might result (Johnston, Kelley, Harris, and Wolf, 1966). They chose climbing as the activity, and for a nine-day baseline observed climbing in general, and upon a particular jungle gym in the school play yard. The baseline rate of climbing on anything averaged well below 5 per cent of the time spent outside. The teachers then shaped a climbing response to the jungle gym, by successive approximation, producing in nine days a rate of climbing exceeding 60 per cent of the time available. Five days of extinction allowed this rate virtually to disappear, but another five days of reinforcement reproduced it almost instantly. The teachers found it easy to generalize this activity to a wide variety of climbing activities. There was also a gratifying change in the amount and quality of social interactions with his peers: now that the boy was effectively elevated from his previous pattern of inactivity, he became a happy and vigorous member of several of the boys' play groups, and blossomed into both physical and verbal social interactions quite readily. An almost identical study, with virtually identical outcomes on all of these dimensions, has been performed by Cooper, Lee, Bierlein, Wolf, and Baer (1966).

We have made a detailed study of the development of such social behaviors when one key response leading to them is singled out for experimental improvement (Buell, Stoddard, Baer, and Harris, 1965). It was pointed out before that the teacher must seek allied agents for reinforcement of the newly established behaviors, so that the child is not left entirely dependent upon the teacher's reinforcers. A 3-year-old girl, quite verbal with adults and sophisticated in the use of play materials inside the pre-school, showed virtually no use of outdoor play equipment, interacted only through parallel play with the other children, and often fell into monosyllabic baby talk. The response class chosen for reinforcement was playing on outdor equipment: if such play could be strengthened, the child might be thrown into numerous social contingencies with her peers, the allies in reinforcement sought by the teacher.

A period of baseline observation was made of verbalization to teachers, verbalizations to children, the use of other children's names, baby talk, touching the teacher, touching another child, parallel play, cooperative play, play on equipment alone, and play on equipment with another child. Only three of these behaviors showed an appreciable rate: parallel play, touching teachers, and baby talk. Play on equipment never exceeded 3 per cent of the time available.

There followed seventeen days of social reinforcemnt for play on equipment. On the first nine days, the teachers relied upon "priming": they forced one occasion of the desired response to each piece of play equipment in the yard. They would lift the child onto a climbing frame, or place her on a swing, or seat her on a tricycle. The teacher would remain close to the child, talking and laughing with her in a warm and appreciative manner. As soon as the child left the piece of equipment, the teacher turned away to some other duty. Under these conditions, the child steadily increased her use of outdoor equipment to about 50 per cent of the time available. For eight more days, the teachers continued this pattern of reinforcement, but without the priming technique. The child's use of equipment dropped to about 25 per cent of the session, then quickly recovered its prior rate of about 50 per cent. After five days of extinction, the rate dropped sharply, but not so low as it had been during the baseline period: it fell to about 20 per cent of the time available. The teachers noted that other children using the equipment were engaging the girl in play with them. The teachers then resumed their own reinforcement of this behavior for another nine days and it increased quickly to about 70 per cent of the time available. They extinguished the behavior again, and the child's use of equipment fell again, but not to its baseline level. Thereupon they once again reestablished the behavior, almost immediately producing extreme rates (90 per cent of the time available), began intermittent reinforcement, and reduced the rate to a more realistic average of 60 per cent. The cycles of reinforcement and extinction were repeated in this study in order to examine thoroughly the failure of the behavior to return to its previous baseline level.

Changes occurred in the other behaviors under observation at the same time. These behaviors were attended to by the teachers in the normal intermittent fashion—neither singled out for intensive reinforcement nor ignored as in extinction. Three other child-oriented behaviors showed an increase during one or another of the reinforcement cycles of the study. There was a marked increase in touching other children, and a steady increase in verbalizing to other children. In a similar but more modest manner, cooperative play emerged from near-zero. None of these behaviors declined systematically during those periods when play on equipment underwent extinction. These behaviors evidently did not depend only on the teacher's stimulation for reinforcement. One component of verbalizing to other children, using their name, appeared during the second extinction period, and may well have served the function of better involving other children in cooperative play, in the absence of a great deal of teacher interaction. Meanwhile, teacher-oriented responses remained unchanged in any systematic manner. Parallel play, greatly variable throughout the study, also showed no systematic relationship to the periods of reinforcement and extinction of equipment play. Baby talk declined steadily as the more mature social behaviors increased. These results may well represent an initial picture of the effects of the teacher's allies in reinforcement, the child's peers, brought into action by the teacher's strengthening of a tactical response.

In summary of these studies, what needs special emphasis is the characterization of the reinforcing stimulus: *the ordinary social responsiveness of the pre-school teacher*. The teacher is doing nothing unusual or alien to her everyday professional behavior; she shows these children the same behavior she typically shows to any child in her pre-school.

What has been controlled in this research is not *what* the teacher does, but *when* she does it. No new stimulus has been introduced; an existent one has been moved from one contingency to another. A preschool is essentially a behavior-modifying environment in which powerful stimuli cannot help but operate, if the teacher is to play any role at all. There seems no choice but that she become a sophisticated student of her own behavior as it falls into contingencies with the behavior of her children. The teacher cannot really choose *not* to shape the behavior of these children; she can only choose not to care and let the contingencies fall where they may; or to begin the systematic analysis of her profession and thereby the systematic education of pre-school children toward specified goals.

An examination of children in the *public schools* shows certain instances in which social reinforcement contingencies deriving from the teachers, family, or peers to reinforce academic achievement, are not operating. One example is a public school system in a section of Kansas City once referred to as a slum but now as an area of cultural deprivation. In that area, many school children can be found who attend school but do little there. Their grades and standardized achievement test scores show that many of them have progressed little if at all since the second grade. They have all the characteristics which correlate highly with future functional illiteracy, dropping out of school, and perpetual unemployability.

It seems worthwhile to study the problem of academic achievement from the point of view of the reinforcement contingency. For the middle-class child, that contingency is ordinarily social, and is usually modestly successful in producing literacy, computational ability, and adequate communication skills. With the culturally deprived child, these social contingencies manifestly do not operate powerfully to produce the same behavior changes.

Montrose Wolf, David Giles, and Vance Hall have begun a research program aimed at developing motivation for academic achievement in sixteen children from this area. These sixth-graders all scored at least two years below the norm for the sixth grade on the reading section of the Stanford Achievement Test. The experimental program involves an extracurricular classroom in which four basic reinforcement contingencies are operative; all are mediated through a point system strongly resembling a trading stamp plan. When the child completes an assignment correctly, he receives "points" which are marked by the experimental teachers on pages in a book which each child has been issued. Filled pages are redeemable, according to their color, for a variety of potential reinforcers somewhat more substantial than social: blue pages are redeemable for weekly field trips; green pages for a daily snack; yellow pages for long-range prizes (requiring weeks or months of achievement) such as clothes, bicycles, or watches; and pink pages for money, which may be spent anywhere, including a store located in the classroom. The children now average about a dollar's worth of rewardable units of *correct* work per day.

The assignments which they must complete correctly to make points are problems derived largely from the many workbooks published for academic exercises suitable to the grade levels of the public schools. These children started largely with second-grade-level problems, and initially received points for every correct problem. As their rate and accuracy increased, the amount of work required was increased accordingly. The experimental sessions conducted after regular school hours involve such assignments, and also homework assigned in the public schools. Students can gain points by bringing in completed work from their public school classrooms, and report card grades from the public school are redeemable for points every six weeks. Thus the contingencies of the experimental classroom tend to infiltrate the public school as well, for these sixteen children.

Preliminary results have been quite encouraging. During the previous *two* years, these children had gained only one-half year in reading and total scores of the academic achievement test used. After one school year in the experimental program, they have gained 1.5 years in total score. Their public school report cards reflect their performance with the sixth-grade material assigned in their regular classrooms. They have increased more than a full grade point, from D to C. A comparable group of children, unsullied by such reinforcement contingencies, has maintained its previous average in report card grade points.

In conclusion, the reinforcement contingency is central to education. In pre-school settings, a social contingency can hardly fail to operate; its mechanics should be recognized, analyzed, and used. In the public schools, some children may not respond to social contingencies. If education is to take place, a stimulus should be found for that contingency which does indeed function as a reinforcer; if that stimulus cannot be a social one, then a more tangible substitute—a difference of detail, after all—can be found.

COURTNEY B. CAZDEN

XI SOME IMPLICATIONS OF RESEARCH ON LANGUAGE DEVELOPMENT FOR PRE-SCHOOL EDUCATION

Courtney B. Cazden (A.B. 1946, Radcliffe College; Bank Street College of Education, 1946–47; M.Ed. 1953, University of Illinois; Ed.D. 1965, Harvard University) is Assistant Professor of Education and Research Fellow in Social Relations, Harvard University. Preparation of this report was partially supported by Public Health Service Research Grant MH7088 from the National Institute of Mental Health to Roger W. Brown, and partially supported by a grant from the Office of Education OE5-10-239 to Harvard University, Center for Research and Development on Educational Differences.

OUR understanding of the role of environmental assistance in language development is tentative and incomplete. We have a growing set of descriptive analyses of the course of language development, and a large body of correlational data on the relation between measures of language and measures of gross features of the child's environment. While these data make group predictions possible, they do not provide a fine-grained analysis of the processes involved. Only a few manipulative experiments exist: Casler (1965); Cazden (1965); Irwin (1960); Rheingold, Gewirtz, and Ross (1959); Weisberg (1963).

Even if we knew what produces healthy language development in natural environments, the difficulty remains of translating this understanding into educational programs. A program modeled closely after particularly beneficial natural environments is not the only possible design. Carl Bereiter's experimental pre-school program (see National Council of Teachers of English, 1965a, pp. 195–203) is an example of a non-natural treatment. Bereiter has gone outside the field of developmental research to draw on a separate body of knowledge about how to change verbal behavior: the teachers in Bereiter's program for socially disadvantaged children talk not like middle-class mothers, but like foreign language teachers.

In discussing language development, I find it helpful to separate aspects of that development which may benefit from different kinds of environmental assistance. This paper will treat the acquisition of grammar or the structure of language, the acquisition of vocabulary, the acquisition of multiple functions of language, and the acquisition of a standard dialect. Then there will be postscripts on the relation of pre-school language development to non-verbal behavior and to beginning reading. I will not try to provide an exhaustive list of worthwhile experiences; fortunately, an excellent description of current programs is available in a publication by the National Council of Teachers of English (1965a). Nor will I review research on subcultural differences in child language (see Cazden, 1966).

The Acquisition of Grammar

Contemporary studies concentrate on the acquisition of grammar. The work of Brown and Bellugi at Harvard, with which I have been associated for three years, is the only one of the language acquisition studies which has protocols of mother-child conversation. Brown has recorded three mothers and their firstborn children—whom we call Adam, Eve, and Sarah—weekly or biweekly from the time the children started putting two words together until they were speaking in complete simple sentences, a period of one to two years. The objective of the project is to describe the developmental sequence of language acquisition and to obtain some hypotheses about environmental influences on that sequence and on developmental rate. We expect to find some features of the acquisition of language which are common across these three children and may be related either to language learning in general or to the learning of English in particular; we expect to find other features which show variation even in our sample of three and may be related either to environmental variables or to individual differences in cognitive style.

Although these analyses won't be complete for another year, I can illustrate the kind of information that is emerging. Speech samples taken at five points (not stages) in the developmental stream are being analyzed. To obtain these five points, the children were equated on linguistic criteria, primarily mean length of utterance, while the age of the children at each of the five points, and the time interval between the points, were allowed to vary freely. Figure 1 gives this data in graph form; Roman numerals indicate the points.

An example of the regularity in sequence which we find is that at

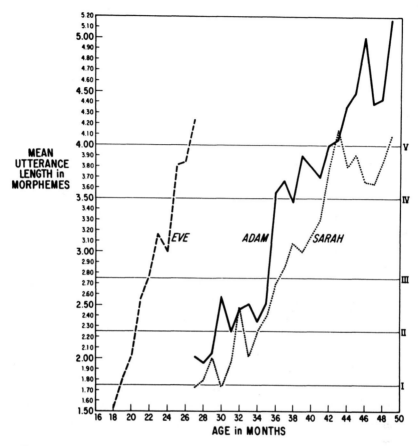

FIGURE 1. MEAN UTTERANCE LENGTH AND AGE IN THREE CHILDREN.

any level noun phrases are more developed in object position than in subject position. An example of variation is the point in the sequence at which plural inflections appear. For Sarah, plural inflections appear midway between I and II; for Adam, it is just after II; for Eve, it is just before III. This variation may be related to the linguistic environment; examination of parent speech shows a striking difference in the density of plurals. In one time-sample, it took the mothers of Adam and Eve ten hours to use 100 plurals, whereas it took Sarah's mother only four hours to use the same number, presumably because a higher percentage of her talking time was used for the naming game: *What's this?* asked about objects in the room or in books.

With two exceptions, immaturities in the child's speech are largely ignored by all three mothers. One set of exceptions, errors in meaning, will be discussed later. The other exceptions are errors of omission, the telegraphic speech of all young children. Parents frequently respond to the child's utterance, for example, "Mommy lunch," with the nearest complete sentence appropriate in the particular situation, for example, "Mommy is having her lunch." Brown named this form of parental response an "expansion" (Brown and Bellugi, 1964).

Expanding looks like an ideal tutorial technique. However, we recognized that an alternative hypothesis was possible—namely, that what is important for language development is not a particular kind of parent-child interaction but simply the amount of well-formed speech that a child hears. When evidence is limited to natural observations it is not possible to separate the effects of these two features of a child's language environment. To separate the effect of expansions from the effect of sheer quantity of speech stimulation, a manipulative experiment was undertaken (Cazden, 1965).

The subjects were twelve Negro children age 28 to 38 months, attending a private day-care center in Boston where the ratio of children under 3½ years to adults was 30 to 1. I assumed that these children were sufficiently linguistically deprived by being in this environment eight to ten hours a day so that the stimulation added in this research should make an observable difference. The children were randomly assigned to three treatment groups: four children received forty minutes per day of deliberate expansions; four were exposed to an equal number of well-formed sentences that were not expansions. Tutors trained for this research talked with each child in these two groups in an individual play session every school day for three months. Four children received no special treatment. Contrary to predictions, the children who received the non-expanding language stimulation gained more on six measures of language development: a sentence imitation test and five measures of spontaneous speech.

Originally I called the non-expanding treatment "modeling" or "exposure," assuming that non-expansion had no special positive quality of its own. An examination of what actually happens shows that this is not the case. If a child says, "Dog bark," when a dog is indeed barking, the expanding adult says, "Yes, the dog is barking." The non-expanding adult who desires to maintain a reasonable discourse sequence has to contribute a related idea: "Yes, he's mad at the kitty," or, "Yes, but he won't bite." Thus a treatment that focuses on grammatical structure tends to limit the ideas to the presumed meaning of the child, and tends to limit the grammatical elements to those used by the child; focus on the idea, by contrast, extends that idea beyond the presumed meaning of the child and introduces more varied grammatical elements to express those related meanings. David McNeill (in press) has named the non-expansion treatment "expatiation."

The finding that expatiations aid the acquisition of grammar more than expansions suggests that richness of verbal stimulation may be a critical feature. There are three sources of support for this interpretation and for its converse, that impoverished language is harder—not easier—to learn.

First, if we consider the learning of inflectional and syntactical skills akin to concept formation, then variation in irrelevant features of the concepts may aid learning. Second, if—as the transformational grammarians argue—the process of first language acquisition is akin to scientific theory construction in which hypotheses are tested against available data, then a meager set of data may be a hindrance: "Rules that hold for selected sets of simple sentences may have to be abandoned in the light of examples of sentences of more complicated types" (Fodor, 1966, p. 120). Third, increased variety of language stimulation may enhance attentional processes in the child. Fiske and Maddi (1961) present evidence for the general value of varied stimulation in effecting arousal.

The Acquisition of Vocabulary

With the exception of proper names, vocabulary items are symbols for concepts. The acquisition of vocabulary involves both learning new words and extending and refining the meaning of words already in use. For example, both Eve and Sarah have said, "I write picture." At some later time, each child will learn the word *draw*. Only then will the meaning of *write* become refined to what one does to letters and numbers.

This process contrasts with the acquisition of grammar in two ways. First, whereas the acquisition of grammar is virtually completed during the pre-school years, the acquisition of vocabulary is never finished. Second, the acquisition of vocabulary seems to benefit from more direct tuition. Evidence comes both from natural observations of parents and from correlational research.

Consider Eve, whose dramatically rapid development is shown in Fig. 1. Once Eve noticed her mother rubbing her face and asked, "What you was having on you nose?" This utterance has no less than four grammatical immaturities: failure to reverse auxiliary and pro-

noun in a question, the wrong auxiliary with *you,* an *-ing* added to a
verb that is never "inged" with this meaning, and failure to add the
possessive inflection on the pronoun. Yet the mother responds, "What
I was having on my nose? Nothing, I was rubbing my eyes." Contrast
that reaction with what happened after a walk to watch construction
on the William James Center for the Behavioral Sciences at Harvard.
Eve, reporting her experience, said, "Watching the men—building
hole." This time the mother said, "Well, they aren't building a hole,
sweetie. They're building a building now. First they dug the hole and
now they're building the building."

The more direct role of parents in teaching vocabulary is also reflected in Stodolsky's research (1965). Her subjects were 56 of the 163
Negro families in Robert Hess's large study of cognitive environments
of pre-school children (Hess and Shipman, 1965). Using data already
available on vocabulary level and teaching styles of the mothers, Stodolsky administered the Peabody Picture Vocabulary Test to the children one year later. She then correlated the children's scores with a
selected set of maternal variables from the year before and obtained a
multiple correlation of .68. The best single predictor of the PPVT scores
was the mother's vocabulary score on the WAIS. The maternal teaching
variables which added most to the prediction equation were amount of
reinforcement and a "discrimination index" which measured the extent
to which the mother isolated task-specific qualities of the environment.

What I am proposing is that the acquisition of grammar and of vocabulary require different kinds of environmental assistance. Learning
the meaning of words and thereby the relations among ideas seems to
benefit from active tuition in the form of conversation between the
child and an interested adult. (Whether it can be done by a more
verbally mature child is still an open question.) Given such tuition, the
acquisition of grammar is aided as well.

One context for such conversation is reading a story to an individual
child. Irwin (1960) induced working-class mothers to read to their
children for twenty minutes a day, and made regular trips to the homes
to provide suitable books; in my research, the non-expanding treatment
included one book read per day. Reading to an individual child may
be a potent form of language stimulation for two reasons. First, it
brings a special physical relationship of close physical contact, with
the adult speaking almost directly into the child's ear. Second, reading
seems inevitably to stimulate interpolated conversation about the pictures to which both adult and child are attending.

The Acquisition of Multiple Functions of Language

The multiple functions of language can be categorized in various ways. One division is between interindividual and intraindividual use, or communication with others and communication with oneself.

We need to know the degree of match or mismatch between the modes of language use required for successful coping with school tasks and the modes of language use which children have learned in their homes, peer groups, etc. Determining the degree of this match requires studies from both ends—in schools and in the natural speech communities from which the children come. We cannot simply conclude, from the observation that children *do* not talk in a certain way in school, that they *can* not do so. Other factors in the school situation may prevent the realization of capabilities for language use which the children do have. (I am indebted to Dell Hymes for this point.)

Research on the intraindividual or mediational use of language is important for pre-school education because the dimension of cognitive growth which brings increased independence of response from immediate stimulation seems to take a qualitative leap in the 5 to 7 age range, just after the pre-school period. S. H. White (1965) has analyzed a large body of research findings on the shift from "associative" to "cognitive" level of functioning during this period. There seems little question that language is part of the story but not all of it, that the availability of a linguistic response in the child's repertoire does not guarantee its use whenever appropriate and helpful. Unfortunately, we do not know how variation in the use of language for interindividual communication affects its intraindividual use, and we don't know what kind of tuition results in what kind of help.

The intrapersonal role of language, or "inner speech," is a primary focus of Soviet psychologists, much of whose work is oriented toward pedagogical applications. I found one suggestion (Slavina, 1957) helpful in first-grade arithmetic. Voya could do simple sums with objects to manipulate but could not do the sums in his head. An intermediate stage was introduced: after manipulating the objects and counting out loud, Voya was asked to do the same operations out loud but without looking at the objects still arrayed before him; that is, he was helped to form a mental schema or representation. Only after this was he asked to try the completely mental process, using the mental schema with covert responses. The key contribution may be finding that intermediate step which can take the child to the acquisition of new behavior. Perhaps some of the experimental conditions in verbal mediation experiments can be converted into treatments. Jensen (1963) has done this with retarded junior high school students. He found that learning of a multiple stimulus response problem improved markedly when the subjects were asked to name the stimuli while learning.

Flavell is doing important research in this area. He and his associates (Flavell, Beach, and Chinsky, 1966) have completed a study of spontaneous verbal rehearsal in a memory task: the experimenter pointed to a series of pictures of readily-nameable objects on a display board, and the subject—either immediately or after a 15-second delay —had to point to the same objects in the same order. A trained observer lip-read and recorded whatever semi-overt verbal behavior the subject engaged in. The percentage of subjects showing such verbalization increased from very few in kindergarten to about half in second grade to nearly all in fifth grade. There was evidence among the second-graders of a relation between presence of verbalization and correct recall. Flavell has now started on a three-year study with three objectives: to see whether spontaneous verbalization is a stable individual characteristic across various memory tasks; to determine the linguistic, cognitive, and personality correlates of such verbalization; and to attempt acceleration of its development by several kinds of systematic training.

The Acquisition of a Standard Dialect

The reason for educational concern about grammar, vocabulary, and language function relates to the use of language for learning and communicating ideas. Concern for a standard dialect, on the other hand, relates to what Joshua Fishman (personal communication) has aptly called "the Pygmalion effect" of language, that is, its role in social mobility.

Current interest in social dialects is reflected in research projects in many cities which are attempting to describe systematically the points of contrast between nonstandard dialects and standard English, and to determine which features create the greatest barrier to acceptance in the dominant culture. Controversy has arisen over the objective of educational intervention: to eradicate nonstandard forms, or inculcate conscious bi-dialectalism. Much of the latest work in this field is reviewed in *Social Dialects and Language Learning* (National Council of Teachers of English, 1965b).

My recommendation is that pre-school teachers concentrate on enlarging the child's linguistic repertoire and not do anything about altering his nonstandard form beyond the provision of models of standard English. With young children, language for social mobility is far less important than language for learning, and the danger that correction will extinguish verbal behavior in general outweighs any possible gains. One first-grade teacher told me that during a science lesson one of her children excitedly told her that, "The magnet brung the paper clips." She tried to explain that we say *brought*, but the child kept saying *brung*. Finally she gave up and told the child that scientists have a special word for what magnets do, they *attract*. My advice is that we all give up the correction even earlier, and concentrate on adding and enlarging and refining (see National Council of Teachers of English, 1965a, p. 70).

The desirability of providing models of standard English raises important questions about pre-school personnel and the composition of the peer group. How much weight should be given to the standardness of the speech patterns of these adults, and how much weight to other reasons for including adults indigenous to lower-class communities, such as on-the-job training for parents and future parents, counteraction of home-school alienation, and the participation of male adults in the schools? And what about the composition of the peer group? We want to maximize the benefits from communication among the children. How much can be gained in desegregated classrooms? Is it worth making a fight against present policies which result in pre-school groups segregated by social class?

Relation of Language to Non-verbal Behavior

If you ask nursery-school teachers working with disadvantaged children what is the outstanding characteristic of these children—particularly if they have previously worked with a more typical nursery school population—the answer is "a short attention span." Along with this goes considerable folklore that disadvantaged children are restless, fidgety, and just very active. We need to know more about the relation of action to language—where it enhances and where it interferes.

I tried to find out if there was any solid evidence that disadvantaged children were, as a group, more active in any sense. The only convincing data I have found is Bayley's (1965) recent summary of mental and motor test scores on a national sample of some fourteen hundred infants, 1 to 15 months old:

> No difference in scores were found for either scale between boys and girls, first-born and later-born, education of either father or mother, or geographic residence. No differences were found between Negroes and Whites on the mental scale, but the Negro babies tended consistently to score above Whites on the motor scale (p. 379).

Bayley interprets this finding as the result of a heightened muscle tone, and reports that other investigators have found comparable data, but only during infancy.

Marcia Guttentag at Yale is studying group differences in quantity and quality of physical movement in pre-school children by observing children in structured situations. She wants to know not only how much gross activity there is, but also how the movements of different children vary in variety, rhythmicity, etc.

In relation to language, three kinds of actions were suggested by my weekly visits to Sarah and my observations in pre-schools: gestures, rhythmic movements, and random activity. Gestures constitute a non-verbal form of representation or communication. Sarah would lift her arms when she wanted to be picked up or point to the refrigerator when she wanted milk; she shivered at the word *cold*, put her fingers to her lips at the word *sleep*, and blew when her mother lit a match to light a cigarette. For more elaborate meaning, gestures supplemented her inadequate language. Attempting to elicit prepositions, we asked her to tell us where her doll was; Sarah answered, "I show you," and ran into her room.

Second, there are the rhythmic motoric activities which have no meaning component, but to which words can be mapped. These include ball bouncing, hand clapping, drum beating, and dancing. There are ready-made chants and newly-made language improvised on the spot. In a pre-school, a little boy deliberately poured a pail of water on the floor. The teacher gave him the mop and together they sang, "This is the way we mop the floor." When their verse had ended, a boy nearby sang by himself, "This is the way we scoop the soup," in perfect time as he did indeed scoop the soup. Teachers differ in how much they use rhythmic activities for this kind of verbal activity. One teacher used so much of it that life at her school had some of the quality of a musical play. At other pre-schools, rich opportunities for a joyful use of language are overlooked in the pressure of preparation for first grade. Guttentag is ultimately interested in designing a language program for disadvantaged children based on associating language with music and with their own motor responses. It will be interesting to see how much conceptual content can be incorporated into such a program.

The third kind of activity raises questions for research. This is the random, non-purposive activity which may interfere with attention and even provide proprioceptive noise for the reception of verbal stimuli. What is the physiological status of such activity? What is its relation to attention? And what, if anything, should be done about it in an educational program?

Beginning Reading

So far I have derived implications for the pre-school program from a backward look at how language develops. The educational objective is to raise the level of oral language of all children as close as possible to that of the most verbal children. One can also derive implications for pre-school language programs from a forward look at the language tasks which will confront the child when he enters first grade.

The most obvious school language task is learning to read. In her analysis of research on beginning reading, Chall (1965) found clear evidence that children are more likely to be successful if they know the names and sound values of the letters and can hear similiarities and differences in spoken words. The correlation of success in beginning reading with these abilities was higher across all the studies than with measures of mental age and oral language ability. In the middle grades, on the other hand, perceptual skills become less important, and intelligence and language ability play a larger role. Reading success is thus correlated with different abilities at successive stages in the long-term task.

This analysis suggests implications for the pre-school curriculum. We have to work on oral language and concept development because they will become critical later, and we have to develop a parallel program for the perceptual skills that will be needed sooner. Pre-school programs usually do include visual and auditory discrimination activities. They can be strengthened by greater use of linguistic materials, namely letters and phonemes, and by taking dialect differences into account.

If a teacher says "Whose name begins like *that?*" and a child says "David," it may be because he doesn't know what she is talking about, or because he knows exactly what she is talking about but neither perceives nor produces a *d-th* contrast. Instruction to attend to sounds which the child does in fact make must be distinguished from instruction in the perception and production of phonemic contrasts which are not part of the child's dialect. It is the first that I am urging here. The second is one aspect of the issue of dialect change raised earlier. It is still an open question whether dialect differences per se interfere with learning to read. Chall's research would tend to dictate *no*, but we don't know how deviant the dialects were in the studies she reviewed. Linguists such as Labov (1965) are also saying *no*. Labov argues that the result of dialect differences in pronunciation is a set of homonyms which are different from the teacher's and may be more numerous than hers. If one has pronounced *during* and *doing* the same way all one's life, learning to read the two words and associate differential meaning with differential spelling is no different from what every English speaker does with *sun* and *son*.

The contrastive linguistic studies mentioned earlier (National Council of Teachers of English, 1965b) have been designed to provide information on the points of maximum contrast between standard English and nonstandard dialects. They should also be useful in indicating the area of overlap, consisting of the sounds and grammatical patterns common to standard English and nonstandard dialects. That area of overlap may provide the best set of materials for reading and prereading programs. (I am indebted to Beryl Bailey for this suggestion.)

XII

INFORMAL EDUCATION DURING THE FIRST MONTHS OF LIFE

Burton L. White (B.S. 1949, Tufts University; B.A. 1955, M.A. 1956, Boston University; Ph.D. 1960, Brandeis University) is Project Director of the Pre-School Program, Center for Research and Development on Educational Differences, and Lecturer, Harvard University; and Chairman of Psychology Area, Harvard Graduate School of Education. At various times, the research reported here has received support from Grant M-3657 from the National Institute of Mental Health, Grant 61-234 from the Foundation's Fund for Research in Psychiatry, Grants HD-00761 and HD-02054 from the National Institutes of Health, the Optometric Extension Program, Grant NSG-496 from the National Aeronautics and Space Administration, Grant AF-AFOSR354-63 from the U.S. Air Force Office of Scientific Research, and the Rockefeller Foundation. The research was conducted at the Tewksbury Hospital, Tewksbury, Massachusetts. The author is grateful for the assistance of Peter Castle, Kitty Riley, Richard Light, and Cherry Collins, and for the consideration and aid given by Drs. John Lu, Solomon J. Fleischman, Peter Wolff, and Lois Crowell and head nurses Helen Efstathiou, Frances Craig, and Virginia Donovan.

I THINK we would all agree that the primary goal of an educational system is to maximize the ability of each student to cope with life's various problems. Until recently, the vast majority of educators have focused their formal efforts on students aged 6 to 16 years. My feeling is that the major reason for the selection of these particular years is the prevalence of an implicit adultomorphism in educational philosophy. We tend to think of the task of educating children as one where we teach them to think as we do. And how do adults think? Well, most everyone knows we use language to form our ideas to ourselves and to transmit them to others. We use formal systems of mathematics to quantify objects and events. We use other formal systems such as logic to relate events to each other and to solve problems, etc. Likewise, everyone knows that children do not respond very well to efforts to teach them language, math, logic, etc., until they get to be at least 6 or 7 years old. Recently, of course, there have been exceptions, such as Bruner and Moore, who show us that by being very clever in curriculum construction, we can start earlier and move faster in these matters (at least with very clever children), but the general procedure of focusing specifically on inculcating adult cognitive skills remains.

But what of the years between birth and age 6? As recently as 1900, except for a few men such as Pestalozzi and Froebel, very few educators had much to say about this period. Then came the influence of Freud. By 1930, child development had come into its own as a field of study, and the first five years of life—at least with respect to personality development—were accorded enormous importance. But the primary effect this seemed to have on educators was to awaken their interest in learning theory and the nature-nurture controversy. From the former grew the tendency to construct educational psychology courses around various theories of conditioning such as Pavlov's and Hull's (much to the dismay of future students of such courses). From the latter came a decade of studies which seemed to show that the rate of acquisition of motor skills was strictly limited by maturation.

In the mid-Thirties, a remarkable book was published. It was called *The Origins of Intelligence in Children*, by Jean Piaget. Unfortunately, partly due to the turgid quality of the writing, the influence of that book is only now coming into its own. In it, Piaget described his view of the ontogenesis of intelligence from its roots in the crude reflex-like behaviors present at birth through the day-by-day sensori-motor explorations of infancy and on to representational or ideational processes. The power of this book derives from its basis in *years of observations* and thousands of small but ingenious tests. It is a tribute to Piaget's genius that with an *n* of 3 (his own children), his findings are remarkably reproducible; furthermore, his book is about *normal* development. How many comparable studies of normal development are there? The nearest facsimile in child development is Lois Murphy's study of Colin reported in *Personality in Young Children*.

Hunt (1961) has made explicit the many implications of Piaget's sensori-motor theory for educators. The fundamental cognitive elements such as the sense of time, causality, space, and object which underlie intelligent activity may or may not evolve as claimed by Piaget. Nor is it necessarily true that the curiosity motive and the capacity for intelligent action may be seriously stunted or maximized as a result of events during the first and second years of life. But can educators afford not to be interested in these possibilities? I don't think so.

Piaget's studies of sensori-motor intelligence therefore involve both issues I place before you. His work, plus other studies such as those dealing with the acquisition of language, show beyond doubt that if we pay little attention to the events occurring in the first years of life, much of the story may be over by the time we begin to "educate" the child, even if we start as early as age 3, let alone age 6. Secondly, his work is monumental largely because it is tied to and documented by gilt-edged observational data. His theorizing by itself is a virtuoso performance, but the fact that it is rooted in and repeatedly tested against reality makes it unparalleled in child development research. For contrast, look at the ratio between theory and empirical material in studies of language acquisition. Roger Brown and Ursula Bellugi's ideas are based on comparatively brief observations on an *n* of 3. What other extensive data exist on the acquisition of language other than vocabulary or phoneme counts? Chomsky, Halle, and Fodor build theories with *n*'s of zero. But we needn't restrict this discussion to topics such as intelligence and language. Aside from Piaget's sensori-motor theory, not a single major theory in child development in this century has been based on observations of human infants and young children. Psychoanalysis was based on data on middle-class female neurotics; learning theory on dogs, mice, and monkeys; Gestalt theory on human adults and mice; and instinct theory on birds and insects. The closest we've come is Gesell's concept of "reciprocal interweaving" and I can't figure out what to do with it.

The research I am going to describe deals with human infants 1 to 6 months of age. I believe that this work is relevant to problems of education for two reasons: first of all, I feel very strongly that educators *must* concern themselves with the *entire* postnatal course of development of adaptive skills rather than events from 6 or even 3 years on; second, I believe that research in child development must be radically reoriented towards careful, expensive, sometimes tedious observation and *inductive* hypotheses. In describing my work I hope I can provide one example of such an approach.

The research I've been involved in the last eight years concerns the behavior of normal human infants from birth through the first half year of life. It has proceeded along three lines. First, we have attempted to trace the development of the major sensori-motor abilities that infants utilize in their first explorations of the postnatal world. These have included visually directed reaching, visual exploration, visual accommodation, and the blink response. We have simultaneously tried to identify environmental or experiential conditions which seem relevant to the abilities in question. Lastly, we have carried out a series of enrichment studies in order to determine whether or not early development was significantly dependent upon rearing conditions. Our results have convinced us that norms of visual-motor development are meaningless without adequate specifications of the rearing conditions. Many of the visual-motor processes we have studied have proven remarkably plastic. We have been able to systematically accelerate and retard the rate of development of behaviors such as visual exploration and visually directed reaching. Moreover, these changes have been of striking magnitude.

SUBJECTS

Reports based on studies of institutionally-reared infants generally include a statement acknowledging the atypicality of the subjects. It is undoubtedly true that such infants are reared under atypical conditions, and in addition they may congenitally constitute a non-representative sample. On the other hand, two factors make such infants unusually suitable for experimental research. First, rearing conditions are virtually identical for each infant, in marked contrast to the highly variable conditions for subjects reared in their own homes. Second, it is possible to institute systematic changes in rearing conditions in the institutional setting and to maintain continuous surveillance over their administration.

Figure 1 illustrates the typical nursery-ward facility for infants between the ages of 1 and 4 months. As you can see, the world of these infants is essentially bland and uniform.

GENERAL PLAN

The lack of knowledge about perceptual development in human infants posed the problem of assessing changes in processes about which no normative data existed. Our first task was therefore to assemble such information as fast as the methodological obstacles could be overcome.

After several years of intensive observation, we are able to describe in detail the development of visually directed reaching, visual attention, visual accommodation, and related behaviors such as the discovery of the hands. We have preliminary information on the de-

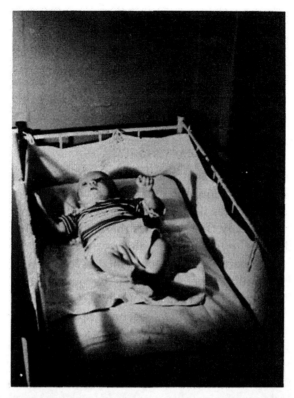

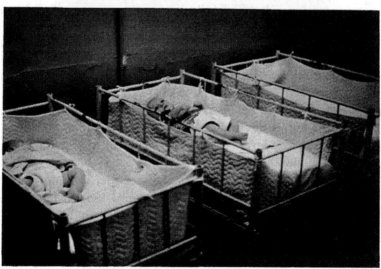

FIGURE 1. CONTROL CONDITION.

velopment of blinking to an approaching visible object and also on visual convergence.

We can also report the results of three attempts to modify the rate of acquisition of visual-motor behaviors by controlled modifications in rearing conditions.

New Normative Data

VISUALLY DIRECTED REACHING

To the best of our knowledge, no one, aside from Piaget, has studied in detail the acquisition of visually directed reaching. However, because Piaget was not centrally concerned with prehension, and also since he used only three subjects, his data—though very provocative—are primarily of suggestive value.

In a recent report we have described a ten-step process which culminates in visually directed reaching by our institutionally reared infants just prior to 5 months of age (White, Castle, and Held, 1964). These behaviors and their rate of occurrence may be seen in Figure 2 and are charted in Table 1.

The relationship of several of the responses to the ongoing development of these infants should be noted. *Swiping,* for example, is a remarkably accurate coordination for a 2-month-old infant. The hand is usually fisted, thereby precluding genuine prehension of the object.

Hands to the midline and clasp is characteristic of the bilateral behavior seen during the fourth month of life as the influence of the tonic neck reflex drops out. *Torso-orienting* reflects the child's growing capacities for gross motor action. What we have called a "Piaget-type" *reach* was described by Piaget as a raising of one hand to the vicinity of the object, followed by alternation of glance between hand and object, a narrowing of the gap between them, and then contact. This response and the "top-level" *reach* reflect a return to unilateral function in the fifth month of life.

We were particularly interested in the fact that swiping at objects appeared as early as the beginning of the third month, but top-level reaching did not appear until almost three months later. Was this delay inevitable?

STIMULUS OBJECT

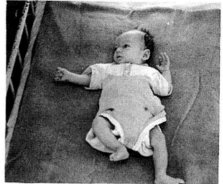

TONIC NECK REFLEX POSITION

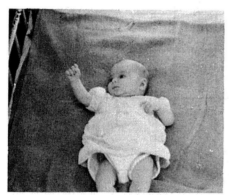

HAND REGARD

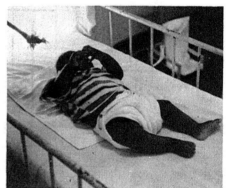

HANDS CLASPED AT MIDLINE

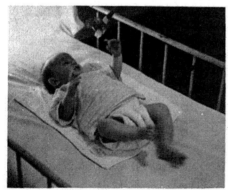

BOTH HANDS RAISED

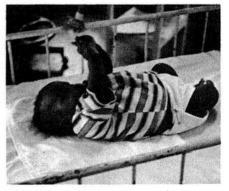

ORIENTED HANDS CLASPED AT MIDLINE

FIGURE 2. VISUALLY DIRECTED REACHING

TABLE 1

CHRONOLOGY OF RESPONSES OF CONTROL GROUP

RESPONSE	OBSERVED IN	TOTAL N	MEDIAN AND RANGE OF DATES OF FIRST OCCURRENCE				
			2M	3M	4M	5M	6M
SWIPES AT OBJECT	13	13	2–5				
UNILATERAL HAND RAISING	15	15	2–17				
BOTH HANDS RAISED	16	18	2–21				
ALTERNATING GLANCES (HAND AND OBJECT)	18	19	2–27				
HANDS TO MIDLINE AND CLASP	15	15		3–3			

Behavior			Age range
ONE HAND RAISED WITH ALTERNATING GLANCES, OTHER HAND TO MIDLINE CLUTCHING DRESS	11	19	3–8
TORSO ORIENTED TOWARD OBJECT	15	18	3–15
HANDS TO MIDLINE AND CLASP AND ORIENTED TOWARD OBJECT	14	19	4–3
PIAGET-TYPE REACH	12	18	4–10
TOP-LEVEL REACH	14	14	4–24

151

THE DEVELOPMENT OF VISUAL ATTENTION

In order to determine the sheer amount of visual exploratory activities exhibited by infants, and also to gain a thorough knowledge of their spontaneous visual-motor behavior, we initiated weekly three-hour observation periods for each of our subjects. Visual attention is defined as the state when the infant's eyes are more than half open, their direction of gaze shifting within thirty seconds.

Figure 3 illustrates the development of this activity from birth through 3 months of age. It is interesting to note the correspondence between rather dramatic changes in the visible environment and the shape of this curve. For example, the sharp increase in slope at about 2 months of age is coincident with the discovery of the hands. For the next 6 weeks or so, the child spends much of his waking time observing his fist and finger movements. The next major change in the visible environment occurred for this group between 3½ and 4 months. They

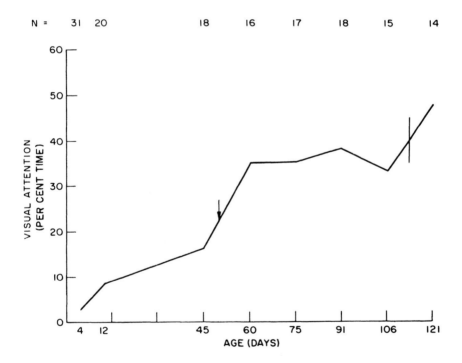

FIGURE 3. THE GROWTH OF VISUAL ATTENTION: CONTROL GROUP.

were transferred to large open-sided cribs. In combination with their greater trunk motility, enabling them to turn from side to side, this relocation suddenly produced a novel visual surround. Coincidentally, the shape of the curve reversed direction and increased markedly.

THE DEVELOPMENT OF VISUAL ACCOMMODATION

No systematic studies have been done of the development of visual accommodation in human infants. Haynes (1963) describes dynamic retinoscopy as a test procedure designed to measure the subject's accommodative ability under conditions more relevant to normal function than those used in traditional opthalmological examinations. The subject is tested in a non-drugged state for accommodative response to a target placed at several distances. He is further tested for his capacity to track the target as it is moved toward and away from his eyes. Dr. Haynes performed 111 dynamic retinoscopy examinations on 25 of our infants. With the use of lenses, objective measures of accommodative performance were obtained at target distances varying from 4 to 60 inches.

Perfect adjustment to changing target distance would be represented by a slope of 0.00, whereas the complete absence of accommodative change would be indicated by a value of +1.00. Prior to 1 month of age, the infant's accommodative response does not adjust to changes in target distance. The system appears to be locked at one focal distance whose median value for the group is 7½ inches. Flexibility of response begins at about the middle of the second month and performance comparable to that of the normal adult is attained by the fourth month, as shown by a median slope value of 0.03. By the time swiping behavior occurs (at about 2 months), the infant is prepared to focus his eyes close to the target.

THE DEVELOPMENT OF THE BLINK RESPONSE TO AN APPROACHING VISIBLE TARGET

In Riesen's studies (1958) young chimps deprived of experience with patterned light failed to develop the blink responses to approaching visible targets. Likewise, in Held and Hein's study (1963) of kittens deprived of self-induced motion in the presence of patterned light, similar deficits developed with respect to this response among others. No such studies have been done with human infants. Even normative data on the development of this function is unavailable.

We have performed a pilot study on ten infants ranging in age from 1 month to 5 months of age. The apparatus we used consisted of a 6-inch bull's eye target with ¼-inch red and white concentric rings. The object was mounted in a frame directly over the head of the supine infant. A plexiglass shield was placed 2 inches above the infant to preclude changes in air pressure as the target was dropped toward the subject. The range of target drop was from 2⅝ to 12½ inches. The sources of light were arranged to minimize brightness changes. Recording procedures were crude in this preliminary effort: one observer dropped the target and reported the magnitude and latency of response, the other recorded the data. The results were remarkably consistent. The median age for the onset of blinking was 2 months. The maximum target drop was necessary to elicit the response, and the responses were often slow and incomplete. By 3½ months, the group exhibited very rapid, completed blinks and even occasional startles in at least seven out of ten trials. A target drop of but 2⅝ inches was sufficient to elicit these responses.

We have described baseline data for the development of four visual-motor functions: visually directed reaching, visual attention, visual accommodation, and blinking to an approaching visible object. Our general research question is, "Are these developmental processes plastic? Is systematic contact with the environment instrumental in their development or does the infant simply grow into these skills?"

Experimental Results

FIRST MODIFICATION OF REARING CONDITIONS

Many recent studies have reported the remarkable effects of postnatal handling on the subsequent development of laboratory-reared lower animals (Denenberg and Karas, 1959; Levine, 1957; G. W. Meier, 1961). Mice, kittens, and dogs, given small amounts of extra early handling, grew up to be "better" animals as measured by a wide variety of tests. They were superior in many physical and adaptive respects. Recent surveys of maternal deprivation studies by Yarrow (1961) and Casler (1961) suggest that early handling is necessary for adequate human development. Sylvia Brody, in her book *Patterns of Mothering* (1951), noted that infants who received moderate handling were consistently more visually attentive than those receiving minimal handling.

TABLE 2

Onset of Sustained Hand Regard Under
Various Rearing Conditions

Condition	N	Median Date of Onset	Significance Levels (Mann-Whitney U 1-Tailed Tests)
Control (C)	16	49	C vs. H — .1469 N.S.
Handled (H)	10	60	C vs. EA — .0571 N.S.
Massive Enrichment (EA)	14	61	C vs. EB — .1867 N.S.
Modified Enrichment (EB)	15	44	H vs. EA — .4168 N.S.
			H vs. EB — .0136
			EA vs. EB — .0016

The following chart indicates the relationship between number of pairs sampled and significance level necessary in order to conclude that the groups come from significantly different (.05 level) parent populations. It was derived from the following formula:

$P = (1 - a_i)n$ where $P = .05$, n = number of pairs compared and
a = the level of significance which must be found for any single pair in order to conclude that there is more than one parent population involved.

N	1	2	3	4	5	6	7
a_i	.050	.025	.017	.012	.010	.008	.007

Would extra handling of our subjects who normally receive minimal amounts result in accelerated visual-motor development?

From day 6 through day 36, nurses administered twenty minutes of extra handling each day to each of the infants. Measures of overall development, physical growth, general health, the development of reaching and visual attention were taken regularly between days 37 and 152. There were no changes found in any developmental process except the growth of visual attention. The handled group was significantly more visually attentive than controls [1] (Fig. 4). Further exploration of the effects of early handling might produce still greater shifts in visual exploratory behavior, but since this problem was not central for us, and because the cost in terms of time and money is so great in research with human infants, we did not pursue this task.

1. In a previous report (White and Castle, 1964), we indicated this increase in visual attention was statistically significant. In fact the analysis used was somewhat inappropriate. In addition, we have added data from one new subject. Subsequent analyses (see Table 3) indicate a strong trend that fails to reach significance at the .05 level.

TABLE 3

Summary of Visual Attention Data

Days	Data				Analyses of Variance							Comparisons of Group Means				
	Group	N$_{ss}$	N scores	X score (% Time)	Groups	Source	ss	df	ms	F	Sign.	Groups	X Scores	t	df	Sign.
37-112	C	45	113	32.1	C	Between	4696	3	1565	3.95	>.01	C vs H	32.1 v 36.8	1.72	213	>.05
	H	11	102	36.8	H	Within	188259	475	396			C vs ME	32.1 32.8			N.S.
	ME	13	118	32.8	ME	Total	192955	478				C vs Mod.E	32.1 40.1	3.10	257	>.005
	Mod.E	14	146	40.1	Mod.E							H vs ME	36.8 32.8			N.S.
												H vs Mod.E	36.8 40.1			N.S.
												ME vs Mod.E	32.8 40.1	2.96	262	>.005
	Totals	83	479		C	Between	987	2	494	1.10	N.S.	Mod.E vs C, H+ ME	40.1 vs 33.8	3.50	477	>.0005
					H	Within	148084	331	447							
					ME	Total	149071	333								
37-75	C	34	59	29.9	C	Between	4550	3	1517	4.56	>.01	C vs H	29.9 v 34.2			N.S.
	H	10	58	34.2	H	Within	86137	259	333			C vs ME	29.9 26.3			N.S.
	ME	13	68	26.3	ME	Total	90687	262				C vs Mod.E	29.9 40.1	3.21	135	>.005
	Mod.E	14	78	36.7	Mod.E							H vs ME	34.2 26.3	2.42	124	>.01
												H vs. Mod.E	34.2 40.1	1.87	134	>.05
												ME vs Mod.E	26.3 40.1	4.56	144	>.0005

AGE (Days)

156

					Between	1615	2	808	2.43	N.S.		ME	26.3		2.97	262	>.01
					Within	63714	192	332				vs	vs.				
					Total	65329	194					C, H+ Mod.E	33.9				
Totals	71		263														
					Between	3560	3	1187	2.87	>.05		C vs H	33.5	41.4	1.73	78	>.05
	C	16	43	33.5	Within	78011	189	413				C vs ME	33.5	46.9	3.06	84	>.005
76-112	H	8	37	41.4	Total	81571	192					C vs Mod.E	33.5	42.5	2.29	111	>.025
	ME	9	43	46.9								H vs ME	41.4	46.9			N.S.
	Mod.E	13	70	42.5								H vs Mod.E	41.4	42.5			N.S.
												ME vs Mod.E	46.9	42.5			N.S.
Totals	46		193		—						—					

(Left group header: C / H / Mod.E with means 33.5 / 41.4 / 46.9 / 42.5)

* In the discussion of the nested ANOVA design (Winer, 1962, pp. 184–85), between subject and within subject mean squares may be pooled if they do not differ significantly. In the data of this study, such was the case. Since we were not interested in either between or within subject variability, we pooled their variances and tested for treatment differences.

** Because 6 significant figures are being calculated in each group, a conservative position would increase the required level of significacnce to $10/K(K-1)$, where K= # of groups. In this case K=4, and the more stringent level required would be .0083. (Ferguson, 1959, p. 238).

157

SECOND MODIFICATION OF REARING CONDITIONS

Several recent studies seem to indicate that visual-motor capacities depend to a significant extent on experience of some kind for their subsequent development. Riesen's early work demonstrated that chimpanzees required exposure to patterned visible stimulation for normal visual-motor development. His later studies have shown that movement within such environment was also required for adequate development (Riesen, 1958). Held and his collaborators (Held, 1961; Held and Bossom, 1961) have repeatedly shown that human adults require the opportunity for *self-induced* motion in dependably structured environments for adaptation to rearranged sensory inputs. More recently they performed a study with kittens which demonstrated the applicability of these findings to developmental processes (Held and Hein, 1963). The results of this study indicated that movement per se in the presence of a dependable surround was insufficient for normal visual-motor

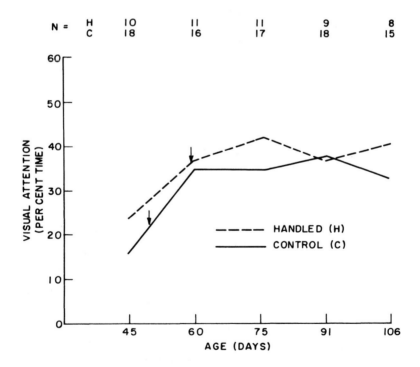

FIGURE 4. COMPARATIVE VISUAL ATTENTION CURVES.

development. Kittens whose movements were *externally produced* rather than *self-induced* did not develop normally. Self-induced movement in a dependable surround was found necessary for adequate development as well as for maintenance of visual-motor behavior.

Our subjects are normally reared under conditions which are obviously less than optimal with respect to such experience. Motility is inhibited by soft mattresses with depressions in them and constant supine posture. The visual surround is poorly figured. Heightened motility in an enriched surround should therefore produce accelerated visual-motor development.

As a first test we enriched the condition of environmental contact of a group of nineteen infants in as many respects as possible.

Increased tactual-vestibular stimulation—Each infant received twenty minutes of extra handling each day from day 6 through day 36.

Increased motility—Infants were placed in the prone posture for fifteen minutes after the 6 A.M., 10 A.M., and 2 P.M. feeding each day from day 37 through day 124. At these times, the crib liners were removed, making the ward activities visible to the child. Movements of the head and trunk in the presence of a figured visual surround resulted from the normal tendency of infants to rear their heads under such circumstances. The crib mattresses were flattened, thereby facilitating head, arm, and trunk motility.

Enriched visual surround—A special stabile featuring highly contrasting colors and numerous forms against a dull white background was suspended over these infants from day 37 through day 124. In addition, printed multicolored sheets and bumpers were substituted for the standard flat white ones (contrast Fig. 5 with Fig. 1). These changes were designed to produce heightened visual interest and increased viewing of hand movements due to the normal tendency of infants to swipe at visible objects nearby.

Weekly measures of prehensory responses and visual attention were made. The rate of development of spontaneous behavior relevant to visual-motor function such as hand regard, hands touching at the midline, mutual fingering and torso turning was assessed from the records of the three-hour observations. Performance on the Gesell tests was recorded at biweekly intervals to determine general developmental progress. Also, records of rate of weight gain and general health were kept.

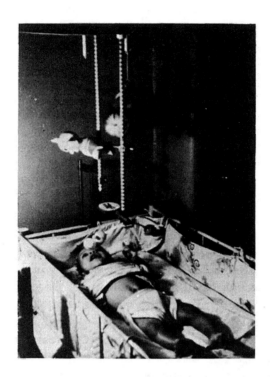

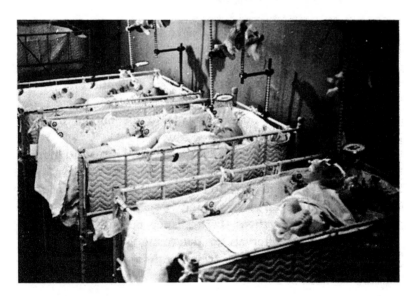

FIGURE 5. MASSIVE ENRICHMENT CONDITION.

Results

HAND REGARD AND SWIPING

Hand regard as such was much less frequently shown by this group as compared with controls. Instead the hands were generally first observed as they contacted portions of the experimental stabile. We called this "pattern-monitored stabile play" and considered it together with monitored bumper play as forms of hand regard. By these criteria, the onset of hand regard was delayed for some two weeks in our experimental group. The onset of swiping was also set back, but by only five days. Figure 6 illustrates the responses to the object leading to reaching for this group. For comparison of this group with the control group, contrast Table 4 with Table 1.

PREHENSION

The median age for the first appearance of top-level reaching was 3 months and 7 days for the experimental group, an advance of some 6½ weeks. ($p < .001$; Mann-Whitney U Test). Some of the types of preliminary responses reported for our control group did not occur prior to the onset of top-level reaching.

VISUAL ATTENTION

The course of development of visual attention was also altered dramatically in our experimental group as illustrated by Figure 6 and Table 3. Concurrent with the unexpected delay in the onset of hand regard (arrows in Fig. 6), was a marked decrease in visual exploratory behavior for the first portion of the test periods. On the other hand, once the group began to engage in prehensory contacts with the stabile and figured bumpers, visual attention increased sharply.

The results of this study clearly demonstrated the plasticity of several visual-motor developments. That the onset of hand regard is in part a function of environmental factors is not a novel notion. Hand regard is a 12-week behavior on the Gesell scale, whereas our control infants, with virtually nothing else to view, discovered their hands at less than 2 months of age. Piaget noted that the onset of this behavior varied by as much as thirty days among his own children, as a function of

TABLE 4

CHRONOLOGY OF RESPONSES OF GROUP REARED UNDER ENRICHED CONDITIONS

RESPONSE	OBSERVED IN	TOTAL N	MEDIAN AND RANGE OF DATES OF FIRST OCCURRENCE				
			2M	3M	4M	5M	6M
SWIPES AT OBJECT	11	14	2–8				
UNILATERAL HAND RAISING	12	13	2–3				
BOTH HANDS RAISED	12	13	2–12				
ALTERNATING GLANCES (HAND AND OBJECT)	10	11		2–21			

HANDS TO MIDLINE AND CLASP	7	10
ONE HAND RAISED WITH ALTERNATING GLANCES, OTHER HAND TO MIDLINE CLUTCHING DRESS	5	9
TORSO ORIENTED TOWARD OBJECT	4	9
HANDS TO MIDLINE AND CLASP AND ORIENTED TOWARD OBJECT	3	9
PIAGET-TYPE REACH	6	9
TOP-LEVEL REACH	9	9

3-2
3-9
3-15
3-28
3-25
3-7

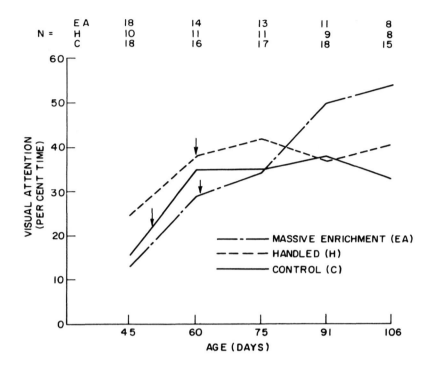

FIGURE 6. COMPARATIVE VISUAL ATTENTION CURVES.

differing environmental circumstances. Therefore, the fact that infants provided with enriched surrounds were late in discovering their hands compared to controls was not totally unexpected.

We were surprised that the group exhibited less visual attention during the first five weeks in the enriched visible surround. In fact, not only did they tend to ignore the stabile and bumpers, but it is my impression that they engaged in much more crying than the control group during the same period. Starting at about 2 months and 12 days of age, the group as a whole began to engage in a great deal of stabile play. As we had suspected, the rattles were repeatedly swiped at, thereby producing far more monitored hand and arm movements than would normally have occurred. Subsequently, in less than one month, the integration of the grasp with approach movements had been completed. You will remember that control infants required almost three months for this transition.

Earlier we had noted that the course of development of visual exploratory behavior seemed to reflect the availability of interesting things to look at. In control and handled groups, the slope of the curve of visual attention increased sharply when the hands were discovered and then decreased during the next six weeks. In this experimental group, it appears that for about a month, starting at 1 month and 7 days, the enrichment was actually ineffective and perhaps even unpleasant. However, once positive responses to the surround began to occur, visual attention increased sharply in striking contrast to the previous groups. The dip seen at 3½ months in both previous groups disappeared.

FURTHER MODIFICATION OF THE ENVIRONMENT

Until day 37, the procedures were the same as in the previous study (Study B), but then—instead of enrichment by prone placement and the stabile and printed sheets and bumpers—there was only one modification from day 37 until day 68: two pacifiers were mounted on the crib rails. These devices were made to stand out visually by appending to them a red-and-white pattern against a flat white background (Fig. 7). The objects were 6 to 7 inches away from the corneal surfaces of the infants' eyes. They were positioned so as to elicit maximum attention from a 6- to 10-week-old infant. The normal tendency of such infants is to accommodate at about 8 to 10 inches. It was assumed that the pacifiers might have the effect of orienting the infant toward the discovery of his own hands. It was further assumed that these objects might provide appropriate anchor points in space intermediate between the locus of spontaneous fixation and the ordinary path of motion of the hand extended in the tonic neck reflex posture.

At 68 days, the infant was then placed in a crib with a stabile similar to that used in the previous study until he was 124 days of age. We hypothesized that these infants would be more consistently precocious in the attainment of visually directed reaching. We also expected consistently higher visual attention from this group.

Results

HAND REGARD AND SWIPING

In the control group, the onset of sustained hand regard occurred at day 49. Infants in the handling study were behind (day 60). Infants in Study B were even later in this respect (day 61), supporting

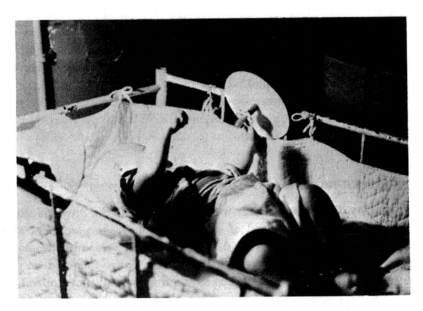

FIGURE 7. MODIFIED ENRICHMENT CONDITION.

the idea (White *et al.*, 1964) that the discovery of the hands is, in part, a function of the availability of interesting visible objects. The modified enrichment of this last study seemed more appropriate for the infant during the second month of life. Study C infants exhibited sustained hand regard at day 44. The onset of swiping responses followed the same general pattern, with Study C infants exhibiting this behavior earlier than all other groups (day 58).

PREHENSION

Apparently, the modified or paced enrichment of the last study was the most successful match of external circumstances to internally developing structures as indicated by the acquisition of top-level reaching at less than 3 months (day 89—significantly earlier than controls at > .001, Mann-Whitney U Test).

VISUAL ATTENTION

Figure 8 shows visual attention data for the subjects of the several studies. The depression of visual interest shown by Study B infants

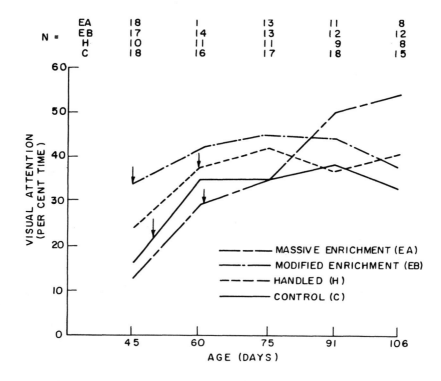

FIGURE 8. COMPARATIVE VISUAL ATTENTION CURVES.

from day 37 to day 74 has been eliminated and the modified enrichment (EB) group is consistently more attentive (sign > .0005)
throughout the test period (see Table 3). Curiously, although the
last group was more consistently attentive than the others, the reduction of such behavior at 3½ months appeared as it had in the first two
groups. It would appear that some uncontrolled variable is interacting
with our various attempts at modifying the function.

Conclusions

THE SIGNIFICANCE OF THE AGE RANGE FROM 1½ TO 5 MONTHS OF AGE

The first major conclusion derivable from our research is that the
age range from 1½ to 5 months is a time of enormous importance for

early perceptual-motor development. According to our findings and those of others, human infants reared under natural conditions show a dramatic surge in both visual activity and development at the middle of the second month of life. During the next 3½ months, the following events occur: (1) the development of flexible accommodative function, culminating in virtually adult-like performance at 3½ months; (2) discovery of the hands and gradual development of manual control by the visual system, culminating in true visually-directed reaching; (3) the initiation and complete development of the blink response to an approaching visible target; (4) the initiation and complete development of visual convergence; and (5) the onset of social smiling.

PLASTICITY IN HUMAN VISUAL-MOTOR DEVELOPMENT

The studies reported above demonstrate that aspects of early visual-motor development are remarkably plastic. As yet, we know neither the limits of this plasticity nor the range of visual-motor functions that fall within this classification. At the very least, the onset of hand regard and visually directed reaching and the growth of visual attentiveness are significantly affected by environmental modification. Infants of both groups B and C developed top-level reaching in approximately 60 per cent of the time required by the control group, a result very much in line with the theory that self-initiated movement with its visual consequences is crucial for visual-motor development. Whether or not visual accommodation, convergence, pursuit, and blinking to an approaching target share this plasticity remains to be seen. Assessment of the extent to which various types of mobility and specific environmental factors contribute to these and other perceptual motor developments is the goal of our continuing research.

I think these studies show clearly that enrichment procedures can produce remarkable effects on the course of early development. It may be said, as Eleanor Maccoby has pointed out before, that we've known for years that short-term effects on development are possible at various stages of growth. And one can ask, "Are there any long-term consequences of such experiences?" My answer would be that the question has usually been posed incorrectly. In education, one doesn't expect to provide instruction to a 6-year-old for six months and then find profound consequences at age 18. We assume that education is a continuing, long-term process. We therefore attempt to design the interventions of each succeeding year so that they mesh with prior events.

Furthermore, we recognize the cumulative nature of the process. A deficit in elementary language or reading skills plagues the student at *every* succeeding grade level.

We will never know very much about the maximal effects of experience on development until we can perform similar cumulative matching studies throughout the developmental years starting from birth. I don't pretend that this is a modest problem. It will take time, and at least a hundred times the knowledge we now have about child behavior.

I believe that any scientific endeavor must start with observations. The more complex the subject, the more extensive the observations required. Since humans and their adaptive abilities are frightfully complex, we need enormous amounts of first-quality observations. In the second phase of such a program, theory enters. The major function of a theory is to bring order to an array of events. I am making a plea for *inductive* theorizing. I maintain that child development and early childhood education is woefully barren with respect to observational data, and until we *recognize* and *remedy* this deficiency we will continue to build castles of sand.

OMAR KHAYYAM MOORE

and

ALAN ROSS ANDERSON

THE RESPONSIVE
ENVIRONMENTS PROJECT

*Omar Khayyam Moore (B.A. 1942, Doane College; M.A.
1946, Ph.D. 1949, Washington University) is Professor of
Social Psychology, Principal Investigator for the Respon-
sive Environments Project, and Head of the Responsive
Environments Laboratory at the Learning Research and
Development Center; and Senior Research Associate, The
Philosophy of Science Center; University of Pittsburgh.
Dr. Moore is also President and Chairman of the Board,
Responsive Environments Foundation, Inc., and an Asso-
ciate in the University Seminar on Basic and Applied
Social Research, Columbia University. Alan Ross Anderson
(Ph.D. 1955, Yale University) is Professor of Philosophy,
Senior Research Associate in the Knowledge Availability
Systems Center, and Senior Research Associate in the Cen-
ter for the Philosophy of Science, University of Pittsburgh.*

OUR purpose is to describe the Responsive En-
vironments Project: to provide an analysis of its structure, to state its
goals, and to give an informal progress report on some of its aspects.

The long-range objective of the Project, which is part of the Learning Research and Development Center at the University of Pittsburgh,
is the creation of an experimentally grounded theory of human problem-solving and social interaction. The present proximate goals are:
(a) to construct new formal systems which, hopefully, will be of use
in formulating such a theory; (b) to design equipment in accordance
with the principles of the theory, both to facilitate testing the theory
and for educational applications; (c) to formulate heuristic principles
which may prove helpful in guiding empirical investigations; and, finally, (d) to test parts of the theory as they are formulated. Our discussion is organized in terms of these four objectives.

[AUTHORS' NOTE: This chapter is severely abridged from a monograph that will
appear eventually either as a book or as an extended journal article; it is intended
to serve as a guide through the bibliography of relevant literature.—O.K.M. and
A.R.A.]

The Formal Sciences

About ten years ago, we undertook the ambitious task of finding out what was wrong with the behavioral sciences; what did these sciences require to accelerate their development? We came to the conclusion that, among other things, the behavioral sciences needed additional formal machinery to handle some of the concepts peculiar to them. In this section we want to consider three kinds of new logical systems which seem to us to be of relevance to the problems under consideration.

1) *Deontic Logic: the logic of obligation, permission, prohibition, and related notions.* Normative aspects, or rules, of the environment are of central importance for the interpretation of human interaction, yet we found almost no mathematical techniques available for treating this idea. To the best of our knowledge, the only inquirers ten years ago who were willing to gamble on the idea that logic in general, and deontic logic in particular, had a direct and immediate bearing on the analysis of social interaction, consisted of a group of us who were then at Yale.[1] Even today, now that deontic logic is a going concern, the motivations of most mathematicians and logicians who work on it outside of our group are either solely formal or solely philosophical. We share these concerns, but we have our eyes on the behavioral sciences as well.

Whenever an experimenter plans a new environment—an environment in which pre-school children learn to read and write, for example—the planner is faced not only with the obvious problems of designing the physical layout, including whatever special equipment is to be employed, but he also faces the fact that he will have some normative system which is to provide the "rules of the game" for entering the environment, for behaving within it once there, and for leaving it.

We contend that if the experimenter does not take the normative aspect into account it will almost always emerge as a major source

1. Nuel D. Belnap, Jr. (philosophy); Frederic B. Fitch (philosophy); Rulon S. Wells (linguistics and philosophy); Conrad Wogrin (electrical engineering); and ourselves. At that time we were working together on a project supported by the Office of Naval Research, Group Psychology Branch, SAR/Nonr-609(16). Also at various times we enlisted the aid of Otomar Bartos (sociology); Morris Berkowitz (sociology); Neil Gallagher (philosophy); Jay Keyser (linguistics); Saul Kripke (mathematics); David Levin (philosophy); Eugene Royster (sociology); Joel Spencer (mathematics); and John Wallace (philosophy).

of unexplained variance in performance. Clearly, for instance, a situation in which the subjects of an experiment are virtually prisoners to the experimental situation, permitted to do *only* what the experimenter orders, is deontically very different from one in which the subjects *may* refuse to come to the laboratory at all, *may* stay as long as they wish, and *may* leave whenever they wish.

There are, both in theory and in practice, considerable variations in the deontic systems that human beings use. Unless we have some way of analyzing the formal structure of these systems, we can characterize neither the norms which subjects bring to a laboratory nor the laboratory's own norms, to say nothing of the possible changes in normative structure which might result from exposure to an experimentally contrived environment.

It develops that the deontic operations referred to at the outset are definable in terms of other modal operations, in particular, what have been called the alethic modes. These have to do with necessity, possibility, contingency, and impossibility. The literature on the topic contains many discussions of how this is to be done. But the leading idea in each case is the same: we say that it is obligatory that *p* just in case the falsity of *p* leads to some violation of the set of norms or rules in which we are interested. Other properties of the deontic concepts then emerge with the help of standard logical techniques.

Given these operations, we can characterize social systems such as *authoritarianism:* one is permitted only to do one's duty, there are no indifferent states-of-affairs, everything is either obligatory or forbidden; *conflated ethics:* what is permitted is what is possible, all states-of-affairs are ethically indifferent or neutral, the only thing that really matters is either what we can do, or else forbidden events are simply ignored. *Cusinism:* what is necessary is, and what is is possible, but what is obligatory is not necessary, and what occurs is not necessarily permitted. Our aim in mentioning these examples is to point out that there exist systems of mathematical logic which might help us better understand the formal properties of various normative systems.

2) *The Logic of Relevance.* A second problem which seemed pressing in the context of analyzing social interaction was the notion of the *relevance* of one proposition to another. Classical truth-functional, alethic, and deontic modal logic take no account whatever of the notion of relevance as between antecedent and consequent of an "if . . . then—" statement. The connection with social interaction is as follows. Certain social situations are less "structured" than others in terms of the relevance of one utterance or action to another. As extreme cases

we might consider the word-salad of psychotics, as compared with a well-conducted criminal trial or an argument contained in a scientific monograph. In the first case almost anything goes; in the second, elaborate preparation is sometimes required to justify the relevance of a certain line of inquiry or reasoning to the issue at hand. We would like to suggest that just as the normative structure of an interactional situation is one important aspect of social interaction, so also are the canons of relevance which help determine the character of the interaction of members of a group.

Building on the work of a fundamental and very important paper by Ackermann (1956), a number of investigators have done work on the problem of relevance from the point of view of mathematical logic.

3) *Erotetic Logic: the logic of questions and answers.* There is another aspect of the problem of characterizing mathematically the forms of social interaction which seems to us of equal importance. Any account of human symbolic interaction should certainly take into account the logic of interrogatives. This field in modern form is very recent; the most definitive study to date is that of Belnap (1963), and though not directly connected with the Responsive Environments Project, it is sufficiently close in spirit that we do not hesitate to claim that Belnap's work has an immediate bearing on the kind of formal work associated with this project.

4) *Projections.* The initial impetus for the development of all these systems was philosophical in character. Yet the formal systems—once set forth—proved of interest from a purely mathematical point of view. Standard mathematical questions about completeness, consistency, decidability, etc., could be asked about them, and in many cases these questions have been answered. Moreover, some of these structures turned out to have close connections with other parts of mathematics which were developed earlier with entirely different motivations.

Those of us associated with the Responsive Environments Project share the philosophical and mathematical interests in the formal systems considered above; such novelty as lies in our approach depends on our belief that the systems could also be useful in constructing some sort of abstract characterization of various important aspects of systems of social interaction. Such applications are largely programmatic, but noticeable progress has been made in relevant areas of alethic modal logic, deontic logic, the logic of relevance, and erotetic logic in the past ten years. We do not see in the immediate future any direct application of these formalisms for the description or construction of systems dealing with human interaction. It may prove that the formal developments are valuable for the behavioral sciences only as heuristic devices which enable us to gain some clarity concerning the concepts involved. But the following considerations may make our projected applications look somewhat plausible.

It seems reasonable to conjecture that anything we would want to consider as a "social group" would consist of individuals who share beliefs about (a) what sort of thing is possible, necessary, etc., (b) what is permitted, obligatory, etc., (c) what is relevant to what, and (d) what sort of questions are to be asked and how they are to be answered. Under (1)–(3) above, we have noted briefly some examples of alethic, deontic, relevant, and erotetic logic which might be applied in describing such a social group.

If we are engaged in contriving, rather than simply describing, an environment, it is our experience that *any* guidance one can get from theoretical considerations such as those outlined above is enormously useful. In this sense these systems have already proved to be helpful as extremely abstract "blueprints" which, when superimposed on one another, give us some guidance in making real the kind of environments which lead to almost unexpectedly dramatic results.

Equipment

1) *Responsive Environments.* Responsive environments were in existence before any of the equipment considered below was available. Automation came later; and before turning to that topic we outline the requirements imposed on an environment in order to qualify it as "responsive."

A person P is said to be in a *responsive environment* R if:

(a) R allows for a variety of actions on the part of P. These actions may be exploratory in character, or may be well thought out ahead of time by P. In either event:

(b) R responds in some reasonably systematic way to P's action, with the result that P is informed immediately—or at some specified interval—of the consequences of his action relative to R.

(c) The pace of the activity is determined principally by P; P is not rushed or delayed in his actions relative to R, although some necessary time lag is allowed for in R's response.

(d) R permits P to use his capacity for discovering constant features of R, relations between the behavior of P and the response of R, etc.

(e) R is sufficiently complex so that the interconnected relations discovered under (d) are generalizable; they shed light for P on general properties of physical, social, or cultural worlds.

It should be clear that not all environments are responsive, and that interactional situations do not fall under the heading of responsive environments as described above; in the course of interaction between two human beings, the general state of both persons is changed as a result of the encounter, but in a responsive environment the "program" of R is left unchanged by the action of P.

2) *Classification of Machines.* For the purposes of guiding the construction of *mechanical* responsive environments, we have been led to a consideration of machines generally, and to an attempt to give a classification of them in terms of the standards we use in evaluating them. We propose the following:

(a) *Tools.* A tool is a machine to be judged primarily in terms of its *efficiency;* most machines are tools. The point of using a tool is to overcome resistance at one point by the application of a force at some other point. Typical simple tools are the lever, the pulley, the screw, and the inclined plane.

(b) *Reproducers.* A mirror is an example of a simple reproducer. More sophisticated examples are the phonograph and the camera. The thing we want to know about a reproducing device is how faithful it is: its *fidelity.*

(c) *Responsive devices.* A responsive device is a machine which meets the requirements of a "responsive environment" as just described above; it is to be judged primarily in terms of a criterion which we shall call *efficacy.* The point of using a responsive machine is to change (hopefully to enhance) the emotional or cognitive state of a human being. An early simple responsive device is the harp. The criterion of efficacy requires disciplines beyond engineering to evaluate such a machine; the behavioral sciences are called upon to judge responsive devices.

(d) *Interactional machines.* At present there are no successful interactional machines in existence. Any machine which can successfully take part in social interaction with human beings is an interactional machine; by "successfully take part" we mean that the human interactors would not recognize or detect that the machine is a machine rather than another human being. An interactional machine is not reproducing or simulating the behavior of any given person, but is a fellow interactor to be taken seriously in its own right. Even though no interactional machines exist, the question can still be asked as to how we would evaluate them if there were any. It would seem that one crucial criterion of adequacy for such machines would be that of *congeniality.*

One of the aims of the Project has been to provide specifications for particular responsive environments with responsive devices, with a view toward accelerating learning. We have chosen what we take to be the most fundamental aspect of the socialization process as material for the initial experimental study of the general notion, namely, the acquisition of a natural language, in both spoken and written form. In the remainder of this section we will describe one example from the potentially very large family of responsive devices currently under investigation: the "talking typewriter."

This device, co-invented by Moore and Kobler (1963; Kobler and Moore, 1966), is in current production under the name of the *Edison Responsive Environment.* One of the things for which it was designed was to enable a person with no knowledge of a particular natural language to learn both the spoken and written forms of that language. It can be used equally well to teach very young children how to cope with the written form of the language they speak (and most of our experience has been with children learning to read and write English), and also to enable adults to learn languages with which they are unfamiliar. If the reader himself wishes to learn Russian, the steps would be roughly as follows (of course, the machine would have to be equipped with the Cyrillic alphabet):

Step 1. The machine is set so that the user may strike any key, after which the keyboard locks until the voice-box gives the user the name and/or the phonetic value of the character. Repeated explorations of the keyboard lead to both visual and auditory command of the alphabet.

Step 2. The machine is reset so that the voice-box names a letter, and the user is to find the corresponding character and strike the appropriate key. Arrangements can be made such that if the machine names a letter—or gives its phonetic value, or both—only the appropriate key can be activated, the rest of the keyboard being locked.

Step 3. The machine is reset so as to display some word, perhaps with an appropriate picture on a screen to the right of the keyboard. A typical sequence of events at this stage might run as follows:

(a) The projection screen displays a picture of a table and directly above the paper carriage there is displayed the Russian word for "table."

(b) The keyboard is locked so that only the keys for the letters of a word in order can be depressed, so that the user may strike the operable keys, and the voice-box will give the phonetic value of each in turn.

(c) The voice-box then repeats the spelling, pronounces the word, and allows the user time to repeat and record the word.

(d) The voice-box may make additional remarks about some words, calling attention to irregularities, etc.

Steps 1–3 simply constitute an example; the talking typewriter can be treated in a variety of subtly different ways, for an indefinitely large number of words. Sentences may be treated relatively to words, in the same way that words are treated relatively to letters; the situation is the same for paragraphs, considered as clusters of sentences.

At each stage, flexibility is maintained. The machine can give or take dictation, with or without the projection screen; the keyboard can be locked or not as the programmer—or the user—wishes, and so on.

To prepare a program the programmer need only do three things, since the keyboard and the recording device are themselves usable as encoding devices. The programmer simply (a) types in the desired material, (b) speaks as desired into the recording system, (c) manipulates a small number of buttons which coordinate the results of (a) and (b), together with any material to be used on the projection screen or exhibitor. The flexibility and simplicity of the encoding procedures make additions or deletions in the program possible with very little time and effort. It is in fact possible to make daily changes with a view to following the interests and progress of the user. The program is not a monolithic affair which begins at the beginning and grinds its way relentlessly to the end. Parts may be skipped or abridged, depending on the user's prior knowledge. And if a user already has some familiarity with the spoken form of the language (as is the case in the uses thus far most extensively investigated—allowing pre-school children to learn to read and write), a large part of what can be learned with the help of the machine is already known, so that the amount to be done by both programmer and user is reduced substantially.

We turn finally to the relationship between the talking typewriter and the notion of a responsive environment. There can be no doubt that the instrument is a "responsive device" in the sense considered under the classification of machines above. Experimental evidence to be discussed below makes it abundantly clear that the machine is "efficacious" in changing the cognitive status of its users.

It should be equally clear that a booth containing such a responsive device, if surrounded by the appropriate autotelic conventions, is a responsive environment in the sense described at the outset of this section. It allows the user a number of actions which may be explored or used systematically; the environment responds promptly and systematically; the pace is determined by the user; the situation permits discoveries by the user; and what is learned is generalizable to other situations in which communication skills are required.

3) *Projections.* Ten years ago there were no automated responsive environments in existence; there were no responsive devices designed specifically for the purpose of facilitating learning, though the concept was available. We envisage, if cooperation between behavioral scientists, formal scientists, and engineers continues, a shelf full of responsive devices from which we may choose those instruments best suited for particular purposes—much as we now have a shelf full of logical systems adaptable to various analytic purposes.

General Substantive Heuristics

The principal thrust in the behavioral sciences since the advent of quasi-scientific methods in these disciplines has been devoted to the study of human *behavior,* individually, in groups, organizations, and societies. We are in sympathy with the studies produced by this army of explorers, but we think it not unreasonable for a small band to split itself off (heuristically) from the main movement, turn around, and march off in the opposite direction in the hope of finding something the others might have missed. This thought may serve as a partial excuse for attending to the *products* of human behavior, with a view to discovering something about the nature of man from his products. These products have been lumped under the heading of "culture"; our attack is to examine the notion of culture in abstraction from users, place, and time of use, etc., and to try to get as clear an abstract conceptualization of the notion as possible. In what follows we will state some views of culture and some related topics, which seem most relevant to the notion of a responsive environment.

1) *Culture.* An item of culture is the kind of thing one person can learn from another; these things include facts, methods, techniques, and abstract structures of various sorts, such as languages. Some sets

(of cultural items) of structural or transformational or generative rules or techniques have aspects in common with what logicians call models.

2) *Models.* We want to distinguish the terms "theory" (a deductively connected collection of propositions designed to explain something) and "model" (a physical or abstract structure or process of which the theory gives an account—a model is said to be a model *of* a theory.) Now the situation in the behavioral sciences generally seems to be that we have no rigorous or satisfactory theories of human behavior; yet it seems that some sort of general guidelines must be part of the equipment of individuals in a society—a set of guidelines which, if not a theory, at least have features which do some of the work we would expect a theory to do. These considerations lead us to our next topic.

3) *Autotelic Folk-models.* Behavioral scientists generally take the stance that the ordinary man has very little in the way of intellectual resources to guide him in managing his affairs beyond folk sayings and aphorisms—which, the social scientist is quick to point out, are often contradictory (for example, "Absence makes the heart grow fonder" and "Out of sight, out of mind").

We would like to suggest, as a heuristic ploy, a different view of people. We are prepared to suppose that early in human history, probably at about the same time natural languages developed, men also created models of the most important features of their environment. These were abstract models which collectively covered relations between man and nature—insofar as nature is not random—man and the random or chancy elements in experience, man in interactional relations with other humans, and man and the normative aspects of group living. Conceptual structures falling within these four classes of models were created by unsung Newtons, and there does not exist a society, however primitive, that does not have cultural objects falling in these four categories of models.

(a) Every society has *puzzles* which stand in an abstract way for man-nature relations; the physical sciences tend to treat nature as a "puzzle" for man to solve.

(b) Every society has some *games of chance* (abstract models of the aleatory aspects of existence).

(c) Every society has *games of strategy* which capture some of the peculiar features of interactional relations among men, relations in which no party to an encounter controls all of the relevant factors upon which the outcome depends, though each controls some of these factors and each participant can take account of the potential actions of others involved in the same situation.

(d) Every society has *aesthetic* entities: art forms, which we suggest give people the opportunity to learn to make normative judgments about their experience.

All societies make use of these cultural objects in the socialization of the young and for the recreation and enjoyment of those who are older. Simple forms of these models are internalized in childhood, and more complex versions of them sustain us in adulthood.

What kind of considerations can be invoked to make these theses sound plausible? We observe that there are only two reasonably deep mathematical theories which have had application in the behavioral sciences: probability theory and the theory of games of strategy. Both of these fields constitute theories, in the sense indicated above, and both have models in a variety of phenomena. Certain kinds of models of particular interest for our present purposes can be suggested: actuarial tables and roulette are models of probability theory; warfare and poker are models of the theory of games of strategy; no suitable general theory analogous to these two is available for puzzles, yet we can extrapolate and see models of a theory of puzzles in maps of the DNA molecule and double-crostics; similarly, and more tenuously, we note that a set of commandments, or Shaw's *Major Barbara*, might be seen as models for some (putative, but as yet nonexistent) theory of aesthetics. Let us, at any rate, suppose that we are correct in these conjectures, and that folk-models do in fact serve as the "theoretical" arm of a society's folk-culture. Considering these constructions, we note that in each pair of models the first have to do with serious concerns in life, and the second appear to have a frivolous character. The distinction we want to draw here is aided by use of the terms "heterotelic" (having purposes or goals extrinsic to the activity) and "autotelic" (cultural products which contain their own goals or sources of motivation).

Our contention is that the appearance of frivolity is specious, that in fact these autotelic folk-models play an important role in the process of socialization. As evidence, we cite the fact that societies with which we are familiar have severe rules designed to keep autotelic activities from becoming heterotelic; for example, the Amateur Athletic Code is designed to distinguish between those athletes who play because it is fun (autotelically) and those professionals who play for money (heterotelically).

The heuristic moral is that if societies have found it feasible, perhaps even necessary, to inculcate what the Greeks would have called "virtue" with the help of folk-models internalized under autotelic circumstances, then perhaps the soundest way of constructing efficacious responsive environments is to surround them with rules designed to keep them autotelic. For example, in our work with the talking typewriter, children are *invited* to come to the laboratory, and they may come or not as they choose; when in the laboratory, they are not told that they *must* do anything, but are left to fool around with the typewriter as they please; they get out of the laboratory when they feel like it, and no one insists that they continue. We hope that these comments will serve to illuminate the fact that we are concerned primarily with *autotelic* responsive environments as aids in learning.

4) *Intelligence, Personality, and Socialization.* Our preceding discussion has emphasized certain differences in heuristic outlook between workers on this project and what we referred to as the "main movement" of the army of professional behavioral scientists. Under the present heading we would like to establish *liaison* with the main party, by indicating where we agree and then indicating where *our* point of view differs from the "new look" in psychology. Accordingly, we list below some assumptions—extracted from the work of Hebb (1949), Hunt (1961), and others, and expressed in a form amenable to our general heuristic strategy—which we shared with a number of other investigators at the inception in 1956 of the project on which we are now reporting:

(a) We distinguish first between *ability* and *capacity* of an organism (or engine, or whatnot). We cannot tell directly from performances what the capacity of the unit is, though we might be able to get a direct test of abilities. Abilities may, under suitable circumstances, be altered radically (for example, we may alter "IQ performances"); it does not seem at present even possible to adequately measure capacities, but presumably these may be altered in as radical ways as abilities.

(b) Early stimulation of a suitable sort has a marked effect on the alterations mentioned above. Evidence seems to indicate that early stimulation increases the ability (and perhaps the capacity) of the adult organism to solve pressing problems. We note, however, that most studies deal with subhuman animals where the stimulation has been of a sensory character; whether the evidence applies to *symbolic* stimulation remains an open question.

(c) Personality development in human organisms does not occur in accordance with a genetically determined timetable (a purely maturational process). The social matrix in which development takes place is a crucial factor in the way in which personalities develop.

(d) In addition to whatever motivation can be attributed to homeostatic needs and specific drives—for example, hunger—the information-processing activities of an organism constitute a motivational system in its own right.

We share these views with a large number of investigators, but we believe that the analysis of folk-models sheds further light. In particular, it seems reasonable to assume that if folk-models play the role in socialization that we have outlined above, then they should play an equally important role in the development of personalities of individuals. Corresponding to the four classes of folk-models we have described above, there should be four aspects of a social personality: four *perspectives*, to which we give the following names:

Perspective (1): that of an *agent;* in Meadean (1934) terminology, an "I"; a unit capable of action relevant to the environment in which he finds himself.

Perspective (2): that of a *patient;* in Meadean terms, a "me"; a unit capable of being the recipient of a perhaps unexpected action on the part of the environment.

Perspective (3): that of *reciprocity;* Mead's "the significant other"; an attempt to see what follows from the point of view of our fellow-interactor, essential to developing a strategy.

Perspective (4): that of an *umpire;* Mead's "generalized other"; the ability to look at the behavior of ourselves and others from the point of view of an impartial inspector.

The four perspectives work together to enable us to look at the same thing in several ways; the fully socialized human being, we suggest, runs his problems through all four of these perspectives in coming to a solution.

In addition to the consideration of personalities from a structural point of view, we ought to say something about the dynamic relations among the four perspectives conceived of as processes.

Plato described "thinking" as an internal dialogue; he, like others in a venerable tradition, thought of language and the logic that is part thereof, as essential parts of "wisdom." We would like to amplify this insight by suggesting that not only is language central to our intercommunication of ideas, but also to the intracommunication; we speak to ourselves continually, now adopting one perspective, now another. Throughout the whole of the internal and external dialogues there runs the continual question as to "what follows from what." We claim, that is, that the formal work described at the beginning of this paper has an immediate bearing on these questions, in the sense that the formal machinery provides us with some sort of apparatus which will enable us to analyze the possible ("What can I do about this?"), the deontic ("What should I do?"), and the erotetic ("How can I phrase the question so as to make sense?"). These aspects of our folk-logic are embodied in our language and are part of what makes communication so interesting, so stimulating. Which brings us to another suggestion: we have a pretty clear idea of what we mean by a "stimulating sensory environment"; what should we mean by a "stimulating symbolic environment"?

We would like to suggest that some measure of symbolic stimulation might be linked to the variety of kinds and combinations of these perspectives available in an environment. A maximally stimulating environment would be one that encompasses as many of these perspectives as possible (that is, puzzles, games of chance and of strategy, art forms). Such considerations have been of first importance in designing *stimulating, autotelic, responsive environments*. And it seems further, that a study of the exceptional cases—where nature has performed cruel experiments, by depriving people of sight, hearing, continuity of experience (as in the case of epilepsy), or with sociocultural deprivations—is likely to shed as much light on the normal ones as is a direct study of the normal cases themselves.

Empirical Studies

We have given hints in the previous section about what we mean by a *stimulating, autotelic, responsive environment*. We want here to discuss a very important, and an easily overlooked, aspect of the Project's empirical work: namely, the set of rules governing the operation of a laboratory. Generally speaking, machines are more accurate than humans, and they take much of the drudgery out of the actual running of a laboratory, but machines are not nearly as essential to the project as the set of rules surrounding the environment. Sensitivity to the *stimulating* and *autotelic* features of an environment requires at least as much managerial skill and concern for the "customer" as is required to run a good restaurant: trained, knowledgeable persons in a position to prepare and dish out intellectual nourishment in a manner sufficiently appetizing so as to get the customers to return of their own volition. The laboratory situation is unlike that in ordinary schools where the law requires attendance. As we mentioned earlier, children are *invited* (not ordered) to come to the laboratory, and we have yet to find a single child among those to whom laboratories under this project have been available, who has persisted in refusing to come. We attribute this fact in part to the truly *invitational* character of the invitation; and it is because (we suspect) the laboratory environment is stimulating, autotelic, and responsive, that the children keep returning without the coercion of a truant officer.

Exploratory Investigations. The period from about 1958 to 1966 has been spent in preparing for large-scale, rigorously designed and executed experimental studies. This preparation has taken the form of numerous "quick and dirty" pilot investigations, designed to answer questions as to the feasibility of the whole enterprise. In order to give the reader a sense of the exploratory studies made to date, we simply list a few briefly:

(a) *Mechanics.* From early 1961 to 1966, the talking typewriter went through many prototypes and three major models, pilot studies being geared to the questions, "Do children like it?" "Is it (nearly) indestructible?" and "Can the laboratory managers operate it?" For each question the answer seems to be, at this writing, "Yes."

(b) *Architecture.* Since 1958 several laboratories have been designed and constructed; four are now in existence, and two more are in the planning stage. Since we are dealing primarily with very young children, it is not feasible at the outset to lecture them on the autotelic character of the laboratory environment; but it has been found very useful to use every possible clue to bring home the point that when they pass through the door they are entering a new environment, where the rules of behavior are different and which is in some sense cut off from their everyday world. This sharp demarcation can be pressed by using different colors, floor textures, temperatures (the laboratories are air-conditioned), and so on. Again, the exploration has been aimed at finding the ideal—so that children on entering the laboratory will know that they are in a "different world."

(c) *Selection and Training of Staff.* For reasons which we do not understand very well, our most successful laboratory assistants have a high degree of interest in matters aesthetic. This seems odd in view of the stereotype according to which interest in aesthetics precludes interest in machines; although, of course, a piano is a sound-producing machine. We hope to speculate on this matter on another occasion; for the moment, we simply note that it guides the selection of trainees and that the fact is compatible with our view of the importance of autotelic folk-models.

Among the other aspects of our training program, we find that professionally trained, experienced teachers meet our needs for laboratory supervisors very well; and in turn they find the connection with the new educational technology to be stimulating and satisfying. We want, also, to stress that very little time is required—a day or so—to master the relevant mechanical details of the machinery itself; what takes time is to internalize the rules designed to ensure that the environment remains stimulating, autotelic, and responsive.

(d) *Curriculum: Content.* A survey of the extensive literature on the topic of reading curricula revealed that on the whole this material was not suitable for our purposes, both because it was not designed for pre-school children, and because it was not sufficiently flexible for use with the wide variety of children (gifted, normal, retarded, culturally affluent or deprived, deaf, epileptic, etc.) whom we hoped to study and possibly help. The tack taken since 1958, then, is to elicit material from the children on an individual basis, making use of their conversations with adults and with other children, and such other ways of expressing themselves (pictures they draw, for example) as can be readily picked up by a sensitive adult's ear or by recorders. The result is a list of topics, sentences, and little stories, derived from a variety of encounters, which are almost bound to match the child's level of sophistication, understanding, and interests. This information is evaluated by the laboratory supervisor, then encoded by the programmer. The child is not, however, confined solely to his own productions; from time to time he is introduced to material outside his ken, and perhaps slightly more difficult than what he creates for himself: he is exposed to the programs of other children in his group, or more advanced groups; and he is given a few "set pieces" chosen by those in charge from appropriate literary classics by such authors as Aesop, Lewis Carroll, Robert Louis Stevenson, and A. A. Milne.

(e) *Curriculum: Organization.* We begin by making some impressionistic observations concerning the four basic aspects of communication with which we are concerned and the social contexts in which these occur, as expressed in the table on page 187.

Our own experience leads us to believe that the bulk of the population is pretty much confined to the lower left quadrant; one of our principal aims has been to try to keep a parallel between writing (as visible speech) and speaking (as audible writing), an attitude de-

	SPEAKING-LISTENING	READING-WRITING
FORMAL	Lectures; after-dinner speeches; set pieces: plays, monologues	Articles and books of an expository nature; non-fiction
INFORMAL	Daily colloquial talk; party chit-chat; use of "ordinary language"	Personal letters; dialogue in fiction; humorous writings; diaries

signed to create in children the view that reading-writing and speaking-listening go hand in hand; one is as natural as the other.

In addition, since 1958 we have been developing and testing various ways of helping a child become familiar with the English notational conventions which will enable him to map orthography onto speech, so that we introduce the child to punctuational conventions and physical arrangement such as spacing between words and paragraphing at the same time as upper- and lower-case letters. Thus the child neither ignores punctuation in learning to read, nor is he faced with the sudden need to sprinkle these marks throughout his sentences when he begins to write.

The environments through which children are led from notational conventions, through words, sentences, and paragraphs, to books, are *stimulating* in the sense described above. At each stage of development, a child is in a position to run his current activity through any of the four perspectives discussed earlier. The aim of the whole program is to organize environments so that in any session a child can take any of the four perspectives, or any combination thereof, independently of the level of sophistication or competence at which he is working.

Some Conjectures and Research Suggestions

In the course of the pilot studies intended to prepare for rigorous experimentation, we have been able to arrive at some conclusions and conjectures, and in this section we will mention a few things we think we have learned about children.

1) The children were uniformly given a battery of examinations before entering the program: general physical examinations, eye examinations, ear examinations, an evaluation of the child's speech develop-

ment, an examination of the child's emotional health by a clinical psychologist, and standard IQ tests. In addition, home interviews were conducted in order to obtain child development histories and information concerning the socioeconomic standing of the families. All tests and examinations were repeated regularly at appropriate intervals, and all were carried out by medical, psychological, and sociological specialists. The baseline data and continuing examinations have thus far indicated no untoward side effects; but we should note that we did not take children who for foreseeable pediatric or other reasons (such as parental disagreement over the advisability of sending the child) might be in some way injured. Evidence seems to show that the primary and secondary effects (of the sort our heuristics would lead us to expect) are positive.

2) Speed of learning reading and writing in the laboratory seems to be positively correlated (as our theoretical views would lead us to expect) with the maturity of the speaking-listening abilities the child brings to the laboratory.

3) Ordinarily there is a high positive correlation between IQ scores and excellence of speech as assessed by speech experts. Children who enter with high ratings on both scales do better than those who enter with lower ones. In the two cases of discrepancies (high IQ and low speech, and low IQ and high speech), under the influence of the program, IQ seems to more rapidly approach speech than speech approaches IQ. The reason apparently derives from (2): if strong speaking-listening habits are available already, and if reading-writing comes more easily as a consequence, then such children will gain rapid access to the material which will influence IQ.

4) With regard to the age at which it is most feasible to start, we are inclined to think the younger the better; by the time a child is 5 or 6, he may well be absorbed with non-autotelic aspects of his everyday world, with the result that his ability to attain the sort of relaxed and exploratory frame of mind required to enable him to make his *own* discoveries is impaired.

5) Observation of convulsive children (those with various forms of epilepsy) suggests that ability may be distributed among them bimodally, with that part of the distribution at the positive end skewed positively and the negative skewed negatively. The occurrence of frequent "subclinical electrical storms," let alone the infrequent clinically observable seizures, would be naturally expected to impair learning by making the child's experience discontinuous—in the direction of chaos. What we had not expected was that some of the most startling

inductive leaps were made by children with occasional mild "storms." It may be that daily practice in tying one's experiences together in spite of small gaps accounts for the development of appropriate abstraction.

6) Experience with the deaf indicates that this is probably the severest of the handicaps (short of severe mental retardation) we have studied, at least as far as the socialization process is concerned. We are inclined to believe that the most effective way of helping those so afflicted is to use a responsive environment properly equipped with tactile, vibratory, and other sorts of signalling devices so as to treat reading and writing as the primary sources of communication and graft on speaking as secondary.

Finally, we want to make some suggestions for improvements of our program which bear centrally on its purposes and interests: we might press for some such program as the Initial Teaching Alphabet or "simplified spelling." Or, in the interest of speed of typing, we might complicate the conventions so as to arrive at something like the output of a stenotype machine. Or, if wedded to traditional orthography, we might at least replace the present standard keyboard by more efficient arrangements of the letters; tests have shown that appreciable gains in efficiency can be made by designing the keyboard more rationally.

If our point is not yet clear, let us stress that if efficiency is the goal, the thing to do, as we have learned from countless cases in almost every branch of human endeavor, is to leave the people alone but change the relevant cultural objects and/or associated equipment. The way to improve the productivity of the man behind the plow is not to give him more training or more exhortation to hard work; the thing to do is to give him a tractor. Efficiency requires a better (cultural or mechanical) mousetrap.

Interest in this project, on the other hand, lies in attempting to understand how the abilities and capacities of human beings can be improved vis-à-vis confidence and ease in a variety of environments, competence in handling cognitive and emotional problems, creativity, and in a host of other directions which are too vague for us to specify carefully. But this much seems clear: any study of the possibilities for improving human abilities and capacities requires not only empirical evidence concerning potentialities, but also some theoretical rationale for constructing a yardstick in terms of which we can measure the ways human beings go about handling symbolic material.

ELEANOR E. MACCOBY

XIV

EARLY LEARNING
AND PERSONALITY:
Summary and Commentary

*Eleanor E. Maccoby (B.S. University of Washington; M.A.,
Ph.D. 1950, University of Michigan) is Professor, Department of Psychology, Stanford University.*

IN trying to bring out the main themes of the
Conference as they bear upon pre-school personality development and
its relation to early teaching and learning, I will occasionally refer to
work which has not been mentioned so far but which seems relevant
to the issues we have been discussing; I will also draw on points raised
informally, as well as material that has come up during our more
formal deliberations.

It is difficult to say just where "personality" leaves off and "cognition" begins. This has been evident especially when we have referred
to cognitive styles, such as the impulsivity-reflectivity dimension, and
have noted their kinship with attributes (such as delay of gratification)
which are traditionally thought of as being in the personality domain.
In the remarks which follow, "personality" will be broadly conceived,
so as to include our discussions on attentiveness, activity level and
curiosity, as well as such aspects of social-emotional development as
impulse control, dependence versus independence, and peer-group social skills.

There seems to be general agreement that efforts to teach intellectual content and skills to very young children are not likely to be
injurious to their social-emotional development. No one has denied
that motor mastery, emotional expressiveness and the acquisition of
social skills through play are important, and no one has proposed
omitting play periods from any pre-school program. There has been
the implication, however, that a shift from a fairly exclusive diet of
free expressive play to programs with more formal teaching content
will probably be beneficial. "Teaching" is not meant to connote a
formal classroom atmosphere, which everyone agrees would be en-

tirely inappropriate for pre-school age children. But age-appropriate teaching, such as structured verbal interactions between children and adults (interactions that are designed specifically to foster language development), and exposure to new materials and new experiences are recommended. Deutsch emphasizes that simple exposure to new experiences (such as trips to the zoo or the harbor) is not enough to produce the desired cognitive growth; she urges the necessity of structuring and interpreting experiences to children in a way that is appropriate to their developmental level, if cognitive assimilation and growth are to be brought about.

It has been argued here that age-appropriate teaching, of both informational content and cognitive skills, will probably foster peer-group social skills, so that we do not have to choose between our values for social and intellectual growth. The reasoning is that the growth of language skills, time concepts, etc., will directly improve social skills by increasing the range of alternatives in the repertoire of behaviors a child has for dealing with interpersonal problems, so that the more immature behavior (such as aggression or withdrawal) can be superseded by bargaining, taking turns and other forms of group problem-solving. Beyond this, there has been an implication that introducing more formal teaching into the pre-school program will foster the growth of certain disciplined temperamental qualities which will benefit both intellectual and social activities. These temperamental qualities include impulse control, frustration tolerance and the focusing of attention. If I interpret the assumptions underlying our discussion correctly, we would be in fairly good agreement that "problem" social behavior is better dealt with by teaching alternative and acceptable modes of coping with difficulties than by encouraging catharsis.

Let us consider in detail some of the aspects of social-emotional functioning which have been mentioned by several participants as important for a child's ability to profit intellectually from pre-school educational programs. One attribute which has been repeatedly mentioned is the ability to focus attention—to resist distraction. While the focusing of attention is clearly a cognitive process, the "attentive-distractible" dimension has also been studied as a personality characteristic, especially as it is related to hyperactivity and impulsiveness. Attentiveness is clearly necessary for task persistence. Eugene Gollin, quoting Wohlwill in part, outlined some of the dimensions of change with cognitive growth, and included an increase in the amount of irrelevant stimulation that can be tolerated without disrupting task-related responses. Bettye Caldwell, Susan Gray, and Cynthia Deutsch all listed increased ability to maintain attention to a task among the goals of their programs. In the Deutsch program, attentive abilities have been measured with a vigilance test as part of the diagnostic testing program. While there is agreement on the fact that it is important to foster attention-focusing ability, little has been said about exactly how one goes about designing a pre-school program to do this. Kohlberg suggested that a program oriented toward free expressive play probably will *not* facilitate the development of attentiveness, because of the high level of distracting stimulation and actual interruption of one child by another which is likely to exist in such a setting. The traditional nursery-school emphasis on social skills may have kept us from setting out to teach children not to interrupt each other, and nursery schools (except possibly Montessori schools) have not been designed to provide any degree of intellectual privacy for children. But it ought to be possible to provide more settings conducive to concentration.

In the discussions on language development, it was suggested that a child's auditory attention span might be improved simply by speaking longer sentences to him—that the child from a depriving environment usually hears truncated verbal communications from those around him and therefore has little practice in having to listen through a long sentence, with subordinate clauses, to get the speaker's meaning. A number of programs include planned verbal interactions with the children in which adults speak longer sentences than the children are accustomed to hearing at home. So far, we do not have evidence that this accomplishes the desired result of increasing the children's attention span, but the approach is promising.

While Donald Baer did not comment directly on the application of his behavior-control techniques to attentiveness, I would assume that he considers attending to be a class of response whose strength could be experimentally increased by reinforcement. No one seems to have tried reinforcing children for increasingly good performance on vigilance tasks, for example, but it would be interesting to see whether daily training in such tasks would improve vigilance and also generalize to other aspects of attention focusing. There seems to have been very little research on the learning conditions which do facilitate attention focusing. There is one study, done by Helen Bee (1964) when she was at Stanford, which is relevant. In this study two groups of children were matched for IQ: one group was able to maintain attention on a school-related task while distracting material was played over earphones, and the other group's performance was considerably disrupted

under the distraction condition. Dr. Bee observed the children in interaction with their parents while the child was working on problems
concerning which the parents had more information than the child
had. She expected that the children who were not very distractible
would have parents who would leave their children alone to solve
problems, seldom interrupting them with suggestions, criticisms, etc.
This expectation was not borne out—the total level of interaction was
the same for the parents of the two groups of children. But there was
a difference in the content of the interaction. The parents of the poor
attenders tended to take the problem solution out of the children's
hands. They would offer highly specific suggestions for solution. The
parents of the children who were skillful attenders, on the other hand,
would suggest new strategies and help the children to abandon an
unproductive approach to a problem without giving them the exact
solution. The solution was the child's own, and the satisfaction of
achieving it might be one element that maintained the child's motivation to "try, try, try again"; the poor attenders tended to become passive, sitting back and waiting for the parents to give them the solution.
The suggestion coming from this study would be that one might be
able to improve task persistence by putting children in problem-solving
situations where they are fed with suggestions about promising strategies and suggestions for restructuring the task so as to improve their
chances for success in the task, while leaving with the child the opportunity to achieve the final solution—to make the desired response,
instead of having it made for him.

In most of our discussion about attentiveness, we have been assuming that there is such a thing as a generally attentive or inattentive
child, and that many culturally deprived children suffer from not having developed the skills that are involved in being "good attenders."
In some of our work at Stanford, we have found that good attentive
performance can be quite situationally specific. As an example: in one
study done by Lance Canon (1963), the level of affiliative motivation
was experimentally varied through social isolation. When working on
an intellectual task, the children who had been previously isolated were
more distracted (their performance impaired) by a human voice
speaking nurturant material; children not previously isolated were
more distracted by nonhuman sounds. Thus brief fluctuations in motivational states will help to determine the kinds of stimuli which will
make a child be "distractible" in a given situation. Other work on selective listening (Maccoby, 1966) has revealed only a moderate level
of intrapersonal consistency in, and a high level of situational control

of, performance in this kind of attention-focusing task. These kinds of findings indicate that we need to do more work to identify just which aspects of attentiveness do reflect stable individual differences, and how transferable attentive skills are between situations. Furthermore, programs designed to improve attention-focusing in children should probably have a dual focus: to train the child in attentive skills which will be applicable in a fairly wide range of situations, and to structure the environment so as to elicit concentration from the children who are capable of it.

In the discussion here, there have been a number of references to activity level (and hyperactivity) as being relevant to cognitive development. Courtney Cazden has particularly stressed the possible importance of activity and its inhibition. Activity and attentiveness are, of course, related—if for no other reason than that the child must be able to sit still in order to concentrate on certain kinds of tasks. There is some early research by Grinsted (1939) that bears upon this point: Grinsted placed children in a "fidget chair" (something like a stabilimeter) which recorded movement, and traced the relationship between body movement and problem-solving. As problem-solving proceeded, the child became more and more still; then, just after the child either achieved a solution or gave the problem up as insoluble, there was a burst of activity. We don't know whether the moment of stillness during the critical moment of problem solving was a cause or an effect of problem-solving success, but it does appear to be clear that the inhibition of activity is at least related to problem solving. Some recent work at Stanford underlines this relationship (Maccoby, Dowley, Hagen, and Degerman, 1965). We measured general activity level during free play by attaching "actometers" to a group of pre-school children. We found that their total level of general activity was not related to measures of intellectual proficiency. We suspect this absence of relationship stems from the fact that a high-level activity in free play can be made up of qualitatively quite different things: impulsive, undirected "nomadic" play (to use Bell's term), which might be negatively related to intellectual development, or directed exploratory activity, which ought to feed positively into intellectual development. We did find, however, that the children's ability to inhibit motor movement on demand *was* related to measures of cognitive performance (both IQ and CFT). Kagan, Moss, and Sigel (1963) have reported similar findings with inhibition tests.

If we agree that the primary importance of the activity dimension lies in the ability to inhibit activity when this is necessary for problem-solving, then when we study activity we are in the larger domain of impulse control, frustration tolerance and delay of gratification. We may regard these personality attributes as part of the same package. As an illustration, imagine that a child wants to play with a particular toy, and finds that another child is playing with it. He doesn't have a temper tantrum or hit the other child and snatch the toy away, but waits his turn to play with it. He has exhibited impulse control and frustration tolerance, and has been able to tolerate delay in gratification. These various names refer to a kind of mature behavior that has to do with waiting and with inhibition.

How do we go about teaching children to inhibit impulsive movement and emotional outbursts, to tolerate frustration, to wait for what they want? We might think back to Skinner's *Walden II;* you'll remember that the children in his utopia had a lollipop on a string around their necks, with instructions not to eat it; the lollipop was coated with powdered sugar, so that covert licks could be detected; only the children who resisted the temptation to lick were allowed to have the whole lollipop later. I'm sure this example could suggest a number of ways and means whereby children could be rewarded for waiting for what they want. How effective such training would be, or how much it would generalize to other aspects of impulse control, we simply do not know. In some early work by Keister and Updegraff (1937) it was found that training in mature reactions to frustration did generalize to new problem situations. The training involved sequencing the difficulty of tasks so the children could have success experiences, and encouraging independence and persistence. Unfortunately, this work has not been followed up in recent years, but it does offer encouragement to program planners who would like to foster frustration tolerance as a temperamental trait conducive to learning.

Walter Mischel and his colleagues have worked extensively on postponement of gratification, and have done some experiments in which they were able to increase children's willingness to wait for reward by allowing them to observe a model who chose delayed rather than immediate reward. One of the interesting findings of this research (Bandura and Mischel, 1965) is that the model need not be physically present for the effect to occur—the experimenter can simply *tell* the children that the model made delayed choices, and this influences them as much as if they have the opportunity to observe the model actually making such choices. Thus it appears that presenting a child with a model can be thought of as a mode of cognitive transmission—what is important is that the child be informed of the behavior of the model and, under some circumstances at least, he will do likewise. Perhaps we should consider including in our pre-school training programs some old-fashioned morality tales, telling children how people get ahead in the world by waiting for a delayed reward!

One of the themes which has come up repeatedly in the papers presented here has been the importance of the adult as the dispenser of attention and affection to the child, and the importance of the child's having developed a trusting relationship to adults. The lists of goals for pre-school programs included the child's development of both trust toward adults (and susceptibility to reinforcement by them) and the ability to work independently. In a sense, these two things would seem to be incompatible. There did seem to be some disagreement as to their relative importance. With respect to a trusting attitude toward adults, it is evidently true that culturally deprived children come into pre-school programs with quite adequate development of affiliative tendencies toward adults. In both Donald Baer's and Susan Gray's work, it is reported that if an adult whom the child has not known very long smiles at him or goes to stand near him, this reinforces the behavior the child is exhibiting at the moment. This certainly suggests some areas of strength in the early socialization experience of these children. It would appear that even though the mothers of deprived children may not be giving them adequate language stimulation or allowing them sufficient opportunties for exploration, they are sufficiently nurturant for the development of affiliation motivation so that their children want the approval of adults. Unhappily, we cannot expect that this open, trusting attitude will remain intact for very long in these particular children. From what many of the Conference participants have said, there comes a time (about the third or fourth grade) when they no longer want to go along with the system. If they are Negroes, they begin to feel that white adults are not really on their side. At the same time, the influence of the peer group increases, so that they would rather behave so as to please the age mates they associate with after school than the teachers or other representatives of authority. So long as this is true, it argues for the importance of the pre-school period as a time when one can still call upon powerful affiliative motivation in getting children to adopt behavior and attitudes which will facilitate school work.

The nature of the disagreement I detect among us concerns the importance of external reinforcement (either material or social reinforcement) versus "intrinsic" motivation. The social-reinforcement people think of keeping behavior going by giving the child candy, money, or more commonly, approval. On the other hand, we have a group who believe that if we provide opportunities for the child to learn at an appropriate level, he will do so, and no externally based motivation will be needed. The followers of Montessori and Piaget would be more in this camp. There is a subsidiary issue: given external "reinforcement," how much difference does the content of the adult's response make? For Donald Baer, the problem is to find a bit of adult behavior which will affect the rate of the child's responses. If simply standing next to the child will serve in this way, then that is the kind of adult response he will use. Cazden and Hess, on the other hand, have been concerned with the content of a socializing agent's verbal response, pointing out that the adult is doing something more than simply reinforcing the child, but is training more complex structures into the child's language by speaking complex sentences, adding interpretations and explanations, expanding his sentences, etc. They would feel, then, that the adult's response is not to be conceived of solely in terms of its reinforcing value. However, the issue of external reinforcement is still an important one. While we will not be able to reconcile the great differences in points of view represented here, we might get some agreement on the following points: in the history of the culturally deprived child, intrinsic reward for learning has often not been sufficient to overcome the elements in his experience that would lead him to avoid, or be afraid of, learning situations. External rewards may be both necessary and desirable to get the child started in the learning process. But some thought must be given to ways and means of weaning the child from external reinforcement. This is necessary partly because he will continue to spend a good deal of his time in the nonreinforcing environment from which he came to pre-school; and we cannot hope that specially designed school programs can be continued for him throughout his school career. If he could be made largely self-rewarding by the time he goes back into the standard public school environment, there might be a better chance of maintaining the gains of an enriched pre-school program.

There was one suggestion that it might be possible to enlist peers to help maintain desired behavior, but others have commented about the poor quality of age-mates as stimulators of intellectual development. All the programs, whether they emphasize the role of the adult as being present to provide social reinforcement for desired behavior or as engaging the child in verbal interaction, do require a very high ratio of trainers to children. If one considers the very large number of children who need enriched pre-school programs, the manpower requirements for adult personnel to staff these programs are staggering. We may be overlooking an important source of manpower in older children. Bronfenbrenner (1962) has reported the ways in which the Russians have been enlisting 11- and 12-year-olds to help teach younger children. Ronald Lippitt (U.S. Office of Education, 1964), at Michigan has recently been making some experimental efforts to train children of that age to work with younger children. He has a training laboratory for children at approximately the sixth-grade level, in which the children observe nursery-school teachers and observe one another in interaction with younger children, and have seminars to discuss desirable and undesirable methods for dealing with various instances of problem behavior the nursery-school children display. Lippitt reports that sixth-grade children can be astonishingly skillful and insightful, but that they need adult guidance to bring out these qualities; one cannot, of course, put an untrained 11-year-old in a nursery school and expect him to be an effective teacher. There might be some important gains in making greater use of older children in our pre-school programs; it is true that it would take time and personnel to train them, but once trained they could increase the total amount of individual attention it is possible to devote to the children in a pre-school program, and there is the further advantage that training older children to act as teachers and helpers might improve their performance as parents and teachers when they are grown.

To return to the list of social-emotional attributes that pre-school programs should try to foster as conducive to intellectual growth: we have discussed task persistence and attentiveness, the importance of impulse control, frustration tolerance, and of trust and affiliative feelings toward adults that will make the child interested in undertaking the learning tasks that the adult puts before him. Another attribute on whose importance we appear to agree is curiosity, and the willingness to explore new situations. Some work done here at Chicago (Schopler, 1964) with ADC mothers and their children involved asking the children to put their hands into a black box to explore and identify by touch what was there. Middle-class nursery-school children enjoy this procedure, but the children from ADC families were afraid to put their hands in the box. This observation underlines the fact that many children coming into our experimental pre-school programs are inhibited and anxious about exploring new situations. Susan Gray has commented that when these children do disinhibit, their response tends to be explosive rather than expressive. One can sometimes see a see-saw between fearful passivity and fairly violent behavior.

It is obvious that children cannot easily profit from the pre-school programs when they are in this emotional state. We have had reports concerning the kinds of home experiences some of these children have had that might be responsible for their fearfulness. Nimnicht says that the Mexican-American mothers he has studied in Colorado, who tend to be affectionate and protective toward their children, do also warn them about "monsters" that may be lurking in places where they do not want the children to go; Strodtbeck similarly reports among ADC mothers in Chicago a high level of threats and warnings; these mothers rely on frightening the child as a means of getting him to comply to the mother's wishes. Beyond this, there is the fact that the mothers themselves are afraid, and their fear is directly communicated to the children. It is difficult to tell whether their fear is a result or a cause of their lack of competence in coping with the large and small problems of daily living. Strodtbeck has given us some poignant examples of ADC mothers being unable to find what they want in a grocery store and being afraid to ask where it is; of their not knowing how to find their way to somewhere they want to go, and not knowing how or where to ask for directions. The result of their ineffectuality in such matters is a remarkable degree of social isolation; they seem to hide within their four walls, cut off from the normal avenues of problem-solving that we all take for granted. It is no wonder that their children are afraid.

What kind of interventions would be most effective in ameliorating the fearfulness of these children? Part of the problem undoubtedly stems directly from the low social status of their families. If a mother is afraid to ask a grocery clerk a question, it is not unlikely that her reluctance has a realistic basis; how many times in her life history have her attempts to get help from people of higher status been met with surly or contemptuous responses, or no response at all? The lower-class person, and especially the person of a minority race, has humiliating experiences in many social interactions, leading him to avoid such interaction. In the long run, the only solution to this would appear to be some real increase in social efficacy, brought about by enfranchisement and a reduction in institutionalized discriminatory practices. It may take some fairly basic changes in existing social-structural relationships to bring about the feeling and actuality of competence in these people who now lack it.

Several people here have implied, however, that there are measures short of "Freedom Now" which could help to increase the coping skills of the families and thereby reduce the anxieties of their children. There has been a difference of opinion concerning whether, and how much, a pre-school program for culturally deprived children should try to involve the families. Moore has explicitly tried to keep the parents away from the nursery school, because it has been his experience that their presence makes it very difficult to develop the game-playing approach to learning that he is trying to achieve. Baer's approach would seem to imply that one can teach the child to discriminate between home and school. The child can be taught to adopt certain kinds of behavior at school—where it is possible to control the contingencies of reinforcement—even though the child may regress when he goes home. One can teach the child, in other words, to live in two different worlds, and let the nursery-school experience simply widen the child's repertoire of behaviors, so that some of the behaviors which facilitate school performance will at least be available to him when he enters school, even if other behaviors continue at home where the social supports are different. It is interesting to note parenthetically that no one has felt it is upsetting to the child to work with him apart from his family. That is, the children in the programs which have been described here have not had noticeable problems in connection with the daily separation from their mothers that nursery school attendance entails. This has been true even of the very young children (2 years old and younger) in the Caldwell program. So in terms of the immediate mental health of the child, it is not necessary to involve mothers in the program.

Nevertheless, several participants in this Conference have urged that one can and must work with families as well as the children. They believe that without such work, the child will be faced with strong pressures to backslide, and may lose whatever gains he achieves in the pre-school program. Relevant to this issue is the experience in literacy programs in developing countries. It is not uncommon to find that children who learn to read during four years of school no longer know how to read when they are tested several years later, after they have stopped school and lived entirely in an illiterate village culture. It is not possible for them to maintain their reading skills in an environment where there is nothing to read and where none of the adults can read. In the case of Head Start programs, the lack of social support at home and the counter-pressures against cognitive development exist not only after the child has "graduated" from the program but while it is going on. A number of people planning pre-school programs have taken the problem seriously enough to start simultaneous programs for parents. Nimnicht has organized literacy training classes for the parents of the Mexican-American children in his pre-school. Susan Gray plans to involve mothers at the nursery school beginning this year. Strodtbeck is working with ADC mothers in an attempt to engender more social activity and more skill in information-seeking, as well as more insight into their children.

While everyone might agree that it would be useful to undertake such work in connection with every Head Start program, there is the problem of the most efficient allocation of limited resources. Is it better to use one's manpower for a smaller number of children, and work with their parents, too, or with a larger number of children apart from their families? We have no agreed-upon answer to this difficult question. It would be a reasonable guess that there are some cognitive skills which a culturally deprived child needs for effective school performance which can be effectively taught in a nursery-school setting not involving the parents. There are other skills and attributes (perhaps especially such attributes as freedom from fear) where it is possible that the greatest gains can be made through total family programs. It would seem desirable to try to recruit sufficient resources so that both approaches can be tried.

SHELDON H. WHITE

XV SOME EDUCATED GUESSES ABOUT COGNITIVE DEVELOPMENT IN THE PRE-SCHOOL YEARS

Sheldon H. White (A.B. 1951, Harvard College; M.A. 1952, Boston University; Ph.D. 1957, University of Iowa) is Associate Professor of Education and Cognitive Psychology, Graduate School of Education, Harvard University.

FIVE or ten years ago, a developmental psychologist asked the important questions which are on the table today would have given generally predictable answers:

—If he were asked whether the IQ can be augmented by pre-school experience, he would have answered that there have been some claims to that effect but that the weight of evidence seemed to discount those claims, the generally accepted, conservative interpretation being that the IQ is fairly constant.

—If he were asked what kinds of pre-school experiences could be used to further intellectual development, he might or might not have made allusion to the somewhat forgotten works of Maria Montessori. He might have argued that such a question was beside the point, that the many pre-schools in every large city existed principally on social justifications, to teach children how to play with other children or to serve as pleasant custodial places for the convenience or the necessity of parents.

—If he were asked to describe what a child learns during the pre-school years, he might have answered by reference to normative studies which compile age-changes in indices of language, motor skills, social attitudes, etc. The aggregate of these normative studies, to be sure, would have amounted to a rather adventitious sampling of the easily measured indices of intellectual growth, not a comprehensive view of the intellectual growth of the child.

—If he were asked how a child learns during the pre-school years, his answer would have been a largely hypothetical account in one or more of the terminologies with which we discuss children's adaptation—the terminology of environmental contingency and habit, the terminology of differentiation and integration, of social and emotional adjustment, of imitation and identification, of self-actualization. Whichever way he chose to answer the question, his answer would have been hypothecated on the basis of studies with animals and adults, very little on the basis of actual observations and experiments done with children of differing ages.

Such questions would have been approached rather casually by most developmental psychologists; it did not seem so urgent to form exact judgment about these questions then. The vagueness of our information about the fundamental questions has not been alleviated noticeably, but there has been a breakthrough in our need for understanding. Society's needs press in upon us suddenly. Placed in the uncomfortable role of experts without expertise, we are all in the business of trying to supply educated guesses about the nature of children's cognitive development.

In the face of the new, strong interest in early learning and cognitive development, this meeting has brought together a number of contemporary attempts to explore and extend our knowledge:

EDUCATIONAL STUDIES

Some studies follow the tradition of Froebel and Montessori. A nursery school is set up and a total educational environment is created in the hope of fostering the intellectual development of the child. There are only the broadest of practical limits on the kinds of material which may be brought to the child, and many behavior patterns are considered in an effort to bring about some enlargement of that pervasive characteristic of the child's behavior which we describe as "intelligence" or "cognitive development." This is the strategy represented in Caldwell's work in the very early years, in the nursery-school work of Gray and the Deutsches, and in the Montessori project reported by Kohlberg.

DEVELOPMENTAL, NATURALISTIC STUDIES

A second group of studies is composed in part of extended observations of developmental sequences, in part of interventive attempts. In this group, there is some focusing on a distinguishable system of behavior and systematic observation or manipulation is made with control over conditions (generally, artificiality) just sufficient to permit the intended observation or manipulation. Such work is represented in Hess's analyses of language interactions between mother and child,

Courtney Cazden's manipulation of children's linguistic environment, Donald Baer's systematic behavioral analysis and subsequent selective reinforcement procedures, Omar Moore's teaching of reading through autotelic, responsive environments, Burton White's observations and manipulations of perceptual development in infants.

HIGHLY CONTROLLED STUDIES

It is peculiar, and not comforting, to reflect that the kind of highly controlled experimentation which is predominant in our psychological journals has deserved such a small part in the deliberations of a Conference such as this. I refer to the large group of experimental studies where highly specified environmental stimuli are presented to the child and highly specified kinds of behavior are recorded as responses, and where, as much as possible, all other features of the environment and behavior of the child are neutralized or controlled. Such studies have not, in fact, yielded a broad understanding of children's learning. Eugene Gollin has made a case for the possible pertinence of such research work for the understanding of intellectual development and, certainly, a number of us have placed bets that such work will ultimately have considerable relevance for the understanding of early learning.

This grouping of studies into three classes is a rough pigeonholing of relatively broader and narrower examination of the questions of early learning. Intelligence is a large and bewildering "thing," and these studies, I think, represent attempts to study the "thing" with greater and lesser degrees of control over conditions, larger and smaller fields of view.

Among the several papers which have discussed efforts to design pre-school education programs, Fowler's work stands somewhat apart in that it has been conducted with relatively advantaged children, and has contained innovative features designed to accelerate what is generally considered to be normal progress through the pre-school years. The bulk of his paper conveys the belief that there are untapped possibilities for cognitive stimulation and advancement during the pre-school years. I must confess I am uneasy about the thesis. We have a way of taking for granted that cognitive development is synonymous with the development of formal symbol systems and, therefore, that any technique which might enable a pre-school child to read, do mathematics, learn a foreign language, is, ipso facto, a good thing. Is this, in fact, true? Certainly the formal symbolic systems and reasoning are generally the most theoretically interesting aspects of man's cognitive repertoire; they distinguish him most sharply from the animals, and thus essays in psychological theory from Hume to Piaget have been most intent on the explanation of man's faculty of reason. We may have overpublicized symbolization and reasoning among ourselves because of this history and, perhaps, because professors have a way of overestimating intellectual prowess as a human necessity or virtue.

One might argue that good pre-school work might advance prodigiousness without producing discomfort, but there are hidden assumptions in the argument to the effect that advance in symbolization is a good thing without end, and that one does not trade this value for other values in the pre-school period. Perhaps because so many irreconcilables are proposed as goals for education, there arises a nice-Nellie tradition which says that one can educate a child to be efficient yet creative, achievement-motivated but not anxious, well-trained and still flexible, etc. In fact, in learning experiments, one cannot get positive transfer without negative transfer. In fact, in most educational goals, one would expect there are cost factors which we are reluctant to admit.

Our most pressing questions about early learning have to do not with the furtherance of the education of the child of average or superior circumstances: we are primarily confronted with the urgent problem of creating an apparatus for supplementary education of the child of poverty. This Conference has reflected serious and continuing concern with the ideological basis of this work, and such concern seems quite justified because we do not stand on sure ground here at all. One of the most distinctly uncomfortable aspects of this work is that it must proceed bravely forward against consensus judgments that are not favorable to it—I refer here to the first few paragraphs of this paper, which reflect what I take to be a consensus among most psychologists just a few years ago which seems distinctly unpromising as an ideological basis for remedial pre-school work. Now we have a few studies, almost all very young, which are proceeding to try to effect intellectual and cognitive development in the pre-school child. How much effect can such early intervention have?

The contemporary move towards new pre-schools is premised upon the belief that the intellectual problem of the lower-class child is already of serious size by the time he reaches the first grade. Some of us believe that the earlier intervention is offered, the better for the child, but such an assumption rests upon analogies from embryology, analogies from folk theories, and not upon any real understanding of the intellectual development of the child and its interaction with environmental stimulation.

Is the lower-class home a deprived environment in the age range from birth to 3? We do, of course, have rather clear evidence that animals raised in bare and monotonous environments are in a number of respects inferior to control animals raised in more stimulating environments. Parallel evidence exists, drawn from studies of human infants in orphanages, which shows similar deleterious effects of what must be similar deprivation. There is some tendency among those who are concerned with slum children to term their environments "deprived," and to make an easy identification between the environments of the lower-class children and the sensorily restricted environments of the psychological deprivation studies. What is fact and what is fiction? Surely, the lower-class infant lives in an environment which offers perceptual change and variety, which offers tactual stimulation, which offers maternal company and affection. One wonders whether the lower-class home is a deprived environment for the intellectual development of the child before age 3—that is, before he has progressed enough in language to need the stimulation of complex language structure which the lower-class parent cannot model for him. There would seem to be some need for more careful analyses of the environments of the "deprived" and the "non-deprived" child, both before 3 and after 3, such as the kind of analysis provided by Hess's work.

The intervention which can be offered in a pre-school program must necessarily differ in a number of ways from the forces acting upon the child in his natural environment. In a pre-school, children must be dealt with in groups; the pre-school can occupy only a limited part of the day; the adults in the pre-school must to some extent be interchangeable figures; the range and emotional intensity of the environment is limited, etc. The pre-school is a special, limited instrument for training the child; it is not necessarily true that because deprivation may exert its maximal effect on the child in very early years, the pre-school experience might have the most weight in counteracting such experiences during the same years; Robinson has made this point. The pre-school is a specialized instrument of training, and it is something of an oversimplification to consider it is a supplementation of the natural environment of the child. It is a specialized world, not a complete world. One question which deserves some thought is the question of what kinds of resources are available to the pre-school.

Several accounts at this conference have described the character of special pre-school programs, notably the accounts by Gray and Deutsch. I am consistently impressed by the sophistication of these accounts, acknowledgment of facets of cognitive development which seem interesting and worthwhile in the current research literature. There is always a question of the relationship between pre-school ideologies and practices. Do we have a terminology which allows us to summarize the content of a pre-school program, to convey the features which in fact distinguish one program from another? There is little enough experimental, innovative pre-school work. We need some way to characterize the differences among programs—the actual, literal differences in manner of treating the children. Without such methods of characterization, it will be difficult to cumulate the experiences derived from experimental pre-school work.

A number of IQ changes have been reported during the present discussions as the result of pre-school intermediation, changes ranging from a gain of 17 points to a decline of 6 points as a result of various pre-school interventions. These IQ changes must, of course, be interpreted against those precautions which it is reflexive in the psychologist to consider. One must know that the changes in a treated group are due to the interventive procedure rather than rapport and familiarization; one must have some reason to believe that the IQ changes will last; one must have some reason to believe that these IQ changes are not test-specific but are valid in the larger universe of intellectual competence. None of the evidence we have considered is unchallengeable on all of these points, although Gray's evidence goes a good distance toward satisfaction. In the long run, we will want considerable amounts of evidence that interventive pre-school work produces changes in intellectual performance indices that are representative of broad-gauge changes, which are lasting, which have implications for the performance of the child in many spheres of his life.

The IQ test cannot be the only measure of the effects of an interventive educational program. There is in fact a consistent need, expressed by each and every person concerned with educational studies, for some better evaluational instrument than the Stanford-Binet; the Binet is considered too broad a sample to be a useful test of the efforts of a pre-school program. We are speaking now of a second kind of evaluation, one involving specialized instruments which will help name the weak points and the strong points of a program. None of us is able to rest content with the intelligence that the intelligence test tests. There is clear need for a new body of useful normative developmental information on the growth of language, of attention span, of representational abilities, against which the experimental pre-school work can measure its efforts. One could, if one liked, call them new intelligence test norms, but what I have in mind is not so much the standardization procedure of Terman as the observational procedures of Piaget and of Burton White.

For the time being, the educational studies are stuck with changes in IQ performance as the prima facie measure of their achievement. As such studies become widespread, another gross measure of the utility of such pre-school work will become available in terms of the grades of children who are graduates of the program, their tendency to stick with school rather than to drop out, etc.

The ultimate importance of the pre-school work may be as much theoretical as practical. Psychology has not yet been successful in establishing a coherent understanding of all the mechanisms of children's learning and cognitive development. We have a series of parallel accounts of the child's adaptation according to reinforcement contingencies, according to psychosexual episodes, according to progressive maturation, each account built on a different aspect of the child's encounters with the world and each somehow valid in its own terms but unreconciled with others. One of the reasons why psychological talk about children has tended to channel into theoretical grooves has been because each psychologist's examinations of children, those which produce the data with which he deals, have been so sharply restricted in time, place, duration, and social definition. The personality theorists give tests and make ratings; the learning theorists perform experiments; within these coded and limited realities, individuals subspecialize. Perhaps the experimental pre-schools, however little gilt-edged data they yield, will provide a wide window for the developmental psychologist. Perhaps individuals who try to weave together experimental data and a pre-school program, as Gray and the Deutsches are doing, can offer fruitful suggestions about how the pieces of the jigsaw puzzle, the many little theories and studies we have, might fit together. I am speaking of course of interesting tie-ins, not the sort of "whole child" everything-depends-on-everything-else-*ism* which is wisdom, but a very resigned and futile sort of wisdom, in psychological discourse.

Burton White has most eloquently set forth the need for more extended and careful naturalistic observation of children, and the point needs to be considered carefully. Certainly, it seems that some open and naive examination of children's behavior might serve as a refresh-

ing counteractive to the great numbers of pro forma studies which
appear in the literature. The power of Piaget's work is unmistakable
and he, like Freud, has constructed his theory out of close, thoughtful
examination of reality without the experiments, the hypotheses, the
statistics.

There is a new trend toward naturalism in psychology, and it is
all to the good. But I do not think the essence of what is needed is
naturalism; there is pedantic and unimaginative observation as there is
pedantic and unimaginative experimentation. The essence of significant
work is the willingness to look broadly, to make the struggle to find
significant pattern and order in events, whether seen first-hand or reflected in that second-order reality which one finds in the reports of
others' observations. Let us remember, also, Piaget's evident compul-
sion to see how reality "puts together," his intelligence, his perseverance.

We have briefly considered Hess's sampling of the flow of language
between mother and child and his analyses of more and less effective
patterns of linguistic communication between mother and child. His
work aligns with Cazden's study in suggesting that a very promising
tactic for pre-school teachers might be to systematically respond to
children's statements with expatiaticn; this sort of technique is, in fact,
indicated in the Deutsches' description of their methods.

There is some interaction today between what appear to be two
emergent camps in the area of cognitive development. One of these,
following Vygotskii, attempts to understand planning, reasoning, and
inference as a derivative of internalized language; the other, following
Piaget, attempts to understand similar phenomena as derivatives of
perceptual sequences decentered, reversible, and grouped. With respect
to the language hypothesis, we are prepared to make considerably more
useful observations following the tactics of Brown, Cazden, and Hess.
Is there a natural ontological sequence of grammatical development?
We are presently led to believe there is. Can this sequence be significantly accelerated by models who expand and explore speech with the
child? Can we find an associated fallout in problem-solving, in learning,
and in concept formation? The nice thing about the language hypothesis is that language is out in the open, and that fairly straightforward
studies can assess linguistic competence and relate it to the quality of
symbolic and inferential activities of the child. Thus, one would like
to see new observational studies which assess not only the quality and
sophistication of children's language, but which assess the functional
characteristics which the language of the child appears to have when
directed at parents, peers, and self.

Perceptual development is much less marked by an observable indicator, like speech. It must be inferred from special experimental situations which, in effect, test various information-processing limits. There is in addition, a subtle reorientation involved in discussing perception. We can speak of language in somewhat familiar additive terms, of the addition of new words, the addition of new grammatical forms, etc. To speak about the relations between perception, attention, and conception, we have to move away from a favorite metaphor which we use in discussing learning, the empty-full metaphor. Learning is very often spoken of as acquisition, assuming always that the child who learns gains something—a skill, an association, a concept, an S-R connection. There is another way of talking about cognitive development, or some significant part of it, which thinks of learning in terms of a blurred-focused metaphor. In ths view, the opposite of "learned" is not "ignorant" but, instead, "confused." Instead of a "tabula rasa" hypothesis, it is a "tabula plena" hypothesis. We think of an unfocused TV screen swirling in confusion, and we think of learning as something that tunes the picture—or better, enables us to pluck something identifiable and meaningful out of it. This is, as I understand it, the essence of Eleanor Gibson's (1963) stimulus differentiation hypothesis—that an important part of learning is to build models of the perceptual or conceptual characters which are distinctive, identifying features, for useful interpretations of the environment.

This kind of perceptual learning can go on from the lowest to the highest levels of intellectual activity. At the lowest level, the child models the distinctive features of what he is going to call "cube," "bigger than," and at the highest level the child gathers, and operates upon, perceptions to identify the earmarks of what he is going to call a "convergent mathematical series," a "monopolistic economy," etc. Interpretations of reasoning are tricky, as we know, and there is very often a way to look at some sophisticated mental operation as either a derivative of linguistic-symbolic operations or, alternately, of sophisticated perceptual categorization. There is, then, a crude sort of rivalry between those two ways of talking about central processing of information.

Improvements in the apparatus of perceptual and conceptual modeling of the environment can best be understood in the experimental procedure which Gollin discusses in his paper. To some extent, we can sample perceptual activity by recording eye movements, or haptic exploration. We can, as Piaget has done, make strong guesses from observational material. Sooner or later, our necessary tactic will be to set up situations where exactly controlled patterns of information are given out to the child and indicator responses outline the characteristics of his ability to take in the information. This is the province of the experimental study.

In his paper, Gollin cites, and slightly amends, Wohlwill's specifications of the dimensions along which perception and conception differ. There is, of course, an implication that the growth of the child from perception to conception involves exactly such improvements in the central modeling processes as will allow him to extract signal from noise in more effective ways. These propositions are excellent examples of the kinds of functional specifications of perceptual-attentional acts which can serve as a basis for fuller translation of Piaget's state-descriptive material into terms of mechanism and processing.

There is evidence indicating a marked improvement in children's ability to single out relevant from irrelevant cues between the ages of 5 and 7 (White, 1966), coincident with other transitions in learning, emotion, perception, language, and IQ factor content. It is interesting that so many studies locate the beginnings of "abstract thought" in this age range. In view of the nature of the research material, one may infer that "abstract thought" involves some of the following functional characteristics:

1) The use of language representations of stimuli as "pure stimulus acts," as second-order cues evoking behavior which the stimuli themselves would not call forth.

2) The ability to maintain orientation toward invariant dimensions of stimuli in a varying surround.

3) The ability to string together internal representations of stimulus-response-consequence into sequences which, projected into the future, allow planning and, projected into the past, allow inference.

4) Relatively more sensitivity to distance receptors of vision and audition, and relatively less sensitivity to near receptors of emotion, touch, pain, proprioception, and kinesthesis (White, 1965).

My belief is that this transition occurs through maturation, perhaps hastened or slowed by differing environments. The transitional signs are seen to reflect the inhibition of a more juvenile level of cognitive function and the superimposition of a new and higher order of function. The dominance of higher education is not stable and irrevocable; fatigue and stress can disinhibit the more juvenile mode of thought.

The complex of behavior changes between the ages of 5 and 7, when explored, may indicate something about what is to be expected from early education. There is a possibility that this transition may be accelerated by favorable early experiences, with beneficial effects for the child. There is another possibility, one which was apparently favored by Maria Montessori. This possibility would be that the transition occurs on a fairly regular schedule, that it is not retarded much or advanced much by experience, that it occurs whether the child is ready or not. If the transition occurs before a child has had favorable pre-school experiences, then there arises the possibility of something like an "educational neurosis." After the transition, the child does not react to experience in the same way: perhaps reality is not so emotion-laden, perhaps there are changes in attention or representation, perhaps that natural stereotypy of behavior which leads the child to repeat and learn sensori-motor experiences has disappeared. After the transition, the child cannot be given missing pre-school experiences, or he can be given them only with great difficulty, by some laborious remedial process which is the educational counterpart of psychotherapy.

Finally, there are the interesting presentations of Omar Moore and of Donald Baer. There is a way in which people have reacted in like ways to the responsive environments work and the operant analysts' work; reactions tend to polarize, with some tending to see panaceas and others tending to dismiss the work as gimmicky.

There is a realistic point of view behind Moore's work which is not talked about often. He points to the universality of play in human societies and he points out that such play has logic, theory, and education in it. In games of chance, games of strategy, puzzles, and aesthetics people inevitably go over, correct, and organize their understanding of the world and of society; there is autotelic learning going on. One might extend the argument further and consider not only the education involved in play, but also that which comes to most people in reading, movies, and television. We tend to be uncomfortable about such education because we sense that there are misinformative transmissions in the material, and because it is the messiest kind of education—we do not know who is teaching what to whom in the babel of popular communication. Still, it seems that this massive public "enrichment" produces significant autotelic learning.

Maybe this kind of education has been implicitly recognized in the organization of our society and formal public education exists primarily to transmit that portion of necessary training which either not enough people will self-elect according to the cafeteria method, or which requires structured and ordered transmission. If so, then the point of Moore's argument is that we may, through ingenuity and new tech-

nology, change over some of our traditional formal education characterized by education under pressure and introduce the same education
to the child in a context where it is spontaneously absorbed.

While Moore's rationale is quite different from Baer's, their methods
converge. Both, through quite different kinds of reasoning, converge on
situations arranged so that the environment reacts instantly and appropriately to what the child does; there is not the blurred kind of
feedback given to the child in the usual kind of classroom procedures.
Baer has given us evidence, part of a large body of such evidence
which is amassing nowadays, indicating that this is an effective procedure in training the child. There is an inexorability about such
demonstrations which buttresses Baer's point that teachers cannot really
choose not to shape the behavior of their children, that they can only
choose to become conscious of the consequences of their behavior. Of
course, this demand for consciousness on the part of the teacher is
somewhat ironic in the face of the fact that the system rather decisively
denies any need for supposing consciousness of the children. Must one
assume that the teacher who is in favor of X will very often behave so
as to get not-X or Y? The psychoanalysts might tend to argue that
there is some sense, then, in which the teacher is covertly in favor of
not-X or Y, but this assumes infallibility of method. The operant analysts have gone some distance in understanding the mechanics of
social psychology and occasionally they have exposed inefficiencies: for
instance, the point that teachers may increase unwanted aggression by
selectively reinforcing it with attention.

If we are talking about the translation of psychology into methods
of early education, then Baer has come forward with an unambiguous
proposal of method and unambiguous evidence of behavior change.
Ambiguity is not a mortal sin of course, and there is a virtue in being
sensitive to vaguely seen variables; they are not necessarily less important than the clear ones. I do not think we are going to get every-
where we want to go in early education on the logic of reinforcement
contingencies and, hence, I believe in the worthwhileness of the
struggle to understand central processes and to improve them through
broad-gauge pre-school work. The significance of such educational
efforts is characteristically underestimated in psychology. Remembering
Caldwell's quote of Lewin, "The best way to understand behavior is to
try to change it," we might do well to think about the significance of
enactive representations of cognitive development.

JOSEPH GLICK

XVI

SOME PROBLEMS IN THE
EVALUATION OF PRE-SCHOOL
INTERVENTION PROGRAMS

Joseph Glick (B.A. 1956, Brandeis University; M.A. 1959, Ph.D. 1964, Clark University) is Assistant Professor, Department of Psychology, Yale University.

TO express doubts about a conference such as this one makes me feel a little like Caliban plotting against a brave new world with such wondrous people in it. But I have doubts and feel a need for more critical and analytic thinking concerning the area of pre-school intervention. By this I mean to indicate that maybe we have not clearly enough identified the problem or assessed the nature and implications of our interventions. My feeling is that we have not learned the lessons of our history well—we might be in danger of eclecticizing when we should be sharpening the issues.

In the following, I should like to formalize these feelings in terms of several dimensions of analysis: (1) a distinction between performance and capability; (2) a distinction between process and achievement; and (3) considerations about the nature of developmental change.

Performance and Capability

The distinction between the performance of a particular act and the capability to perform that act is a commonsense distinction which may have profound consequences for assessment and attempts at improvements of the "deficits" of the culturally disadvantaged.

If we do not pay serious attention in our thinking to the probable discrepancies between performance and the ability to perform, we are likely to make several interrelated assumptions which may be in error. First, we are likely to interpret performance measures such as intelligence test scores as reflecting some underlying cognitive structure

215

which we call intelligence. Second, we are likely to interpret changes in test score to reflect some change in underlying ability. Third, we are likely to relate this "change in ability" to the interventions that we have specifically planned.

In keeping with these assumptions, we have been regaled with reports of IQ changes of substantial degree which are presumed to reflect some change in intellectual capacity achieved by our intervention programs. To be sure, many of these programs have been so broad-scaled as to not allow for the particular assessment of the particular kinds of experiences provided and their particular effects on IQ. Nonetheless, we all react with a good deal of optimism when presented with such data.

Perhaps, however, this optimism may be a bit tempered by considerations as to what has been changed by our interventions. Is it an underlying ability? If so, of what type? Or is it rather the "non-underlying ability" of being motivated to look good on IQ tests?

If we keep in mind the distinction between performance and capability, these questions arise. Some recent work by Zigler and his associates has suggested that Binet scores are not necessarily measures of cognitive abilities alone. They may, in fact, be looked at as being multiply determined by cognitive capabilities and other (possibly) motivational factors. In a recent and as yet unpublished study, Zigler and Butterfield (1967) have shown that Binet scores for underprivileged children vary by a mean of 10 points depending upon whether the child is tested under standard testing conditions or under conditions designed to draw out the child and thus to obtain his optimal level of performance. In addition to assessing the difference between optimal and standard forms of testing IQ, Zigler and Butterfield compared both of these measures on children prior to their entering a preschool nursery program and after seven months in that program. The rather striking finding of this study was that tested IQ (under standard test conditions) showed a rise during the course of the year, while optimal IQ measures showed no corresponding increase. Data such as this suggests the importance of the distinction between performance on a test and capability to perform. If we take the optimal testing condition as a rough estimate of "underlying ability," the data show that there is no change in ability as a function of the pre-school intervention. Where the changes have occurred however, is in the area of the *relationship* between *ability* and *performance*. Here it was shown that the difference between standard tests and optimal tests decreased as a function of the pre-school intervention. These data caution us against being overoptimistic in our assessments of changes in intellectual struc-ture coincident with pre-school intervention programs.

This observation in no way detracts from the presumably beneficial effects of pre-school intervention. It does suggest however, that our optimism may be misplaced. It appears that we are not producing "supermen" or restoring "normalcy" to "deficient" men by instilling cognitive factors which normally would not occur. We may, in fact, merely be producing children who are well motivated to "play the game." In the school situation, this is extremely important. However, I believe we should recognize that many false conflicts are introduced by interpretation of IQ changes due to pre-school intervention as fundamental changes in cognitive structure. (Additionally, with the current changes of our concepts of cognition, it becomes more and more difficult to see either change or lack of changes in IQ scores as having relevance to statements about cognitive structures).

Process versus Achievement

A second analytic dimension to keep in mind in evaluating pre-school programs is a distinction that was made by Heinz Werner in 1937 between behavioral achievement and the process or structure underlying the achievement. This distinction is closely allied to the performance-capability distinction described above. It differs from it, though, in significant ways. While the "performance-capability" dis-tinction refers to the possibility that different behavioral outcomes (for example, changes in IQ scores) might be subserved by the same cogni-tive structures, the process-achievement distinction refers to the pos-sibility that the "same" behavioral outcome may be subserved by different structures.

The basic notion focused on in the process-achievement distinction is that a given outcome in behavior can be achieved by means of a variety of analagous processes. These processes may be ranked from developmentally *more primitive* to developmentally more advanced, although in restricted situations the behavioral outcomes may in fact be identical.

Two examples might be offered here. First, let us consider the behavioral "achievement" of locomoting between point A and point B. If we take as our criterion measure of this achievement the time taken in traversing the distance between these points, we might be able to show that there is little difference between a child of 1 year and a child of 2 years of age. Of course, what is obscured in this analysis is that one child traverses the distance by crawling and the other by walking. While this example is intentionally gross, the distinction between process and achievement can be applied more subtly, as is attested to in Gollin's paper.

A second example might serve to drive this point home. There is a current controversy in the child development literature, centered around Piaget's work, about the age at which concrete transitivity of length is achieved. Originally, the achievement of the ability to integrate two propositions of the form $A > B: B > C$ into a transitive series $(A > B > C)$ so that $A > C$, had been placed at about the age of 7 years. Braine, utilizing arguments derived from a performance-competence distinction (Braine, 1959) ostensibly showed that when sources of verbal confusion are eliminated, children are able to make concrete transitive judgments by about the age of 5 years. Smedslund (1963), arguing from a process-achievement distinction, attempted to show that the criterion performance which Braine interpreted as indicating transitivity could be subserved by a developmentally lower process which *in restricted situations* yields results which look like transitive judgments. By introducing a slightly different set of conditions, Smedslund was able to demonstrate that a "transitive" judgment may in fact be achieved on the basis of a "non-transitive" hypothesis. More recent work by Glick and Wapner (1966) tends to substantiate this claim. Although the issues at stake have not been resolved, this controversy has served to indicate the centrality of both the performance-competence distinction, and the process-achievement distinction for developmental analysis (Smedslund, 1965).

These illustrations indicate potential sources of difficulty in evaluating the effects of any pre-school program. One may be able to show, for example, that in achievement on certain criterion performances there may be vast "beneficial" effects of either pre-school intervention in a remedial sense or in terms of making younger kids precocious. However, until investigation is made which is oriented toward uncovering the basic processes underlying the achievement, one must take this evidence in a rather critical vein. It is not enough to simply demonstrate that criterion performances (that is, achievements) increase with age or are changed by intervention. What is necessary in order to make any argument which is basic to developmental questions is to show that the processes underlying the achievements have in fact been shifted up to a higher developmental level. Evidence for such "process" changes may be obtained by use of multisituational designs oriented toward the investigation of any shift in factors that determine behavior, or from close analysis of the *patterns* of responses in any given situation.

The Nature of Developmental Change

The issues involved in the process-achievement distinction may be extended in terms of their implications for our notions of developmental change, and particularly for our notions of change induced by pre-school interventions.

From the previous analysis of the process-achievement distinction, the possibility may be raised that intervention programs may lead to achievement gains, but without any real changes in process. Children may improve "achievements" simply because developmentally primitive processes have been brought out. At any rate, there have been few, if any, investigations oriented toward this question—few transfer designs have been used, and few studies have gone into detailed analysis of the patterns of response.

This ambiguity in previous data must be resolved, since one of the critical issues in the analysis of developmental change is involved. This issue may be phrased in terms of a question—"To what extent does the availability of primitive means of achieving criterial performance hinder or help the development of developmentally more advanced means of achieving that performance?"

There is evidence on this issue from the field of perceptual pathologies. Goldstein (1939) and S. C. McLaughlin (1964) have indicated that in cases of amblyopia, adaptation to this condition is hindered by attempts to maintain function in the weaker eye. It is in this case the persistence of an earlier mode of adaptation that hinders attempts at achieving a new level of adaptation. Similar deficits in higher functioning due to the maintaining of developmentally more primitive means of adaptation have been reported by Luriia (1960) in the case of a subject with a well-developed memory based upon perceptual imagery, and by Luriia and Yudovitch (1959) in the case of language development in twins which was retarded by the availability of more primitive means of communication. What we have in these examples is an "einstellung" problem phrased in developmental terms.

These examples would suggest that achievements based on developmentally primitive means are something that must be overcome rather than encouraged by our intervention programs. It therefore becomes quite important to analyze changes in criterion performances in order to determine the processes being used. If we have made kids "look smarter" by encouraging the use of lower means, we may, in the end, have defeated our own purpose. For example, let us suppose we are able to teach children arithmetic at a very early age, by showing them the use of such primitive means as counting on fingers. Within a narrow range of problems, we might be quite impressed by their precocity, and, accordingly would congratulate ourselves on a stunning educational achievement. However, this optimism might be a bit tempered when we begin to wonder whether the too facile use of this means of calculation, at too early an age, might serve to impede the adoption of more sophisticated means of calculation, or the use of number systems that are not to the base 10.

An appropriate model of developmental change must take into account the "transformational characteristics" of change. Rather than development being the gradual acquisition of more and more "adult-like" behaviors, it seems to be governed by a set of different structural levels which fundamentally transform and subordinate previous levels. In addition to the remarkable observations of Piaget, a particularly striking example of this type of change may be seen in the ontogenesis of the use of strong and weak verb forms.

Observations suggest that children first learn the appropriate form of strong verb conjugations, for example "I have"—"I had," etc. Here their performance is like that of the adult. However, in subsequent development, this appropriate usage is "transformed" by the application of the weak verb rules, so that subsequently children conjugate, "I have"—"I haved," etc. Only later is this regularizing form superseded by correct usage again.

If the analysis of development in terms of a series of structural transformations is applicable, then one of our duties as researchers is to investigate the fundamental problem of whether specific training of performance at one level will retard or advance the transformation to the next level of functioning. An ancillary question which applies specifically to the problem of the underprivileged concerns the question of whether the "undertraining" of performance at a lower level hinders subsequent transformations.

I believe that questions such as these should occupy a considerable part of our research effort. The analysis of criterion performances alone is insufficient to answer this question. We should shift away from being satisfied solely with change in criterion performances. We should shift toward the development of means of analysis of the processes underlying performance and changes in performance.

At this stage of the game, we need a good deal of basic research. The decisions being made now will be central to the course of the social evolution of the underprivileged, and cannot help but have radical implications for educational practices throughout society.

We are thus obligated to answer questions about what the nature of our interventions are. What kind of education are we offering, and what are our best estimates of its probable effects? Here is the area where our responsibilities as social scientists constrain our role as social engineers. Accordingly our statements must be based on research rather than well-intentioned optimism.

XVII
ISSUES IN EARLY LEARNING
AND PRE-SCHOOL EDUCATION:
*A Summary of the
Conference Discussions*

Roberta Meyer Bear (B.A. 1963, Mills College; Ph.D. 1967, University of Chicago) is Research Associate (Assistant Professor), Committee on Human Development, University of Chicago.

IN planning the publication of the formal papers of the Social Science Research Council Conference on Pre-School Education, the editors felt it important to share with the reader some of the content and flavor of the discussions which the presentations stimulated among the Conference participants.

A major purpose of the Conference was to provide an opportunity for participants—from varied backgrounds in research, education, and the administration of educational-research programs, yet all concerned with the programming and assessment of early learning—to exchange information and opinions on the current status of pre-school education, on theory and methodology in child development research.

In his welcome to Conference participants, Lloyd Morrisett touched on three issues with which the conferees were expected to deal. First, the conference was concerned not with providing a set of suggestions for pre-school curriculum, or with finding *the* answers to contemporary problems of educational technique and assessment, but with examining the evidence relevant to current educational practices. By confronting accumulated experience in educational programs with empirical evidence on the processes of early learning, some evaluation could be made of the fruitfulness and validity of current orientations, and some suggestions could be made for the direction of future efforts in both research and its application. Morrisett's second point was that the Conference was concerned with all children and not solely with the disadvantaged—although it may be noted that the Conference was convened in an environment of concern with the disadvantaged. Finally, the focus of the conference was on the environmental conditions facilitating *mental* growth—as opposed to social or emotional growth, intertwined though they be—during the specific time period from *birth to 6 years of age.*

Provision had been made in the Conference schedule for formal summaries by William Fowler and Halbert B. Robinson of theory and past research, and conclusions reached and issues raised within the research reports were synthesized by Sheldon H. White and Eleanor Maccoby at the final session of the Conference. Interlaced with the first-session panel of research reports, and the two sets of summary papers, were wide-ranging discussions sparked by the papers. The Conference schedule was organized to stimulate as informal an exchange as possible among the participants. The resulting discussions, while coherent to those attending, were not only too lengthy but too informally organized to be meaningfully published in total as an appendix to this volume. Accordingly, the task of this final chapter is to present, in semi-chronological order, a paraphrased description of the Conference sessions, highlighting those questions and issues not already presented at length in the chapters of this volume.

The discussion following the initial presentation of research papers by Robert D. Hess, Bettye M. Caldwell, Donald M. Baer, Susan Gray, and Lawrence Kohlberg, and stimulated by the immediately preceding paper by William Fowler, centered on the issue of instrumentation in assessing formal educational programs at the pre-school level. Questioning the validity and fruitfulness of using standardized measures such as IQ tests, the participants raised several separate yet intertwined issues. The fact that an IQ score is a good predictor of academic achievement has supported the use of standard intelligence tests; because these tests also meet such practical requirements as the existence of normative data or limitations on time, standardized tests have been used to a great extent in past and current research. Yet many professionals are dissatisfied with standard IQ tests, for the dilemma of finding acceptable instruments of assessment involves more than the practical issues of time and prediction of school success. Assessment of an individual's level of functioning implies some knowledge of what is desirable or effective cognitive behavior. Assessment of progress made through experimental treatment, intervention, or any type of learning situation, requires prior statement of the goals of intervention.

Some positive goals for education and desirable outcomes for individuals were suggested: intrinsic rather than extrinsic motivation for learning; emphasis on socialization and cooperative peer-interaction rather than on isolated individual problem-solving; self-knowledge and self-expression rather than rote-learning and a regurgitative intellect;

curiosity, creativity, and adaptive intelligence rather than task-specific skills; and a clinical concern with the total personality of the child rather than with the verbal expression of cognitive behavior.

Because standard intelligence test items concern rather specific knowledge and are generally highly verbal in content, their use is necessarily associated with some of the options listed above as undesirable. A general measure of verbal cognitive functioning does not permit diagnosis of development in specific areas, nor—although standard intelligence tests as used in most research provide information on the general level of functioning—does it assess the creative adaptive intelligence which has become the concern of many child-development professionals.

If the goal of intervention is to raise the achievement level of the individual, then the collection of less restricted data from wide-ranging, open-ended interviews, or naturalistic observation, should allow more complete and specific evaluation of the individual's potential and an assessment of his progress in a variety of areas. Finally, if the focus of interest is creative intelligence, new tests and new techniques are required to measure this behavior.

The use of standard assessment techniques such as the IQ was discussed in terms of the goals of educational programs on a more general level: Does the value of an educational program lie in its ultimate results at adulthood or in its achieving *any* progress beyond the individual's original level? Is the goal of an educational program (whether it concerns intervening with the deprived, or working with children from more normal or enriched environmental circumstances) to change intellectual processes, to increase the cognitive level at which the individual goes about solving a problem, or to increase facility at a specific skill?

If the goal is increasing the cognitive level in a general sense, are the data on changes in IQ following intervention a valid indication of what such programs are accomplishing and of what occurs in their absence? Is an increase in IQ points a sign of successful intervention, an indication that the level of functioning in the broad sense has been raised—or is it specious, due to a combination of increased rapport with adult teacher-examiners, socialization into test-taking behaviors, and familiarity with testing situations? Is the progressive drop in IQ points which has been observed among lower-class children in the absence of intervention a reflection of a real progressive decline in cognitive abilities, or is it a function of the age-differential in the factorial content of standard IQ tests, and a reflection of poor development in specific surface skills such as verbal ability?

If standard IQ measures do not fit present needs, their replacement might take one of two forms: batteries of tests to measure retardation and growth in specific skills (in order to assess programs which concentrate upon training in specific areas); or techniques to assess that creative intelligence expected to emerge from less task-specific programs (designed to increase the range and adaptability of behavior).

The importance of constructing instruments to assess the effectiveness of educational methods, however, was pointed out to be only secondary to the task of finding criteria for educational programs, to finding out what needs to be learned and how best to go about teaching it.

As evidenced in the Conference reports, researchers tend to focus on specific behavioral areas for study; yet many of the conferees felt that creating programs to develop creativity and adaptability was an important ultimate goal. The lack of techniques and methods for fostering and measuring creative adaptability, however, introduced a new issue: the need for more coordinated research and sharing of efforts and findings among those concerned with various specific skills. To shift emphasis from general intelligence or specific skills and behaviors (such as reading, perceptual discrimination, or learning sets) to curiosity, creativity, intrinsic motivation, and cognitive styles would require increased communication among researchers and educators in order to develop a common fund of methods and findings upon which attempts to measure and foster creative adaptive intelligence might be based.

Robinson's presentation served to heighten discussion of the criteria of evaluation, especially within the realm of longitudinal examination of behavior; in addition, examining normally developing behavior in order to provide a baseline for intervention studies is another approach to the problem of establishing that fund of basic knowledge necessary for experimental programs. Longitudinal studies are important in evaluating short-term programs: are pre-test and immediate post-test data enough to evaluate intervention, or need one assess the long-term effects of an educational program? Longitudinal study is important, too, to the issue of the generality of experience: does stimulation in a single, discrete area affect only the target skill? Does deprivation in a single area affect only the behaviors associated with that area? Or is experience manifested more generally, having a broad effect on behavior in all areas?

A discussion of the generality of effects in such enrichment programs as those described by Cynthia Deutsch and Burton White led to consideration of the notion of *process*—the underlying nature of an executed behavior—as the prime dependent variable to be investigated in child development research. The theoretical model assumed in most pre-school education is that of stage theory, which defines development as change through time. It was suggested that the emphasis on stages or levels of growth might mask the plasticity of the developing organism. If the notion of development is divorced from the notion of temporal sequence, it becomes possible to study development not by longitudinal naturalistic observation, but by forcing the appearance of a behavior or skill at an "inappropriate time" (that is, out of sequence). The purpose of such forcing is not to accelerate normal growth— although this might be an additional accomplishment—but to allow comparison of the processes involved in the successful appearance of a behavior at different chronological and mental ages, thus allowing examination of the conditions of success and failure at a task. Attempts to stimulate the emergence of a skill which normally appears at a later age should aid the understanding of the bases of behavior at different ages, the styles or strategies which underlie the development of all skills.

With this approach, the goal of developmental study is specifying the resources needed to understand a concept or to successfully execute a skill. Yet, with behavior divorced from time, a framework is still needed to relate behaviors occurring regularly in temporal sequence— and, more importantly, a framework is needed for differential assessment of behavior: If order in time is not used, what are the criteria for defining behaviors in relationship to one another, for assessing and ranking individuals on a given behavior? Those who emphasize process would define the criteria for high- and low-order behaviors as dependent upon the nature of the behavior but independent of the chronological sequence in which the behaviors occur.

The majority of the research reports having been heard, and some of the current theoretical concepts examined, the group turned its attention to the practical question of where and how time and effort are best spent in educational programs, particularly those involving intervention with the disadvantaged. To answer this question, it was necessary to discuss the nature of development and of deprivation.

Two sets of alternative hypotheses were offered as to the nature of the effects of deprivation on developing intelligence. The *deficit model* asserts that lack of stimulation leads to retardation in time or even the lack of appearance of a certain skill; this model is associated with the notion of critical periods. Opposing it is the *cumulative model* which asserts that the damage done by deprivation is not specific, but that the degree of retardation and the nature of the deficit change with prolonged deprivation, just as the nature of behavior changes in the normal development of any particular skill. A variant of the cumulative model is the *socialization model,* which asserts that the child doesn't fail to learn or to develop through time, but that he learns the wrong behaviors and develops inappropriate skills. Intervention would involve, alternately, the application of the type of stimulation which was lacking at some point in the past, or a more individualized and broad program of stimulation, including attempts to alter existing skills through resocialization, the specific content of which would depend not only upon the area of deprivation (for example, verbal, perceptual, motivational) but also upon the immediate functional level of the organism in all areas.

The general issue of the nature of the effect of deprivation, whether it represents a deficiency in a specific skill or affects the total growth potential of the child, was raised again and expressed in another set of alternative hypotheses about the nature of intelligence. The *differentiation hypothesis* asserts that the child has its total intellectual potential at birth and that development involves the progressive appearance and elaboration of specific skills. Opposed to this model is the *agglutination hypothesis,* which conceptualizes development as a progressive addition of skills and abilities to the child's repertoire.

It is clear that these two sets of alternatives lead to different kinds of intervention. On the one hand, empirical studies of the skill required at a given age or school-grade level become the basis of specific training in the pre-school years. This type of work has dominated the field and represents a practical answer to the question of how best to spend time and effort.

On the other hand, if the plasticity of the human organism is emphasized, then an educational program would demand decisions about such potential outcomes as the options listed earlier. With these options as the basis, lengthy training might result in the creatively adaptive individual. Such a program would be complex and difficult to undertake, since the goals are not observable behaviors like reading skills and abstract conceptualization, but are themselves concepts not yet examined in detail by child-development professionals.

Finally, the importance of matching training to the future expected environment, of intervening at a variety of levels across the developmental process, was noted: The criterion of successful intervention is not the outcome or level of achievement of its subjects per se, but whether the resulting behaviors provide a basis upon which to build and shape later skills. Ideally, then, intervention—and education in general—continues so long as the organism is vulnerable to change.

Eleanor Gibson introduced Courtney Cazden's presentation by noting that the previous discussions had asked what an educational program should be trying to achieve. Once the criterion skill is specified, analysis of the skill is the necessary next step. Ultimately, the only way to educate is to know what it is the child should be learning. It is in language that the greatest gain has been made recently, from a breakdown of the skill into units, processes, and rules, to the discovery of complex structures. The basic units of language are acquired informally by any child in a linguistic environment, but there are obviously more formal variables involved.

The discussion which followed Cazden's paper began with the question of the dialect differences between the lower-class child and the middle-class teacher. It was noted that it is possible to have a vocabulary which is not used, to understand a dialect which one does not speak; yet, despite the development of a "classroom dialect" native to neither teacher nor child, the basic dialect differences between the two can disrupt teacher-pupil interaction. (There are other sources of disruption in this interaction, such as those on the non-verbal level of affect and attitudes.)

The relationship of auditory discrimination to reading ability was seen as an important factor linking dialect differences with the lower-class child's poor achievement in verbal skills. It was suggested that auditory discrimination training should precede formal training in reading and that such training begin with sounds the child already discriminates; the child should be made aware of what he already discriminates as well as being taught new discriminations. Among other suggestions for improving verbal skills were teaching reading aloud, thus bypassing the problem of auditory discrimination; using a phonetic alphabet; and working to eliminate proprioceptive noise in language learning, using the methods of recent Russian work with motor mediation to facilitate verbal behavior.

In addition to comments on the summary papers of Sheldon White and Eleanor Maccoby (which have been incorporated into their chapters in this volume), the final discussion session dealt with two basic issues: the importance of defining the goal of education not in terms of skills but as processes allowing flexibility and adaptability; and the responsibility of the researcher-educator to attend to the child's social environment. The first issue had been dealt with in some detail in previous discussions, as described earlier in this chapter, and it led to the paper submitted to the editors by Joseph Glick after the Conference and included in this volume.

The second issue, however, had not been stressed at any length in the Conference thus far. In Robert Hess's introduction to this volume (Chapter I), he emphasizes that professionals in child development and education must become concerned and involved in the revolution now occurring in American education. No less importantly, the family—especially the disadvantaged family—must be considered as a source in understanding early development, and included in programs with the child who becomes the subject of an educational intervention program.

The theoretical bases of applied research are intricately linked with the practical issues of planning future pre-school programs. Although the concern of this conference was not solely with the problems of educating the disadvantaged child, that group was of particular interest to many of the participants; in addition, the disadvantaged present special problems to both researchers and educators. It became clear that no easy answers were readily available to the question of how best to work with these children. The general optimism accompanying the discussion of fostering creative intelligence necessarily wanes when the educator is confronted with the immediate and overwhelming problem of educating the disadvantaged.

In addition to the learning problems manifested by the disadvantaged, there are social problems and problems of attitude towards education, the schools, authority, and adults. It was noted that one often sees in such a child a progressive withdrawal from the influence of adults, both parents and teachers. This schism in the adult-child relationship cannot be overlooked in planning long-term educational programs or in evaluating the long-range effects of such programs. Two possible solutions to this problem were suggested; first, the child might be encouraged to seek more information and aid from his teachers, attempting to perpetuate the close relationship initially established between the pre-school child and adults who express interest in him. An equally important step would be to increase the amount and degree of contact between families—especially mothers, who are probably the most significant adult to the pre-school child—and social institutions such as the school, attempting to establish a better foundation in the home environment for generalization of the behaviors which intervention programs aim to produce in the child.

The need for child development psychologists and educators to attend to the broader societal context within which the child spends his earliest years seemed a fitting issue with which to end the Conference discussions: pre-school education cannot practically exist in isolation from the economic, social, and emotional climate with which the young child constantly interacts.

BIBLIOGRAPHY

ABEL, H., and SAHINKAYA, R. Emergence of sex and race friendship preferences. *Child Develpm.*, 1962, 33, 939–943.

ACKERMANN, W. Bergründung einer strengen Implikation. *J. symbolic Logic*, 1956, 21, 113–128.

———. Uber die Beziehung zwischen strikter und strenger Implikation. *Dialectica*, 1958, 12, 213–222.

ADAMS, E. M. Hall's analysis of "ought." *J. Phil.*, 1958, 55, 73–75.

ADAMS, JEANNE C. Teaching scientific programming assisted by the computer. *Computers and automation*, 1967, 16, 20–22.

ADJUKIEWICZ, K. *Logiczne podstawy nauczania.* Warszawa, Poland: 1943.

ALLEN, K. EILEEN, HART, BETTY M., BUELL, JOAN S., HARRIS, FLORENCE R., and WOLF, M. M. Effects of social reinforcement on isolate behavior of a nursery school child. *Child Develpm.*, 1964, 35, 511–518.

ALLEN, L. E. Symbolic logic: a razor-edged tool for drafting and interpreting legal documents. *Yale law J.*, 1957, 66, 833–879.

———. Logic, law and dreams. *Law libr. J.*, 1959, 52, 131–144.

———. Deontic logic. In *Modern uses of logic in law*, 1960, 2, 13–27.

ALMY, MILLIE C. *New views on intellectual development: A renaissance for early childhood education.* Unpublished manuscript, Teachers College, Columbia University, New York, 1963.

ALTUS, W. D. Birth order and its sequelae. *Science*, 1966, 151, 44–49.

AMBROSE, ALICE. On entailment and logical necessity. *Proc. of the Aristotelian Soc.*, 1955, 56 n.s., 241–258.

ANASTASI, ANNE. *Differential psychology.* (3rd ed.) New York: Macmillan, 1958.

ANDERSON, A. R. The formal analysis of normative systems. Tech. Rep. No. 2, Contract SAR/Nonr-609(16). New Haven: Office of Naval Research, Group Psychology Branch, 1956. (a) To appear in N. Rescher (Ed.), *The logic of action and decision* (Pittsburgh: University of Pittsburgh Press, 1967).

———. Review of Prior and Feys. *J. symbolic Logic*, 1956, 21, 379. (b)

———. Review of Wilhelm Ackermann, Bergründung einer strengen Implikation. *J. symbolic Logic*, 1957, 22, 327–328.

———. The logic of norms. *Logique et analyse*, 1958, 1 n.s., 84–91. (a)

———. Mathematics and the "language game." *Rev. of Metaphysics*, 1958, 11, 446–458. (b) Also in P. Benacerraf and H. Putnam (Eds.), *Philosophy of mathematics; selected readings* (Oxford: Blackwell's, Prentice-Hall Philosophy Series, 1964).

————. A reduction of deontic logic to alethic modal logic. *Mind*, 1958, *67* n.s., 100–103. (c)

————. On the logic of "commitment." *Phil. Stud.*, 1959, *10*, 23–27.

————. Completeness theorems for the systems E of entailment and EQ of entailment with quantification. Tech. Rep. No. 6, Contract SAR/Nonr-609(16). New Haven: Office of Naval Research, Group Psychology Branch, 1960. Reprinted in *Zeitschr. f. Math. Logik und Grund. d. Math.*, 1960, *6*, 201–216.

————. Reply to Mr. Rescher. *Phil. Stud.*, 1962, *13*, 6–8.

————. Some open problems concerning the system E of entailment. *Acta philosophica fennica*, 1963, fasc. 16. (Helsinki)

————, and BELNAP, N. D., JR. A modification of Ackermann's "rigorous implication." *J. symbolic Logic*, 1958, *23*, 457–458. (Abstract)

————. A simple proof of Gödel's completeness theorem. *J. symbolic Logic*, 1959, *24*, 320–321. (Abstract) (a)

————. Modalities in Ackermann's "rigorous implication." *J. symbolic Logic*, 1959, *24*, 107–111. (b)

————. A simple treatment of truth functions. *J. symbolic Logic*, 1959, *24*, 301–302. (c)

————. Enthymemes. *J. Phil.*, 1961, *58*, 713–723. (a)

————. The pure calculus of entailment. *J. symbolic Logic*, 1961, *27*, 19–52. (b)

————. Tautological entailments. *Phil. Stud.*, 1961, *13*, 9–24. (c)

————. First degree entailments. Tech. Rep. No. 10, Contract SAR/Nonr-609(16). New Haven: Office of Naval Research, Group Psychology Branch, 1963. Also in *Math. Annalen*, 1963, *149*, 302–319.

————, and WALLACE, J. R. Independent axiom schemata for the pure theory of entailment. *Zeitschrift für mathematische logik und grundlagen der mathematik*, 1960, *6*, 93–95.

ANDERSON, A. R., and MOORE, O. K. The formal analysis of normative concepts. *Amer. sociol. Rev.*, 1957, *22*, 1–17.

————. Autotelic folk models. Tech. Rep. No. 8, Contract SAR/Nonr-609(16). New Haven: Office of Naval Research, Group Psychology Branch, 1959. Also in *The soc. quarterly*, 1960, *1*, 203–216.

————. Toward a formal analysis of cultural objects. *Synthese*, 1962, *14*, 144–170.

APOSTEL, L. Game theory and the interpretation of deontic logic. *Logique et analyse*, 1960, *3* n.s., 70–90.

APPEL, M. H. Aggressive behavior of nursery school children and adult procedures in dealing with such behavior. *J. exp. Educ.*, 1942, *11*, 185–199.

AQVIST, L. A note on commitment. *Phil. Stud.*, 1963, *14*, 22–25. (a)

————. Postulate sets and decision procedures for some systems of deontic logic. *Theoria*, 1963, *29*, 154–175. (b)

————. Interpretations of deontic logic. *Mind*, 1964, *73*, 246–253.

ARONFREED, J. The nature, variety, and social patterning of moral response to transgression. *J. abnorm. soc. Psychol.*, 1961, *63*, 223–241.

ARONFREED, J., and REBER, A. The internationalization of social control through punishment. *J. Pers. soc. Psychol.*, 1961, *1*, 1.

AUSUBEL, D. P. Teaching strategy for culturally deprived pupils: cognitive and motivational considerations. *Scholastic Rev.*, 1963, *71*, 454–463.

BACON, J. Entailment and the modal fallacy. *Rev. of Metaphysics*, 1965, *18*, 566–571.

BAER, D. M. Escape and avoidance response of pre-school children to two schedules of reinforcement withdrawal. *J. exp. anal. Behav.*, 1960, *3*, 155–159.

BALDWIN, A. L. The effect of home environment on nursery school behavior. *Child Develpm.*, 1949, *20*, 49–62.

———. A is happy—B is not. *Child Develpm.*, 1965, *36*, 583–600.

———, KALHORN, JOAN, and BREESE, FAY H. The appraisal of parent behavior. *Psychol. Monogr.*, 1949, *63*, No. 4 (Whole No. 299).

BALDWIN, CLARE M. The role of verbal interaction in the cognitive development of pre-school children. Paper presented to Conference on Improvement of Nursery School Curriculum, May, 1963.

BAMBERGER, JEANNE. Montessori. *Instrumentalist*, 1965, *20* (3), 54–58.

BANDURA, A., and MISCHEL, W. Modification of self-imposed delay of reward through exposure to live and symbolic models. *J. Pers. soc. Psychol.*, 1965, *2*, 698–705.

BARMAN, MRS. MATHEW. *A statement on the teaching of reading to preschool children.* Winnetka, Ill.: North Shore Mental Health Association, no date. (Printed statement)

BARRETT, HELEN E., and KOCH, HELEN L. The effect of nursery-school training upon the mental test performance of a group of orphanage children. *J. genet. Psychol.*, 1930, *37*, 102–122.

BARRY, H., BACON, MARGARET K., and CHILD, I. L. A cross-cultural survey of some sex differences in socialization. *J. abnorm. soc. Psychol.*, 1957, *55*, 327–332.

BARRY, H., CHILD, I. L., and BACON, MARGARET K. Relation of child training to subsistence economy. *Amer. Anthrop.*, 1959, *61*, 51–63.

BAYLEY, NANCY. Consistency and variability in the growth of intelligence from birth to eighteen years. *J. genet. Psychol.*, 1949, *75*, 165–196.

———. Some increasing parent-child similarities during the growth of children. *J. educ. Psychol.*, 1954, *45*, 1–21.

———. Comparison of mental and motor test scores for ages 1–15 months by sex, birth order, race, geographical location and education of parents. *Child Develpm.*, 1965, *36*, 379–411.

———, and SCHAEFER, E. S. Correlations of maternal and child behaviors with the development of mental abilities: data from the Berkeley growth study. *Monogr. Soc. Res. Child Develpm.*, 1964, *29*, No. 6 (Whole No. 97).

BEAR, ROBERTA M., HESS, R. D., and SHIPMAN, VIRGINIA C. Social class differences in maternal attitudes toward school and the consequences for cognitive development in the young child. Paper read at Amer. Educ. Res. Assn., Chicago, February, 1966.

BECKER, O. Zur logik der modlälitaten. *Jahrbuch für philosophie und phänoenomlogische forschung*, 1930, *11*, 4.

BEE, HELEN L. The relationships between parent-child interaction and distractibility in fourth-grade children. Unpublished doctoral dissertation, Stanford University, 1964.

BELLER, E. K. Dependency and independence in young children. *J. genet. Psychol.*, 1955, *87*, 25–35.

———. The impact of pre-school experience on intellectual development in educationally deprived children. Paper read at the Amer. Educ. Res. Assn., Chicago, February, 1966. (a)

———. Teacher behavior and intellectual functioning in deprived kindergarten children. Paper read at the Amer. Educ. Res. Assn., Chicago, February, 1966. (b)

————, and NASH, ALAN. Research with educationally deprived pre-school children. Paper read at the Amer. Educ. Res. Assn., Chicago, February, 1965.

BELLER, E. K., and YOUNG, ARNOLD. Type of reinforcement and prior experience in the learning of lower class Negro children. Paper read at the Eastern Psychol. Assn., New York, April, 1966.

BELLUGI, URSULA, and BROWN, R. The acquisition of language. *Monogr. Soc. Res. Child Develpm.*, 1964, 29, No. 1 (Whole No. 92).

BELNAP, N. D., JR. Pure rigorous implication as a 'Sequenzenkalkül.' *J. symbolic Logic*, 1959, 24, 282–283. (Abstract) (a)

————. Tautological entailments. *J. symbolic Logic*, 1959, 24, 316. (Abstract) (b)

————. Entailment and relevance. *J. symbolic logic*, 1960, 25, 144–146. (a)

————. EQ and the first order functional calculus. *Zeitschrift für mathematische Logik und Grundlagen der Mathematik*, 1960, 6, 217–218. (b)

————. First degree formulas. *J. symbolic logic*, 1960, 25, 388–389. (Abstract) (c)

————. A formal analysis of entailment. Tech. Rep. No. 7, Contract SAR/Nonr-609(16). New Haven: Office of Naval Research, Group Psychology Branch, 1960. (d)

————. *An Analysis of questions: preliminary report.* Santa Monica: System Development Corp., 1963.

————, and WALLACE, J. R. A decision procedure for the system E_I of entailment with negation. Tech. Rep. No. 11, Contract SAR/Nonr-609(16). New Haven: Office of Naval Research, Group Psychology Branch, 1961. Also in *Zeitschr. f. math. Logik und Grund. d. Math.*, 1965, 11, 277–289.

BENNETT, J. F. Meaning and implication. *Mind*, 1954, 63 n.s., 451–463.

————. On a recent account of entailment. *Mind*, 1958, 67 n.s., 393–395.

BEREITER, C., and ENGELMANN, S. *Teaching disadvantaged children in the preschool.* New York: Prentice-Hall, 1966.

————, OSBORN, JEAN, ENGELMANN, S., and REIDFORD, P. A. An academically-oriented preschool for culturally deprived children. Paper read at the Amer. Educ. Res. Assn., Chicago, February, 1965.

BERG, J. A note on deontic logic. *Mind*, 1960, 69 n.s., 566–567.

BERNSTEIN, B. Language and social class. *Brit. J. Sociol.*, 1960, 11 (1), 271–276.

————. Social class and linguistic development: a theory of social learning. In A. H. Halsey, Jean Floud, and C. A. Anderson (Eds.), *Education, economy, and society.* New York: Free Press, 1961.

BEYER, EVELYN. Let's look at Montessori. *J. nursery Educ.* 1962, 18, 4–9.

BIBER, BARBARA. Premature structuring as a deterrent to creativity. *Amer. J. Orthopsychiat.*, 1959, 29, 280–290.

————. Preschool education. In R. Ulich (Ed.), *Education and the idea of mankind.* New York: Harcourt, Brace, 1964.

————, and MARGERY B. FRANKLIN. The relevance of developmental and psychodynamic concepts to the education of the preschool child. *J. Amer. Acad. Child Psychiat.*, 1967, 6, 5–24.

BIJOU, S. W., and BAER, D. M. Some methodological contributions from a functional analysis of child development. In L. P. Lipsitt and C. C. Spiker (Eds.), *Advances in child development and behavior.* New York: Academic Press, 1963.

————. *Child development*, vol. 2. New York: Appleton-Century-Crofts, 1965.

BING, ELIZABETH. Effect of childrearing practices on development of differential cognitive abilities. *Child Develpm.*, 1963, *34*, 631–648.

BISHOP, LEILA. Some relationships between the frequency of infants' vocalizations and mothers' behaviors. *Amer. Psychol.*, 1960, *15*, 394. (Abstract)

BLATT, B., and GARFUNKEL, F. A field demonstration of the effects of non-automated responsive environments on the intellectual and social competence of educable retarded children. Tech. Rep., Proj. D-014, Coop. Res. Branch, U.S.O.E. Boston: Boston University, 1965.

BLOOM, B. S. *Stability and change in human characteristics.* New York: Wiley, 1964.

BLOOM, R., WHITEMAN, M., and DEUTSCH, M. Race and social class as separate factors related to social environment. *Amer. J. Sociol.*, 1965, *70*, 471–476.

BOBBIO, N. Considerations introductives sur le raisonnement des juristes. *Rev. intern. de Phil.*, 1954, *8*, 67–83.

BODY, MARGARET K. Patterns of aggression in the nursery school. *Child Develpm.*, 1955, *26*, 3–11.

BOHNERT, H. G. The semiotic status of commands. *Phil of Sci.*, 1945, *12*, 302–315.

BOWER, E. M. *Early identification of emotionally handicapped children in school.* Springfield, Ill.: Charles C Thomas, 1960.

BOWERS, PATRICIA, and LONDON, P. Developmental correlates of role-playing ability. *Child Develpm.*, 1965, *36*, 499–508.

BOWLBY, J. The nature of the child's tie to his mother. *Int. J. Psychoanal.*, 1958, *39*, 350–373.

BOYD, G. F. Levels of aspiration of white and Negro children in a non-segregated elementary school. *J. soc. Psychol.*, 1952, *36*, 191–196.

BRAINE, M. D. S. The ontogeny of certain logical operations: Piaget's formulation examined by nonverbal methods. *Psychol. Monogr.*, 1959, *73*, No. 5 (Whole No. 475).

BRAZZIEL, W. F., and TERRELL, MARY. An experiment in the development of readiness in a culturally disadvantaged group of first grade children. *J. Negro Educ.*, 1962, *31*, 4–7.

BRICKER, W. A. Speech training with autistic and mentally retarded children. Paper read to the Biennial Meeting of the Soc. Res. Child Develpm., Minneapolis, March, 1965.

BRODY, GRACE F. Relationship between maternal attitudes and behavior. *J. Pers. soc. Psychol.*, 1965, *2*, 317–323.

BRODY, SYLVIA. *Patterns of mothering.* New York: International Universities Press, 1951.

BRONFENBRENNER, U. Socialization and social class through time and space. In Eleanor E. Maccoby, T. M. Newcomb, and E. L. Hartley (Eds.), *Readings in social psychology.* New York: Holt, 1958.

BRONFENBRENNER, U. Soviet methods of character education: some implications for research. *Amer. Psychol.*, 1962, *17*, 550–564.

BROPHY, J., HESS, R. D., and SHIPMAN, VIRGINIA C. Teaching behavior of mothers in structured interaction with their four-year-old children: a study in frustration. Paper read at 38th Annual Meeting of the Midwest. Psychol. Assn., Chicago, May, 1966.

BROTTMAN, M. A. Kenneth Montgomery research nursery school, research design. Unpublished manuscript. Chicago: Institute for Juvenile Research, Sept. 3, 1965.

BROWN, B. R. The assessment of self concept among four-year-old Negro and white children: a comparative study using the Brown-IDS Self Concept Reference Test. Paper presented at East. Psychol. Assn., New York, 1966.

BROWN, R. W. A study in language and cognition. *J. abnorm. soc. Psychol.*, 1954, *49*, 454–462.

BROWN, R. W. *Words and things*. Glencoe, Ill.: Free Press, 1958.

———, and BELLUGI, URSULA. Three processes in the child's acquisition of syntax. *Harvard Educ. Rev.*, 1964, *34*, 133–151.

———, and BERKO, JEAN. Word association and the acquisition of grammar. *Child Develpm.*, 1960, *31*, 1–14.

BRUNER, J. S. *The process of education*. Cambridge: Harvard University Press, 1960.

———. The act of discovery. *Harvard Educ. Rev.*, 1961, *31*, 21–32.

———. *Toward a theory of instruction*. Cambridge: Harvard University Press, 1966.

———, GOODNOW, JACQUELINE J., and AUSTIN, G. A. *A study of thinking*. New York: Science Editions, 1962.

BUELL, JOAN S., STODDARD, PATRICIA, BAER, D. M., and HARRIS, FLORENCE R. Patterns of social development collateral to social reinforcement of one form of play in an isolate nursery school child. Unpublished manuscript, University of Kansas and University of Washington, 1965.

BURRELL, D. B. Entailment: "E" and Aristotle. *Logique et analyse*, 1964, *27* n.s., 111–129.

BURT, C. The inheritance of mental ability. *Amer. Psychol.*, 1958, *13*, 1–15.

BURTON, R. V., MACCOBY, ELEANOR E., and ALLINSMITH, W. Antecedents of resistance to temptation in four-year-old children. *Child Develpm.*, 1961, *32*, 689–710.

BURTT, H. E. An experimental study of early childhood memory. *J. genet. Psychol.*, 1932, *40*, 287–295.

———. An experimental study of early childhood memory: final report. *J. genet. Psychol.*, 1941, *58*, 435–439.

CALDWELL, BETTYE M. Stimulus potential in the home. Paper read at Amer. Psychol. Assn., Los Angeles, September, 1964.

———. Preschool inventory. (Manual and Form) CAP-HS Form 42, Budget Bur. No. 116–504. 1965.

———, HERSCHER, L., LIPTON, E. L., RICHMOND, J. B., STERN, G. A., EDDY, EVELYN, DRACHMAN, R., and ROTHMAN, A. Mother-infant interaction in monomatric and polymatric families. *Amer. J. Orthopsychiat.*, 1963, *33*, 653–664.

———, and RICHMOND, J. B. Programmed day care for the very young child—a preliminary report. *J. Marriage Fam.*, 1964, *26*, 481–488.

CAMPBELL-SMITH, NORMA, and McFARLAND, MARGARET B. The role of the nursery school teacher in the development of child personality. *J. nursery Educ.*, 1963, *19*, 5–18.

CANON, L. Social isolation and susceptibility to distraction. Unpublished master's thesis, Stanford University, 1963.

CANTOR, G. N. Effect of three types of pretraining on discrimination learning in preschool chlidren. *J. exp. Psychol.*, 1955, *49*, 339–342.

CAREY, JANICE E., and GOSS, A. E. The role of mediating verbal responses in the conceptual sorting behavior of children. *J. genet. Psychol.*, 1957, *90*, 69–74.

CARPENTER, J. A., MOORE, O. K., SNYDER, C. R., and LISANSKY, EDITH S. Alcohol and higher-order problem solving. *Quart. J. Stud. on Alcohol*, 1961, *22*, 183–222.

CARR, V. S. The social and emotional changes in a group of children of high intelligence during a program of increased educational stimulation. Unpublished master's thesis, University of Iowa, 1938.

CASE, D., and COLLINSON, J. M. The development of formal thinking in verbal comprehension. *Brit. J. educ. Psychol.*, 1962, *32*, 103–111.

CASLER, L. Maternal deprivation: a critical review of the literature. *Monogr. Soc. Res. Child Develpm.*, 1961, *26*, No. 2 (Whole No. 80).

———. The effect of supplementary verbal stimulation on a group of institutionalized infants. *J. child Psychol. and Psychiat.*, 1965, *6*, 19–27. (a)

———. The effects of extra stimulation on a group of institutionalized infants. *Genet. Psychol. Monogr.*, 1965, *71*, 137–175. (b)

CASTANEDA, H. N. La lógica general de las normas y la ética. *Univer. de San Carlos* (Guatemala), 1955, *30*, 129–196.

———. Un sistema general de lógica normativa. *Dianoia*, 1957, *3*, 303–333. (a)

———. On the logic of norms. *Methodos*, 1957, *9*, 207–216. (b)

———. Imperatives and deontic logic. *Analysis*, 1958, *19*, 42–48.

———. The logic of obligation. *Phil. Stud.*, 1959, *10*, 17–23.

———. Obligation and modal logic. *Logique et analyse*, 1960, 3 n.s., 40–48. (a)

———. "Ought" and assumption in moral philosophy. *J. Phil.*, 1960, *57*, 791–804. (b)

CAUDLE, F. M. Prereading skills through the talking typewriter. *The Instructor*, 1965, *75*, 39–40.

CAZDEN, COURTNEY B. Environmental assistance to the child's acquisition of grammar. Unpublished doctoral dissertation, Harvard University, 1965.

———. Subcultural differences in child language. *Merrill-Palmer Quart.*, 1966, *12*, 185–219.

CHALL, JEANNE. Learning to read: the great debate. Final report of the City College–Carnegie reading study, New York, 1965. New York: McGraw-Hill, in press.

CHISHOLM, R. Contrary-to-duty imperatives and deontic logic. *Analysis*, 1963, *24*, 33–36.

CHITTENDEN, GERTRUDE E. An experimental study in measuring and modifying assertive behavior in young children. *Monogr. Soc. Res. Child Develpm.*, 1942, 7, No. 1 (Whole No. 31).

CHOMSKY, N. *Syntactic structures*. The Hague: Mouton, 1957.

CHRISTIANSON, HELEN M., ROGERS, MARY M., and-LUDLUM, BLANCHE A. *The nursery school: adventure in living and learning*. Boston: Houghton Mifflin, 1961.

CHURCH, A. The weak theory of implication. *Kontrolliertes denken*. Munich: 1951. (a)

———. Minimal logic. *J. symbolic Logic*, 1951, *16*, 239. (b)

CHURCH, J. Some procedures for the study of cognitive functioning and development in infancy and early childhood. Mimeographed. Vassar College, 1964.

CLARK, K. B. Educational stimulation of racially disadvantaged children. In

A. H. Passow (Ed.), *Education in depressed areas.* New York: Bureau of Publications, Teachers College, Columbia University, 1963.

————, and CLARK, M. K. Skin color as a factor in racial identification of Negro pre-school children: a preliminary report. *J. soc. Psychol.*, 1940, *11*, 159–169.

COHEN, F. S. What is a question? *Monist*, 1929, *39*, 350–364.

COHEN, J. Three-valued ethics. *Phil.*, 1951, *26*, 208–227.

COLBY, MARTHA G. Instrumental reproduction of melody by preschool children. *J. genet. Psychol.*, 1935, *47*, 413–430.

COMMITTEE ON DIAGNOSTIC READING TESTS, INC. *Diagnostic reading tests.* New York: The Committee, 1963.

CONTE, A. G. Bibliografia di logica giuridica. *Riv. int. de Filo. del diritto*, 1961, *38*, 119–144.

COOPER, MARGARET L., LEE, CONSTANCE J., BIERLEIN, MARCILEE W., WOLF, M. M., and BAER, D. M. The development of motor skill and consequent social interaction in a withdrawn nursery school child by social reinforcement procedures. Unpublished manuscript, University of Kansas, 1966.

CRANDALL, V. J., ORLEANS, SONYA, PRESTON, ANNE, and RABSON, ALICE. The development of social compliance in young children. *Child Develpm.*, 1958, *29*, 429–444.

D'ASARO, M. J., and JOHN, VERA P. A rating scale for evaluation of receptive, expressive, and phonetic language development in the young child. *Cerebral Palsy Rev.*, 1961, *22* (5) 3–4.

DAVIDSON, HELEN P. An experimental study of bright, average, and dull children at the four-year mental level. *Genet. Psychol. Monogr.*, 1931, *9*, 119–289.

DAVIS, ALLISON, *Social-class influences upon learning.* Cambridge: Harvard University Press, 1961.

DAWE, HELEN C. A study of the effect of an educational program upon language development and related mental functions in young children. *J. exp. Educ.*, 1942, *11*, 200–209.

DAWSON, E. E. A model for deontic logic. *Analysis*, 1959, *19*, 73–78.

DELACATO, C. H. *The treatment and prevention of reading problems: the neuro-psychological approach.* Springfield, Ill.: Charles C Thomas, 1959.

————. *The diagnosis and treatment of speech and reading problems.* Springfield, Ill.: Charles C Thomas, 1963.

DEMBER, W. N. The new look in motivation. *Amer. Sci.*, 1965, *53*, 409–427.

DENENBERG, V. H. Critical periods, stimulus input and emotional reactivity: a theory of infantile stimulation. Psychol. Rev., 1964, *71*, 335–351.

————, and KARAS, G. G. Effects of differential infantile handling upon weight gain and mortality in the rat and mouse. *Science*, 1959, *130*, 629–630.

DENNIS, W. The effect of restricted practice upon the reaching, sitting, and standing of two infants. *J. genet. Psychol.*, 1935, *47*, 17–32.

————. Causes of retardation among institutional children: Iran. *J. genet. Psychol.*, 1960, *96*, 47–59.

————, and DENNIS, MARSENA G. The effect of cradling practices upon the onset of walking in Hopi children. *J. genet. Psychol.*, 1940, *56*, 77–86.

DENNIS, W., and NAJARIAN, P. Infant development under environmental handicap. *Psychol. Monogr.*, 1957, *71*, No. 7 (Whole No. 436).

DENNIS, W., and SAYEGH, YVONNE. The effects of supplementary experiences upon the behavioral development of infants in institutions. *Child Develpm.*, 1965, *36*, 81–90.

DEUTSCH, CYNTHIA P. Auditory discrimination and learning: social factors. *Merrill-Palmer Quart.*, 1964, *10*, 277–296.

DEUTSCH, M. *Annual report: Institute for Developmental Studies.* New York: New York University, 1965. (a)

————. The role of social class in language development and cognition. *Amer. J. Orthopsychiat.*, 1965, *35*, 78–88. (b)

————, and BROWN, B. Social influences in Negro-white intelligence differences. *J. soc. Issues*, 1964, *20* (2), 24–35.

DEWEY, J. *The school and society.* Chicago: University of Chicago Press, 1899.

————. *The child and the curriculum.* Chicago: University of Chicago Press, 1902.

DIETZE, DORIS. The facilitating effect of words on discrimination and generalization. *J. exp Psychol.*, 1955, *50* (4), 255–260.

DODWELL, P. C. Children's understanding of number and related concepts. *Canad. J. Psychol.*, 1960, *14*, 191–205.

————. Children's understanding of number concepts: characteristics of an individual and of a group test. *Canad. J. Psychol.*, 1961, *15*, 29–36.

————. Relations between the understanding of the logic of classes and of cardinal number in children. *Canad. J. Psychol.*, 1962, *16*, 152–160.

DOLBEAR, KATHERINE E. Precocious children. *Pedagog. Sem.*, 1912, *19*, 461–491.

DOMAN, G. J., STEVENS, G. L., and OREM, R. C. You can teach your baby to read. *Ladies Home J.*, 1963, *80*, 62–63.

————. *How to teach your baby to read; the gentle revolution.* New York: Random House, 1964.

DOUVAN, ELIZABETH. Social status and success strivings. *J. abnorm. soc. Psychol.*, 1956, *52*, 219–223.

DREGER, R. M., and MILLER, K. S. Comparative psychological studies of Negroes and whites in the United States. *Psychol. Bull.*, 1960, *57*, 361–402.

DUBIN, ELISABETH R. The effect of training on the tempo of development of graphic representation in preschool children. *J. exp. Educ.*, 1946, *15*, 166–173.

DUNCAN, C. P. Description of learning to learn in human subjects. *Amer. J. Psychol.*, 1960, *73*, 108–114.

DUNNINGTON, MARGARET J. Behavior differences of sociometric status groups in a nursery school. *Child Develpm.*, 1957, *28*, 103–111. (a)

————. Investigation of areas of disagreement in sociometric measurement of preschool children. *Child Develpm.*, 1957, *28*, 93–102. (b)

DURKIN, DOLORES. *Phonics and the teaching of reading.* New York: Bureau of Publications, Teachers College, Columbia University, 1962.

————. Children who read before first grade. In W. G. Cutts (Ed.), *Teaching young children to read.* Washington: U.S. Govt. Printing Office, 1964. (a)

————. A fifth-year report on the achievement of early readers. *Elem. Sch. J.*, 1964, *65*, 76–80. (b)

EARL, R. W. A theory of stimulus selection. Special document SD 61–132. Fullerton, Calif.: Hughes Aircraft Company Ground Systems. Sept. 8, 1961.

ELKIND, D. The development of quantitative thinking: a systematic replication of Piaget's studies. *J. genet. Psychol.*, 1961, 98, 37–46.

EL'KONIN, D. B. Nekotorye itogi izucheniia psikicheskogo razvitiia detei dosh kol'nogo vozrasta. *Psikhologicheskaiia nauka v SSSR.* (Some results of studying the mental development of pre-school age children. *Psychological Science in the USSR.*) Acad. Educ. Sci. RSFR. Inst. Psychol., Moscow, 1960, 2, 249–261.

EMMERICH, W. Young children's discriminations of parent and child roles. *Child Develpm.*, 1959, 30, 403–419.

ENGEN, T., LIPSITT, L. P., and KAYE, H. Olfactory responses and adaptation in the human neonate. *J. comp. physiol. Psychol.*, 1963, 56, 77–81.

ENGLUND, F. W. A report on employment and education program for high school dropouts. Paper read to Subcommittee on Employment and Manpower of the Committee on Labor and Welfare of the U.S. Senate, 1963.

ERIKSON, E. H. *Childhood and society.* New York: Norton, 1950.

ERVIN, SUSAN M. Changes with age in the verbal determinants of word-association. *Amer. J. Psychol.*, 1961, 74, 361–372.

———. Imitations in the speech of two-year-olds. Paper read at Amer. Psychol. Assn., Philadelphia, August 29, 1963.

———, and MILLER, W. R. Language development. *Yearb. nat. soc. Stud. Educ.*, 1963, 62, Part I.

FABREGUETTES, P. *La logique judiciare et l'art de juger.* Paris: Librairie générale de droit et de jurisprudence, 1962.

FANTZ, R. L. Pattern vision in young infants. *Psychol. Rec.*, 1958, 8, 43–47.

FARIS, R. E. L., and DUNHAM, H. W. *Mental disorders in urban areas.* Chicago: University of Chicago Press, 1939.

FAULS, LYDIA B., and SMITH, W. D. Sex-role learning of five-year-olds. *J. genet. Psychol.*, 1956, 89, 105–117.

FELDMANN, SHIRLEY. A preschool enrichment program for disadvantaged children. *New Era*, 1964, 45, 79–82.

FENSTAD, J. E. Notes on normative logic. *Avhandlinger utgitt av det norske vindenskapsakademi i Oslo. 2. Historisk-filosofisk klasse*, 1959, 1, 1–25.

FERGUSON, G. A. *Statistical analysis in psychology and education.* New York: McGraw-Hill, 1959.

FEYS, R. Expression modale du "devoir-être." *J. symbolic Logic*, 1955, 20, 91–92.

———. Reply (untitled) to A. N. Prior. *Rev. phil. de Louvain*, 1956, 54, 88–89.

———, and MOTTE, MARIE-THÉRÈSE. Logique juridique, systemes juridiques. *Logique et analyse*, 1959, 2 n.s., 143–147.

FISHER, M. A three-valued calculus for deontic logic. *Theoria*, 1961, 27, 107–118.

———. A system of deontic-alethic modal logic. *Mind*, 1962, 71 n.s., 72–78.

———. A contradiction in deontic logic? *Analysis*, 1964, 25, 12–13

FISHMAN, J. A., DEUTSCH, M., KOGAN, L., NORTH, R., and WHITEMAN, M. Guidelines for testing minority group children. *J. soc. Issues*, 1964, 20, 129–145.

FISKE, D. W., and MADDI, S. R. *Functions of varied experience.* Homewood, Ill.: Dorsey Press, 1961.

FLAVELL, J. H. *The developmental psychology of Jean Piaget.* Princeton: Van Nostrand, 1963.

———. Role-taking and communication skills in children. *Young Child.*, 1966, 21, 164–177.

————, BEACH, D. R., and CHINSKY, J. M. Spontaneous verbal rehearsal in a memory task as a function of age. *Child Developm.*, 1966, 37, 283–299.

FODOR, J. A. How to learn to talk: some simple ways. In F. Smith and G. A. Miller (Eds.), *The genesis of language: a psycholinguistic approach.* Cambridge: M.I.T. Press, 1966.

FOWLER, W. Cognitive stimulation, IQ changes, and cognitive learning in three-year-old identical twins and triplets. *Amer. Psychologist*, 1961, 16, 373. (Abstract)

————. Cognitive learning in infancy and early childhood. *Psychol. Bull.*, 1962, 59, 116–152. (a)

————. Teaching a two-year-old to read: an experiment in early childhood learning. *Genet. Psychol. Monogr.*, 1962, 66, 181–283. (b)

————. Structural dimensions of the learning process in early reading. *Child Develpm.*, 1964, 35, 1093–1104.

————. A study of process and method in three-year-old twins and triplets learning to read. *Genet. Psychol. Monogr.*, 1965, 72, 3–89. (a)

————. Concept learning in early childhood. *Young Child.*, 1965, 21, 81–91. (b)

FOXWELL, HELEN R., THOMSON, CAROLINE L., COATS, BETTY A., BAER, D. M., and WOLF, M. M. The development of social responsiveness to other children in a nursery school child through experimental use of social reinforcement. Unpublished manuscript, University of Kansas, 1966.

FRUTIGER, P. Logique necessaire et logique obligatoire. In *Proc. 10th int. Cong.* Amsterdam: North Holland Publishing Co., 1949.

FURTH, H. G. Conservation of weight in deaf and hearing children. *Child Develpm.*, 1964, 35, 143–150.

————. *Thinking without language.* New York: Free Press, 1966.

————, and YOUNISS, J. Effect of overtraining on three discrimination shifts in children. *J. comp. physiol. Psychol.*, 1964, 57, 290–293.

GARDNER, D. B., HAWKES, G. R., and BURCHINAL, L. G. Noncontinuous mothering in infancy and development in later childhood. *Child Develpm.*, 1961, 32, 225–234.

GARDNER, R. W. Cognitive styles in categorizing behavior. *J. Pers.*, 1953, 22, 214–233.

————, HOLZMAN, P. S., KLEIN, G. S., LINTON, HARRIET, and SPENCE, D. P. Cognitive controls: a study of individual consistencies in cognitive behavior. *Psychol. Issues*, 1959, 1, No. 4 (Whole No. 4).

GARDNER, R. W., JACKSON, D. N., and MESSICK, S. J. Personality organization in cognitive controls and intellectual abilities. *Psychol. Issues*, 1960, 2, No. 4 (Whole No. 8).

GEACH, P. T. Entailment. *Aristotelian soc. suppl. volume*, 1958, 32, 157–172. (a)

————. Imperative and deontic logic. *Analysis*, 1958, 18, 49–56. (b)

GESELL, A. Maturation and infant behavior pattern. *Psychol. Rev.*, 1929, 36, 307–319.

————, and THOMPSON, HELEN. Learning and growth in identical infant twins. *Genet. Psychol. Monogr.*, 1929, 6, 1–124.

————. Twins T and C from infancy to adolescence: a biogenetic study of individual differences by the method of co-twin control. *Genet. Psychol. Monogr.*, 1941, 24, 3–121.

GETZELS, J. W. Creative thinking, problem-solving, and instruction. *Yearb. Nat. soc. Stud. Educ.*, 1964, 63, Part I.

————, and JACKSON, P. W. *Creativity and intelligence: explorations with gifted students.* New York: Wiley, 1962.

GEWIRTZ, J. L. Three determinants of attention-seeking in young children. *Monogr. soc. Res. Child Develpm.*, 1954, *19*, No. 2 (Whole No. 59).

————. A factor analysis of some attention-seeking behaviors in young children. *Child Develpm.*, 1956, *27*, 17–37.

————. A learning analysis of the effects of normal stimulation, privation and deprivation on the acquisition of social motivation and attachment. In B. M. Foss (Ed.), *Determinants of infant behaviour.* New York: Wiley, 1961.

————, and BAER, D. M. Deprivation and satiation of social reinforcers as drive conditions. *J. abnorm. soc. Psychol.*, 1958, *57*, 165–172. (a)

————. The effect of brief social deprivation on behaviors for a social reinforcer. *J. abnorm. soc. Psychol.*, 1958, *56*, 49–56. (b)

GIBSON, ELEANOR J. Development of perception: discrimination of depth compared with discrimination of graphic symbols. In J. C. Wright (Ed.), Basic cognitive processes in children. *Monogr. soc. Res. Child Develpm.*, 1963, *28*, No. 2 (Whole No. 86). (a)

————. Perceptual development. *Yearb. nat. soc. Stud. Educ.*, 1963, *62*, Part I. Pp. 144–195. (b)

GIORGIANNI, V. Logica matematica e logica quiridica. *Rev. int. di Filo. del diritto*, 1953, *30* (3rd s.), 462–486.

GLICK, J., and WAPNER, S. Ontogenetic changes in transitivity. Paper read at Eastern Psychol. Assn., New York, April 14–16, 1966.

GODA, S., and SMITH, KAY. Speech stimulation practices among mothers of preschool children. *J. Speech Hearing Disorders*, 1959, *24*, 150–153.

GOLDFARB, W. The effects of early institutional care on adolescent personality. *J. exp. Educ.*, 1943, *12*, 106–129.

————. Psychological privation in infancy and subsequent adjustment. *Amer. J. Orthopsychiat.*, 1945, *15*, 247–255.

————. Variations in adolescent adjustment of institutionally reared children. *Amer. J. Orthopsychiat.*, 1947, *17*, 449–457.

————. Emotional and intellectual consequences of psychologic deprivation in infancy: a reevaluation. In P. H. Hoch and J. Zubin (Eds.), *Psychopathology of childhood.* New York: Grune and Stratton, 1955.

GOLDSTEIN, K. *The organism.* New York: American Book Co., 1939.

GOLDSTEIN, L. S. A partial overview of process research at the Institute for Developmental Studies. Unpublished manuscript, Institute for Developmental Studies, New York University, December, 1964.

————. Evaluation of an enrichment program for socially disadvantaged children. Unpublished manuscript, Institute for Developmental Studies, New York University, June, 1965.

GOLLIN, E. S. Tactual form discrimination: a developmental comparison under conditions of spatial interference. *J. exp. Psychol.*, 1960, *60*, 126–129.

————. Tactual form discrimination: developmental differences in the effects of training under conditions of spatial interference. *J. Psychol.*, 1961, *51*, 131–140.

————. Reversal learning and conditional discrimination in children. *J. comp. physiol. Psychol.*, 1964, *58*, 441–445.

————. A developmental approach to learning and cognition. In L. P. Lipsitt and C. C. Spiker (Eds.), *Advances in child development and behavior.* Vol. 2. New York: Academic Press, 1965.

GORDON, E. W. A review of programs of compensatory education. *Amer. J. Orthopsychiat.*, 1965, *35*, 640–651.

GOTKIN, L. G. The machine and the child. *Audio visual commun. Rev.*, in press.

———, and FONDILLER, FAY. Listening centers in the kindergarten. *Audio-visual Instruction*, 1965, *10*, 24–25.

GOTKIN, L. G., and GOLDSTEIN, L. S. Programed instruction in the schools: innovation and innovator. In M. B. Miles (Ed.), *Innovation in education.* New York: Bureau of Publications, Teachers College, Columbia University, 1964.

GOTTESMAN, I. I. Genetic aspects of intelligent behavior. In N. R. Ellis (Ed.), *Handbook of mental deficiency.* New York: McGraw-Hill, 1963.

GRAY, P. H. Theory and evidence of imprinting in human infants. *J. Psychol.*, 1958, *46*, 155–166.

GRAY, SUSAN W., and KLAUS, R. A. An experimental preschool program for culturally deprived children. *Child Develpm.*, 1965, *36*, 887–898.

GREEN, P. C., and GORDON, M. Maternal deprivation: its influence on visual exploration in infant monkeys. *Science*, 1964, *145*, 292–294.

GRELLING, K. Zur logik der sollsätze. *Unity of sci. forum*, Jan. 1939, 44–47.

GRIM, P., KOHLBERG, L., and WHITE, S. Relations between resistance to temptation and stability of attention. *Child Develpm.*, 1967, in press.

GRINSTED, A. D. Studies in gross bodily movement. Unpublished doctoral dissertation, Louisiana State University, 1939.

GUILFORD, J. P. The structure of intellect. *Psychol. Bull.*, 1965, *53*, 267–293.

———. Three faces of intellect. *Amer. Psychologist*, 1959, *14*, 469–479.

HALLDEN, S. On the logic of "better." Kobenhavn: E. Musksgaard, 1957.

HAMBLIN, C. L. Questions. *Austral. J. Phil.*, 1958, *36*, 159–168.

———. Questions aren't statements. *Phil. Sci.*, 1963, *30*, 62–63.

HARE, R. M. *The language of morals.* Oxford: Clarendon Press, 1952.

HARLOW, H. F., and HARLOW, MARGARET K. Social deprivation in monkeys. *Sci. Amer.*, 1962, *207* (5), 136–146.

———, ———, RUEPING, R. R., and MASON, W. A. Performance of infant Rhesus monkeys on discrimination learning, delayed response, and discrimination learning set. *J. comp. physiol. Psychol.*, 1960, *53*, 113–121.

HARRAH, D. A logic of questions and answers. *Phil. Sci.*, 1961, *28*, 40–46.

———. *Communication: a logical model.* Cambridge, Mass.: M.I.T. Press, 1963.

HARRIS, FLORENCE R., JOHNSTON, MARGARET K., KELLEY, C. SUSAN, and WOLF, M. M. Effects of positive social reinforcement on regressed crawling of a nursery school child. *J. educ. Psychol.*, 1964, *55*, 35–41.

HART, BETTY M., REYNOLDS, NANCY J., BRAWLEY, ELEANOR, HARRIS, FLORENCE R., and BAER, D. M. Effects of contingent and non-contingent social reinforcement on the isolate behavior of a nursery school girl. Unpublished manuscript, University of Kansas and University of Washington, 1965.

———, ALLEN, K. EILEEN, BUELL, JOAN S., HARRIS, FLORENCE R., and WOLF, M. M. Effects of social reinforcement on operant crying. *J. exp. Child Psychol.*, 1964, *1*, 145–153.

HARTUP, W. W. Nurturance and nurturance-withdrawal in relation to the dependency behavior of preschool children. *Child Develpm.*, 1958, *29*, 191–201.

———. Friendship status and the effectiveness of peers as reinforcing agents. *J. exp. Child Psychol.*, 1964, *1*, 154–162.

————. Early pressures in child development. *Young Child.*, 1965, *20*, 270–283.

————, and HIMENO, Y. Social isolation vs. interaction with adults in relation to aggression in preschool children. *J. abn. soc. Psychol.*, 1959, *59*, 17–22.

HARTUP, W. W., and KELLER, E. D. Nurturance in preschool children in its relation to dependency. *Child Develpm.*, 1960, *31*, 681–689.

HARTLEY, RUTH E., FRANK, L. K., and GOLDENSON, R. M. *Understanding children's play.* New York: Columbia University Press, 1952.

HAYNES, H. M. Development of accomodative behavior in infants. Paper read at Conf. on Theor. Optometry and Visual Train., St. Louis, January, 1963.

HEATHERS, G. Acquiring dependence and independence: a theoretical orientation. *J. genet. Psychol.*, 1955, *87*, 277–291. (a)

————. Emotional dependence and independence in nursery school play. *J. genet. Psychol.*, 1955, *87*, 37–57. (b)

HEBB, D. O. The effects of early experience on problem-solving at maturity. *Amer. Psychologist*, 1947, *2*, 306–307. (Abstract)

————. *The organization of behavior: a neuropsychological theory.* New York: Wiley, 1949.

————. Alice in Wonderland, or psychology among the biological sciences. In H. F. Harlow and C. N. Woolsey (Eds.), *Biological and biochemical bases of behavior.* Madison: University of Wisconsin Press, 1958.

HECHINGER, F. M. (Ed.). *Pre-school education today.* New York: Doubleday, 1966.

HELD, R. Exposure-history as a factor in maintaining stability of perception and coordination. *J. nerv. ment. Dis.*, 1961, *132*, 26–32.

————, and BOSSOM, J. Neonatal deprivation and adult rearrangement: complementary techniques for analyzing plastic sensory-motor coordinations. *J. comp. physiol. Psychol.*, 1961, *54*, 33–37.

————, and HEIN, A. Movement-produced stimulation in the development of visually-guided behavior. *J. comp. physiol. Psychol.*, 1963, *56*, 872–876.

HENTON, C. L., and JOHNSON, E. E. Relationship between self concepts of Negro elementary school children and their academic achievement, intelligence, interests, and manifest anxiety. Coop. Res. Proj. No. 1592. Washington: U.S.O.E., May, 1964.

HESS, R. D. Preschool projects (II): inventory of compensatory education projects. Unpublished manuscript, University of Chicago, Urban Child Center, 1965.

————, and HANDEL, G. *Family worlds: a psychosocial approach to family life.* Chicago: University of Chicago Press, 1959.

————, and SHIPMAN, VIRGINIA C. Early experience and the socialization of cognitive modes in children. *Child Develpm.*, 1965, *36*, 869–886.

————. Cognitive elements in maternal behavior. *Minnesota Sympos. on Child Psychol.*, Vol. 1. Minneapolis: University of Minnesota Press, 1967.

————. Maternal attitude toward the school and the role of pupil: some social class comparisons. In A. H. Passow (Ed.), *Teaching and learning in depressed areas.* New York: Teacher's College Press, 1967.

HEYNS, R. W., and LIPPITT, R. Systematic observational techniques. In G. Lindzey (Ed.), *Handbook of social psychology.* Vol. 1. Cambridge, Mass.: Addison-Wesley, 1954.

HICKS, J. A., and RALPH, DOROTHY W. The effects of practice in tracing the Porteus Diamond Maze. *Child Develpm.*, 1931, 2, 156–158.

HIGGINS, C., and SIVERS, CATHRYNE H. A comparison of Stanford-Binet and Colored Raven Progressive Matrices IQs for children. *J. consult. Psychol.*, 1958, 22, 465–468.

HIGHBERGER, RUTH. The relationship between maternal behavior and the child's early adjustment to nursery school. *Child Develpm.*, 1955, 26, 49–61.

HILGARD, JOSEPHINE R. Learning and maturation in preschool children. *J. genet. Psychol.*, 1932, 41, 31–56.

HILL, S. D. The performance of young children on three discrimination-learning tasks. *Child Develpm.*, 1965, 36, 425–435.

HISSEN, IRENE. A new approach to music for young children. *Child Develpm.*, 1933, 4, 308–317.

HIZ, H. Questions and answers. *J. Phil.*, 1962, 59, 253–265.

HOFFMAN, LOIS W. Effects of maternal employment on the child. *Child Develpm.*, 1961, 32, 187–197.

————, ROSEN, S., and LIPPITT, R. Parental coerciveness, child autonomy, and child's role at school. *Sociometry*, 1960, 23, 15–22.

HOFFMAN, M. L. Parent discipline and the child's consideration for others. *Child Develpm.*, 1963, 34, 573–588.

————, and HOFFMAN, LOIS W. (Eds.). *Review of child development research*. Vols. 1 and 2. New York: Russell Sage Foundation, 1964 and 1967.

HOFSTADTER, A., and McKINSEY, J. C. C. On the logic of imperatives. *Phil. of Sci.*, 1939, 6, 446–457.

HONZIK, MARJORIE P., MACFARLANE, JEAN W., and ALLEN, LUCILLE. The stability of mental test performance between two and eighteen years. *J. exp. Educ.*, 1948, 17, 309–324.

HOROWITZ, FRANCES D. Incentive value of social stimuli for preschool children. *Child Develpm.*, 1962, 33, 111–116.

————. Social reinforcement effects on child behavior. *J. nursery Educ.*, 1963, 18, 276–284.

HUNT, J. M. *Intelligence and experience*. New York: Ronald Press, 1961.

————. The psychological basis for using pre-school enrichment as an antidote for cultural deprivation. *Merrill-Palmer quart.*, 1964, 10, 209–248.

————. Intrinsic motivation and its role in psychological development. In D. Levine (Ed.), *Nebraska symposium on motivation*. Vol. 13. Lincoln: University of Nebraska Press, 1965.

HYMES, J. L. Excellence in teacher education. *J. nursery Educ.*, 1963, 18, 168–171.

INSTITUTE FOR DEVELOPMENTAL STUDIES. Index and description of tests. New York: New York University, March, 1962; revised, 1965.

IRWIN, O. C. Infant speech: effect of systematic reading of stories. *J. Speech Hearing Res.*, 1960, 3, 187–190. (a)

————. Language and communication. In P. H. Mussen (Ed.), *Handbook of research methods in child development*. New York: Wiley, 1960. (b)

IVASHCHENKO, F. I. An experimental study of the relationships between words heard, seen and pronounced. *Pavlov J. Higher nerv. Activity*, 1958, 8, 168–174.

JAAKO, J., and HINTIKKA, K. Quantifiers in deontic logic. *Sociatas scientiarum fennica*, 1958, 23, 1–23.

JACKSON, P. *Life in classrooms*. New York: Holt, Rinehart, 1967.

JAHODA, G. Child animism: a critical survey of cross-cultural research. *J. soc. Psychol.*, 1958, *47*, 197–212.

JEFFREY, W. E., and COHEN, L. B. Response tendencies of children in a two-choice situation. *J. exp. Child Psychol.*, 1965, *2*, 248–254.

JEGARD, SUZANNE, and WALTERS, R. H. A study of some determinants of aggression in young children. *Child Develpm.*, 1960, *31*, 739–747.

JENSEN, A. R. Learning abilities in Mexican-American and Anglo-American children. *Calif. J. educ. Res.*, 1961, *12*, 147–159.

―――. Learning ability in retarded, average, and gifted children. *Merrill-Palmer quart.*, 1963, *9*, 123–140.

―――. Varieties of individual differences in learning. In R. M. Gagne (Ed.), *Learning and individual differences*. Columbus, Ohio: Merrill, 1966.

JERSILD, A. J., and BIENSTOCK, SYLVIA F. The influence of training on the vocal ability of three-year-old children. *Child Develpm.*, 1931, *2*, 272–291.

―――. A study of the development of children's ability to sing. *J. educ. Psychol.*, 1934, *25*, 481–503.

―――, and MARKEY, FRANCES V. Conflicts between preschool children. *Child Develpm. Monogr.*, 1935, No. 21.

JOHN, VERA P. The intellectual development of slum children. *Amer. J. Orthopsychiat.*, 1963, *33*, 813–822.

JOHNSTON, MARGARET K., KELLEY, C. SUSAN, HARRIS, FLORENCE R., and WOLF, M. M. An application of reinforcement principles to development of motor skills of a young child. *Child Develpm.*, 1966, *37*, 379–387.

JONES, H. E. The environment and mental development. In L. Carmichael (Ed.), *Manual of child psychology*. (2nd ed.) New York: Wiley, 1954.

KAGAN, J., and MOSS, H. A. Parental correlates of child's IQ and height: a cross-validation of the Berkeley Growth Study results. *Child Develpm.*, 1959, *30*, 325–332.

―――. The stability of passive and dependent behavior from childhood through adulthood. *Child Develpm.*, 1960, *31*, 577–591.

―――. *Birth to maturity: a study in psychological development*. New York: Wiley, 1962.

―――, ―――, and SIGEL, I. E. Psychological significance of styles of conceptualization. In J. C. Wright and J. Kagan (Eds.), Basic cognitive processes in children. *Monogr. Soc. Res. Child Develpm.*, 1963, *28*, No. 2 (Whole No. 86).

―――, ROSMAN, BERNICE L., DAY, DEBORAH, ALBERT, J., and PHILLIPS, W. Information processing in the child: significance of analytic and reflective attitudes. *Psychol. Monogr.*, 1964, *78*, No. 1 (Whole No. 578).

KALINOWSKI, J. Théorie des propositions normatives. *Stud. logica*, 1953, *1*, 147–182.

―――. Interpretation juridique et logique des propositions normatives. *Logique et analyse*, 1959, 2 n.s., 128–142. (a)

―――. Y a-t-il une logique jurisdique? *Logique et analyse*, 1959, 2 n.s., 48–53. (b)

―――. *Introduction a la logique juridique*. Bibliotheque de philosophie du droit, Vol. 3, 1965.

KAPLAN, B. The "Latent Content" of Heinz Werner's comparative-developmental approach. In S. Wapner and B. Kaplan (Eds.), *Heinz Werner*

(*1890–1964*): *papers in memoriam.* Worcester, Mass.: Clark University Press, 1966.

KARP, JOAN M., and SIGEL, I. E. Psycheducational appraisal of disadvantaged children. *Rev. educ. Res.*, 1965, *35*, 401–412.

KEISTER, M. E., and UPDEGRAFF, R. A study of children's reactions to failure and an experimental attempt to modify them. *Child Develpm.*, 1937, *8*, 241–248.

KENDLER, H. H., and D'AMATO, MAY F. A comparison of reversal shifts and nonreversal shifts in human concept formation behavior. *J. exp. Psychol.*, 1955, *49*, 165–174.

———, and KENDLER, TRACY S. Vertical and horizontal processes in problem solving. *Psychol. Rev.*, 1962, *69*, 1–16.

KENDLER, TRACY S. Development of mediating responses in children. In J. C. Wright and J. Kagan (Eds.), Basic cognitive processes in children. *Monogr. Soc. Res. Child Develpm.*, 1963, *28*, No. 2 (Whole No. 86).

———, and KENDLER, H. H. Reversal and nonreversal shifts in kindergarten children. *J. exp. Psychol.*, 1959, *58*, 56–60.

———, ———, and WELLS, DORIS. Reversal and nonreversal shifts in nursery school children. *J. comp. physiol. Psychol.*, 1960, *53*, 83–88. Urbana: University of Illinois Press, 1958.

KIRK, S. A. *Early education of the mentally retarded: an experimental study.*

———, and McCARTHY, J. J. *The Illinois Test of Psycholinguistic Abilities: an approach to differential diagnoses.* Urbana: University of Illinois Press, 1961.

KLATSKIN, ETHELYN H. Intelligence test performance at one year among infants raised with flexible methodology. *J. clin. Psychol.*, 1952, *8*, 230–237.

KLINEBERG, O. Negro-white differences in intelligence test performance: a new look at an old problem. *Amer. Psychologist*, 1963, *18*, 198–203.

KLUG, U. *Juristische logik.* Berlin: Springer Verlag, 1951.

KLUGH, H. E., and ROEHL, KAREN. Developmental level and concept learning: interaction of age and complexity. *Psychonomic Sci.*, 1965, *2*, 385–386.

KOBLER, R., and MOORE, O. K. *Educational system and apparatus*, U.S. Patent No. 3,281,959. 1966.

KOCH, HELEN L. The relation of "Primary Mental Abilities" in five- and six-year-olds to sex of child and characteristics of his sibling. *Child Develpm.*, 1954, *25*, 209–223.

KOHLBERG, L. Sensori-motor intelligence test. Unpublished mimeographed manuscript, Yale University, 1958.

———. Stages in children's conceptions of physical of social objects in the years 4 to 8. Unpublished mimeographed manuscript, Center for Advanced Studies in the Behavioral Sciences, 1962.

———. The development of children's orientation toward a moral order: I. Sequence in the development of moral thought. *Vita Humana*, 1963, *6*, 11–33.

———. A cognitive-developmental analysis of children's sex-role concepts and attitudes. In Eleanor E. Maccoby (Ed.), *The development of sex differences.* Stanford: Stanford University Press, 1966. (a)

———. Moral education in the schools: a developmental view. *School Rev.*, 1966, *74*, 1–30. (b)

———. Cognitive stages and pre-school education. *Human Develpm.*, 1966, *9*, 5–17. (c)

————. The cognitive-developmental approach to early education. In D. Elkind and J. Flavell (Eds.), *Contributions of Jean Piaget.* New York: Van Nostrand, 1967.

KOHN, M. L. Social class and the exercise of parental authority. *Amer. sociol. Rev.,* 1959, *24,* 252–366.

————. The importance of the beginning: kindergarten. *Nat'l. Elem. Prin.,* 1962, *41,* 18–22.

KOLTSOVA, M. M. *On the formation of higher nervous activity in children.* Leningrad: State Medical Literature Pr., 1958. Cited by Yvonne Brackbill, Experimental research with children in the Soviet Union. *Amer. Psychologist,* 1960, *15,* 226–233.

————. Cited by Yvonne Brackbill. Research and clinical work with children. In R. A. Bauer (Ed.), *Some views on Soviet psychology.* Washington: Amer. Psychol. Assn., 1962.

KREBS, R. Relations between attention, moral judgment, and moral behavior. Unpublished doctoral dissertation, University of Chicago, 1967.

KRIPKE, S. A. A completeness theorem in modal logic. *J. symbolic Logic,* 1959, *24,* 1–15. (a)

————. Distinguished constituents. *J. symbolic Logic,* 1959, *24,* 323. (Abstract) (b)

————. The problem of entailment. *J. symbolic Logic,* 1959, *24,* 324. (Abstract) (c)

KUENNE, MARGARET R. Experimental investigation of the relation of language to transposition behavior in young children. *J. exp. Psychol.,* 1946, *36,* 471–490.

LABOV, W. Linguistic research on the non-standard English of Negro children. Paper read at N.Y. Soc. Exp. Study of Educ., New York, April, 1965.

LAMBERT, W. E., and TAGUCHI, Y. Ethnic cleavage among young children. In J. M. Seidman (Ed.), *The child: a book of readings.* New York: Rinehart, 1958.

LANDRETH, CATHERINE. *Education of the young child.* New York: Wiley, 1949.

LANGFORD, LOUISE M. *Guidance of the young child.* New York: Wiley, 1960.

LEMMON, E. J., and NOWELL-SMITH, P. H. Escapism: the logical basis of ethics. *Mind,* 1960, *69* n.s., 289–300.

LENNEBERG, E. H. Understanding language without ability to speak: a case report. *J. abnorm. soc. Psychol.,* 1962, *65,* 419–425.

LENROW, P. What price acceleration? Paper presented at the Society for Research in Child Development, New York, March 29, 1967.

LEONARD, H. S. *Principles of right reason.* New York: Henry Holt, 1957.

LEVINE, S. Infantile experience and resistance to physiological stress. *Science,* 1957, *126,* 405.

LEVIT, S. G. Twin investigations in the U.S.S.R. *Charact. Pers.,* 1935, *3,* 188–193.

LEVY, D. Maternal overprotection. In M. L. Haimowitz and Natalie R. Haimowitz (Eds.), *Human development: selected readings.* New York: Crowell, 1960.

LING, B. Form discrimination as a learning cue in infants. *Comp. Psychol. Monogr.,* 1941, *17,* No. 2 (Whole No. 86).

LIPPITT, P., and LOHMAN, J. Cross-age relationships—an educational resource. *Children,* 1965, *12,* 113–117.

LIPPITT, R. Report on cooperative research project No. E-001. Washington: U.S.O.E., June, 1964.

LIPSITT, L. P. Learning in the first year of life. In L. P. Lipsitt and C. C. Spiker (Eds.), *Advances in child development and behavior.* Vol. 1. New York: Academic Press, 1963.

———, and SPIKER, C. C. (Eds.) *Advances in child development and behavior.* New York: Academic Press, 1963–64. 2 vols.

LIUBLINSKAYA, A. A. The development of children's speech and thought. In B. Simon (Ed.), *Psychology in the Soviet Union.* Stanford: Stanford University Press, 1957.

LONG, E. The effect of programmed instruction in special skills during the preschool period on later ability patterns and academic achievement. Terminal progress report. U.S. Office of Educ. Proj. No. 1521, University of North Carolina, 1966.

LOTT, A. J., and LOTT, BERNICE E. *Negro and white youth.* New York: Holt, Rinehart, 1963.

LUCCO, A. The curiosity behavior of four-year-old children: an exploratory study. Unpublished doctoral dissertation, University of Chicago, 1965.

LURIIA, A. R. Memory and the structure of mental processes. *Voprosy Psikhol.,* 1960, 1–2, 81–93.

———. *The role of speech in the regulation of normal and abnormal behaviour.* New York: Pergamon Press, 1961.

———, and YUDOVICH, F. I. *Speech and the development of mental processes in the child.* London: Staples Press, 1959.

LYAMINA, G. M. K voprosu o Makhanizme Ovladeniya Proiznosheniem Slov u Detei Vtorogo i Tret'ego Goda Zhisni. (On the mechanism of mastery of pronunciation of words by children in the second and third years of life.) *Voprosy Psikhol.,* 1958, 6, 119–130.

———. Razvitie Ponimaniya Rechi u Detei Vtorogo Goda Zhizni. (Development of speech comprehension in children the second year of life.) *Voprosy Psikhol.,* 1960, 3, 106–121.

McCANDLESS, B .R. The effect of enriched educational experiences upon the growth of intelligence of very superior children. Unpublished master's thesis, University of Iowa, 1940.

———, BILOUS, CAROLYN B., and BENNETT, HANNAH L. Peer popularity and dependence on adults in preschool-age socialization. *Child Develpm.,* 1961, 32, 511–518.

———, and HOYT, JUNE M. Sex, ethnicity, and play preferences of preschool children. *J. abnorm. soc. Psychol.,* 1961, 62, 683–685.

———, and MARSHALL, HELEN R. A picture sociometric technique for preschool children and its relation to teacher judgments of friendship. *Child Develpm.,* 1957, 28, 139–147. (a)

———. Sex differences in social acceptance and participation of preschool children. *Child Develpm.,* 1957, 28, 421–425. (b)

McCARTHY, DOROTHEA. Language development in children. In L. Carmichael (Ed.), *Manual of child psychology.* (2nd Ed.) New York: Wiley, 1954.

McCLELLAND, D. C., RINDLISBACHER, A., and deCHARMS, R. Religious and other sources of parental attitudes toward independence training. In D. C. McClelland (Ed.), *Studies in motivation.* New York: Appleton-Century-Crofts, 1955.

MACCOBY, ELEANOR E. Role-taking in childhood and its consequences for social learning. *Child Develpm.,* 1959, 30, 239–252.

————. Selective auditory attention in children. In L. P. Lipsitt and C. C. Spiker (Eds.), *Advances in child development and behavior.* Vol. 3. New York: Academic Press, 1966.

————, Dowley, Edith M., Hagen, J. W., and Degerman, R. Activity level and intellectual functioning in normal preschool children. *Child Develpm.,* 1965, *36,* 761–770.

McCurdy, H. G. The childhood pattern of genius. *J. Elisha Mitchell Sci. Soc.,* 1957, *73,* 448–462.

McGraw, Myrtle B. *Growth: a study of Johnny and Jimmy.* New York: Appleton-Century, 1935.

————. Later development of children specially trained during infancy: Johnny and Jimmy at school age. *Child Develpm.,* 1939, *10,* 1–19.

Mackay, D. M. The informational aspects of questions and commands. *London sympos. inform. theory,* 1961, 469–476.

McKee, J. P., and Leader, Florence B. The relationship of socioeconomic status and aggression to the competitive behavior of preschool children. *Child Develpm.,* 1955, *26,* 135–142.

McLaughlin, R. N. Further problems of derived obligation. *Mind,* 1955, *64* n.s., 400–402.

McLaughlin, S. C. Visual perception in strabismus and amblyopia. *Psychol. Monogr.,* 1964 *78,* No. 12 (Whole No. 589).

McNeill, D. Developmental psycholinguistics. In G. Lindzey (Ed.), *Handbook of social psychology.* (2nd ed.) Reading, Mass.: Addison-Wesley, in press.

Mallitskaya, M. K. On the use of pictures to develop speech understanding in children at the end of the first and during the second year of life. *Voprosy. Psikhol.,* 1960, *3,* 122–126.

Mann, N. Dependency in relation to maternal attitudes. Unpublished master's thesis, University of Iowa, 1959.

Markey, F. V. Imaginative behavior of young children. *Child Develpm. Monogr.,* 1935, No. 18.

Marshall, Helen R. Relations between home experiences and children's use of language in play interactions with peers. *Psychol. Monogr.,* 1961, *75,* No. 5 (Whole No. 509).

————, and McCandless, B. R. Relationships between dependence on adults and social acceptance by peers. *Child Develpm.,* 1957, *28,* 413–419. (a)

————. A study in prediction of social behavior of preschool children. *Child Develpm.,* 1957, *28,* 149–159. (b)

Martin, J. H. *Freeport public schools experiment on early reading using the Edison responsive environment instrument.* Englewood Cliffs, N.J.: Responsive Environments Corp., 1964.

Mattick, Ilse. Adaptation of nursery school techniques to deprived children: some notes on the experience of teaching children of multi-problem families in a therapeutically oriented nursery school. *J. Amer. Acad. of Child Psychiatry,* 1965, *4* (4), 670–700.

Mattson, Marion L. The relation between the complexity of the habit to be acquired and the form of the learning curve in young children. *Genet. Psychol. Monogr.,* 1933, *13,* 299–398.

Mayer, M. The prodiges. *Esquire,* 1964, *61* (5), 106–107.

Mayers, F. A study of prognostic factors for a therapeutic program for children. Unpublished doctoral dissertation, University of Chicago, 1965.

MEAD, G. H. *Mind, self and society.* Chicago: University of Chicago Press, 1934.

MEIER, G. W. Infantile handling and development in Siamese kittens. *J. comp. physiol. Psychol.,* 1961, *54,* 284–286.

MEIER, J. H. Innovations in assessing the disadvantaged child's potential. In J. Helmuth (Ed.), *The disadvantaged child.* Seattle: Special Child Publishers, in press.

MENGER, K. A logic of the doubtful; an optative and imperative logic. *Rep. math. Colloq.* (Notre Dame), 2nd series, 1939, *1,* 53–64.

MENYUK, PAULA. Syntactic rules used by children from preschool through first grade. *Child Develpm.,* 1964, *35,* 533–546.

MERBAUM, ANN D. Need for achievement in Negro and white children. Unpublished doctoral dissertation, University of North Carolina, 1961.

MEREDITH, D. A correction to von Wright's decision procedure for the deontic system P. *Mind,* 1956, *65* n.s., 548–550.

MEYERS, C. E., and DINGMAN, H. F. The structure of abilities at the preschool ages: hypothesized domains. *Psychol. Bull.,* 1960, *57,* 514–532.

———, ———, ORPET, R. E., SITKEI, E. G., and WATTS, C. A. Four ability-factor hypotheses at three preliterate levels in normal and retarded children. *Monogr. Soc. Res. Child Develpm.,* 1964, *29,* No. 5 (Whole No. 96).

———, ORPET, R. E., ATWELL, A. A., and DINGMAN, H. F. Primary abilities at mental age six. *Monogr. Soc. Res. Child Develpm.,* 1962, *27,* No. 1 (Whole No. 82).

MILES, CATHERINE C. Gifted children. In L. Carmichael (Ed.), *Manual of child psychology.* New York: Wiley, 1954.

MILLER, W., and ERVIN, SUSAN. The development of grammar in child language. In Ursula Bellugi and R. Brown (Eds.), The acquisition of language. *Monogr. Soc. Res. Child Develpm.,* 1964, *29,* No. 1 (Whole No. 92).

MILNER, ESTHER. A study of the relationship between reading readiness in grade one school children and patterns of parent-child interaction. *Child Develpm.,* 1951, *22,* 95–112.

MITCHELL, F. D. Mathematical prodigies. *Amer. J. Psychol.,* 1907, *18,* 61–143.

MOH SHAW-KWEI. The deduction theorems and two new logical systems. *Methodos,* 1950, *2,* 56–75.

MONTESSORI, MARIA. *The Montessori method.* New York: Frederick A. Stokes, 1912. (New York: Schocken Books, 1964.)

———. *Dr. Montessori's own handbook.* Cambridge: Bentley, 1964. (New York: Schocken Books, 1965.)

———. *Spontaneous activity in education.* New York: Schocken, 1965.

MOORE, C. E. External and internal relations. *Proc. of the Aristotelian Soc.,* 1920, *20* n.s., 40–62.

MOORE, O. K. Nominal definitions of "culture." *Phil. Sci.,* 1952, *19,* 245–256.

———. Divination—a new perspective. *Amer. Anthrop.,* 1957, *59,* 69–74.

———. Problem solving and the perception of persons. In R. Tagiuri and L. Petrullo (Eds.), *Person perception and interpersonal behavior.* Palo Alto: Stanford University Press, 1958.

———. Orthographic symbols and the preschool child—a new approach. In E. P. Torrence (Ed.), *Creativity: 1960 proceedings of the 3rd conference on gifted children.* Minneapolis: University of Minnesota, Center for Continuation Studies, 1961.

————. *Autotelic response environments and exceptional children.* (Report) Hamden, Conn.: Responsive Environments Foundation, 1963.

————. Technology and behavior. In *Proc. invitational conference on testing problems.* Princeton: Educational Testing Service, 1964.

————. From tools to interactional machines. In *New approaches to individualizing instruction.* Princeton: Educational Testing Service, 1965. (a)

————. The responsive environments project and the deaf. *Amer. Ann. of the Deaf,* 1965, *110,* 604–614. (b)

————, and ANDERSON, A. R. *Early reading and writing* (motion picture). Pittsburgh: Basic Education, Inc., (Washington Plaza, Apt. 2004), 1960. 3 parts. (Copyright Mp. 10361. LC Fi A 60-3067).

————. Some puzzling aspects of social interaction. In J. H. Criswell, H. Solomon, and P. Suppes (Eds.), *Mathematical methods in small group processes.* Stanford: Stanford University Press, 1962.

————, and KOBLER, R. *Educational apparatus for children.* U.S. Patent No. 3,112,569. 1963.

————, and LEWIS, D. J. Learning theory and culture. *Psychol. Rev.,* 1952, *59,* 380–388.

MOORE, SALLIE B., and RICHARDS, PHYLLIS. *Teaching in the nursery school.* New York: Harper, 1959.

MOORE, SHIRLEY G. Displaced aggression in young children. *J. abnorm. soc. Psychol.,* 1964, *68,* 200–204.

————, and UPDEGRAFF, RUTH. Sociometric status of preschool children related to age, sex, nurturance-giving, and dependency. *Child Develpm.,* 1964, *35,* 519–524.

MORENO, FLORENCE B. Sociometric status of children in a nursery school group. *Sociometry,* 1942, *5,* 395–411.

MORPHETT, MABEL V., and WASHBURNE, C. When should children begin to read? *Elem. Sch. J.,* 1931, *31,* 496–503.

MOSS, H. A., and KAGAN, J. Maternal influences on early IQ scores. *Psychol. Rep.,* 1958, *4,* 655–661.

MOUSTAKES, C. E., and BERSON, MINNIE P. *The young child in school.* New York: Morrow, 1956.

————, SIGEL, I. E., and SCHALOCK, H. D. An objective method for the measurement and analysis of child-adult interaction. *Child Develpm.,* 1956, *27,* 109–134.

MUMMERY, DOROTHY V. A comparative study of the ascendant behavior of Northern and Southern nursery school children. *Child Develpm.,* 1950, *21,* 183–196.

————. Family backgrounds of assertive and non-assertive children. *Child Develpm.,* 1954, *25,* 63–80.

MUSSEN, P., URBANO, P., and BOUTOURLINE-YOUNG, H. Esplorazione del motivi per mezzo di un reattivo: II. Classi sociali e motivazione fra adolescenti di origine italiani. *Arch. Psicol. Neuro. Psichiat.,* 1961, *22,* 681–690.

MUSSEN, P. H. Differences between the TAT responses of Negro and white boys. *J. consult. Psychol.,* 1953, *17,* 373–376.

MUSSEN, P. and DISTLER, L. Child rearing antecedents of masculine identification in kindergarten boys. *Child Develpm.,* 1960, *31,* 89–100.

MUSTE, MYRA J., and SHARPE, DORIS F. Some influential factors in the determination of aggressive behavior in preschool children. *Child Develpm.,* 1947, *18,* 11–28.

MYHILL, J. On the interpretation of the sign " ". *J. symbolic Logic*, 1953, 18, 60–62.

NAESS, A. La validité des normes fondamentales. *Logique et analyse*, 1958, 1 n.s., 4–13.

————. Do we know that basic norms cannot be true or false? *Theoria*, 1959, 25, 31–53.

————. We still do know that norms cannot be true or false: a reply to Dag Oesterberg. *Theoria*, 1962, 28, 205–209.

NATIONAL COUNCIL OF TEACHERS OF ENGLISH. *Language programs for the disadvantaged.* Champaign, Ill.: Author, 1965. (a)

————. *Social dialects and language learning.* Champaign, Ill., Author, 1965. (b)

NELSON, E. J. Intensional relations. *Mind*, 1930, 39 n.s., 440–453.

NELSON, M. J., and DENNY, E. C. *Nelson-Denny Reading Test.* Boston: Houghton Mifflin, 1960.

NEWELL, A., SHAW, J. C., and SIMON, H. A. Elements of a theory of human problem solving. *Psychol. Rev.*, 1958, 65, 151–166.

NEWMAN, H. H., FREEMAN, F. N., and HOLZINGER, K. J. *Twins: a study of heredity and environment.* Chicago: University of Chicago Press, 1937.

NEWTON, EUNICE S. Planning for the language development of disadvantaged children and youth. *J. Negro Educ.*, 1964, 33, 264–274.

NIMNICHT, G. P., and MEIER, J. H. A first year partial progress report of a project in an autotelic responsive environment nursery school for environmentally deprived Spanish-American children. *J. Res. Serv.*, 1966, 5, 3–34.

NORCROSS, KATHRYN J., and SPIKER, C. C. The effects of type of stimulus pretraining on discrimination performance in pre-school children. *Child Develpm.*, 1957, 28, 79–84.

OESTERBERG, D. We know that norms cannot be true or false. Critical comments on Arne Naess: Do we know that basic norms cannot be true or false? *Theoria*, 1962, 28, 200–204.

OLIM, E. G. Mothers' language and children's cognitive styles. Unpublished doctoral dissertation, University of Chicago, 1965.

————, HESS, R. D., and SHIPMAN, VIRGINIA C. Maternal language styles and their implications for children's cognitive development. Paper read at Amer. Psychol. Assn., Chicago, September, 1965.

OPIE, IONA, and OPIE, P. The lore and language of schoolchildren. *Brit. J. Sociol.*, 1960, 11, 178–181. (Abstract)

OREM, R. C. (Ed.). *Montessori for the disadvantaged.* New York: G. P. Putnam, 1967.

ORLANSKY, H. Infant care and personality. *Psychol. Bull.*, 1949, 46, 1–48.

OSGOOD, C. E. A behavioristic analysis of perception and language as cognitive phenomena. In R. J. C. Harper, C. Anderson, C. M. Christensen, and S. M. Hunka (Eds.), *The cognitive processes.* Englewood Cliffs, N.J.: Prentice-Hall, 1964.

OURTH, LYNN, and BROWN, K. B. Inadequate mothering and disturbance in the neonatal period. *Child Develpm.*, 1961, 32, 287–295.

PALERMO, D. S., and LIPSITT, L. P. (Eds.). *Research readings in child psychology.* New York: Holt, Rinehart, 1963.

PAPOUŠEK, H. Conditioned head rotation reflexes in infants in the first months of life. *Acta Paediatr.*, 1961, 50, 565–576.

————. The development of higher nervous activity in children in the first half-year of life. *Monogr. Soc. Res. Child Develpm.*, 1965, *30*, No. 2 (Whole No. 100).

PARRY, W. T. Ein Axiomensystem für eine ne neue art von implikation (analytische implikation). *Ergebnisse einer mathematischen kolloquiums,* 1933, *4*, 5–6.

PARTEN, MILDRED, and NEWHALL, S. M. Social behavior of preschool children. In R. G. Barker, J. S. Kounin, and H. F. Wright (Eds.), *Child behavior and development.* New York: McGraw-Hill, 1943.

PASAMANICK, B., and KNOBLOCH, HILDA. Epidemiologic studies on the complications of pregnancy and the birth process. In G. Caplan (Ed.), *Prevention of mental disorders in children.* New York: Basic Books, 1961.

PEARL, A., and RIESSMAN, F. *New careers for the poor.* New York: Free Press, 1965.

PECK, L., and WALLING, R. A preliminary study of the eidetic imagery of preschool children. *J. genet. Psychol.,* 1935, *47*, 168–192.

PEISACH, ESTELLE C. Children's comprehension of teacher and peer speech. *Child Develpm.,* 1965, *36*, 468–480.

PERRYMAN, LUCILE C. Dramatic play and cognitive development. *J. nursery Educ.,* 1962, *17*, 185–188.

PETERS, C. C., and McELWEE, A. R. Improving functioning intelligence by analytical training in a nursery school. *Elem. Sch. J.,* 1944, *45*, 213–219.

PETTIGREW, T. F. Negro American intelligence: a new look at an old controversy. *J. Negro Educ.,* 1964, *33*, 6–25.

PIAGET, J. *The psychology of intelligence.* New York: Harcourt Brace, 1950.

———. *The origins of intelligence in children.* New York: International Universities Press, 1952. (a)

———. *Play, dreams and imitation in childhood.* New York: Norton, 1952. (b)

———. *The construction of reality in the child.* New York: Basic Books, 1954.

———. Response to Brian Sutton-Smith. *Psychol. Rev.,* 1966, *73*, 111–112.

POULTON, E. C. British courses for adults on effective reading. *Brit. J. educ. Psychol.,* 1961, *31*, 128–137.

PRAWITZ, D. *Natural deduction.* Stockholm: 1965.

PRIOR, A. N. The interpretation of two systems of modal logic. *J. computing Systems,* 1954, *1*, 201–208. (a)

———. The paradoxes of derived obligation. *Mind,* 1954, *63* n.s., 64–65. (b)

———. *Formal logic.* Oxford: Clarendon Press, 1955.

———. A note on the logic of obligation. *Rev. phil. de Louvain,* 1956, *54*, 86–87.

———. Escapism: the logical basis of ethics. In A. J. Melden (Ed.), *Essays in moral philosophy.* Seattle: University of Washington Press, 1958.

PRIOR, M., and PRIOR, A. N. Erotetic logic. *Phil. Rev.,* 1955, *64*, 43–59.

PROJECT HEAD START. Community Action Program. Daily Program I for a child development center. Washington: U.S. Office of Economic Opportunity, 1965.

RADIN, NORMA L., and WEIKART, D. A home teaching program for disadvantaged preschool children. Unpublished manuscript, Ypsilanti Public Schools, Ypsilanti, Michigan, 1966.

RADKE, MARIAN J. The relation of parental authority to children's behavior and attitudes. *Inst. Child Welf. Monogr.,* 1946, No. 22.

RAMBUSCH, NANCY M. *Learning how to learn: an American approach to Montessori.* Baltimore: Helicon, 1962.

RAPIER, JACQUELINE L. Measured intelligence and the ability to learn. *Acta Psychol.*, 1962, 20, 1–17.

RAPPOPORT, L. Detecting a cognitive schema in a young child. *Psychol. Rep.*, 1964, 14, 515–518.

RAYMONT, T. A. A history of the education of young children. London: Longmans, Green, 1937.

READ, KATHERINE H. *The nursery school: a human relationships laboratory.* (3rd ed.) Philadelphia: Saunders, 1960.

REESE, H. W. Transposition in the intermediate-size problem by preschool children. *Child Develpm.*, 1961, 32, 311–314.

———. Discrimination learning set in children. In L. P. Lipsitt and C. C. Spiker (Eds.), *Advances in child development and behavior.* New York: Academic Press, 1963.

RESCHER, N. An axiom system for deontic logic. *Phil. Stud.*, 1958, 9, 24–30.

———. Conditional permission in deontic dogic. *Phil. Stud.*, 1962, 13, 1–6.

———. *The logic of commands.* London: Routledge and Kegan Paul, 1966.

RÉVÉSZ, G. The indivisibility of mathematical talent. *Acta Psychol.*, 1940, V (2), 1–21.

RHEINGOLD, HARRIET L. The modification of social responsiveness in institutional babies. *Monogr. Soc. Res. Child Develpm.*, 1956, 21, No. 2 (Whole No. 63).

———. The measurement of maternal care. *Child Develpm.*, 1960, 31, 565–575.

———. The effect of environmental stimulation upon social and exploratory behaviour in the human infant. In B. M. Foss (Ed.), *Determinants of infant behaviour.* New York: Wiley, 1961.

———, and BAYLEY, NANCY. The later effects of an experimental modification of mothering. *Child Develpm.*, 1959, 30, 363–372.

———, GEWIRTZ, J. L., and ROSS, HELEN W. Social conditioning of vocalizations in the infant. *J. comp. physiol. Psychol.*, 1959, 52, 68–73.

RICCIUTI, H. N. Object grouping and selective ordering behavior in infants 12 to 24 months old. *Merrill-Palmer quart.*, 1965, 11, 129–148.

———, and JOHNSON, L. J. Developmental changes in categorizing behavior from infancy to the early preschool years. Paper read at the Society for Research in Child Development, Minneapolis, March, 1965.

RICHARDS, T. W., and SIMONS, MARJORIE P. The Fels Child Behavior Scale. *Genet. Psychol. Monogr.*, 1941, 24, 259–309.

RICHMOND, J. B., and CALDWELL, BETTYE M. Development of a demonstration day care center for young children. Research proposal, Children's Bureau, U.S. Dept. of Health, Education, and Welfare. Syracuse: Upstate Medical Center, State University of New York, 1964.

RIESEN, A. H. Plasticity of behavior: psychological series. In H. Harlow and C. N. Woolsey (Eds.), *Biological and biochemical bases of behavior.* Madison: University of Wisconsin Press, 1958.

RIESSMAN, F. *The culturally deprived child.* New York: Harper, 1962.

RIPPLE, R. E. (Ed.) *Readings in learning and human abilities: educational psychology.* New York: Harper, 1964.

ROEPER, ANNEMARIE, and SIGEL, I. Finding the clue to children's thought processes. *Young child.*, 1966, 21, 335–349.

ROOT, W. T. A socio-psychological study of fifty-three supernormal children. *Psychol. Monogr.*, 1921, 29, No. 4 (Whole No. 133).

ROSE, A. M. (Ed.) *Mental health and mental disorder.* New York: Norton, 1955.

ROSEN, B. C. The achievement syndrome: a psychocultural dimension of social stratification. In J. W. Atkinson (Ed.), *Motives in fantasy, action, and society.* Princeton, N.J.: Van Nostrand, 1958.

———. Race, ethnicity, and the achievement syndrome. *Amer. sociol. Rev.,* 1959, *24,* 47–60.

———, and D'ANDRADE, R. The psycho-social origins of achievement motivation. *Sociometry,* 1959, *22,* 185–218.

ROSENBLITH, JUDY F. Learning by imitation in kindergarten children. *Child Develpm.,* 1959, *30,* 69–80.

RUDOLPH, MARGUERITA. *Living and learning in nursery school.* New York: Harper, 1954.

RUSSELL, R. W. Studies in animism: II. The development of animism. *J. genet. Psychol.,* 1940, *56,* 353–366.

SANTOSTEFANO, S. G. A developmental study of the cognitive control "leveling-sharpening." *Merrill-Palmer quart.,* 1964, *10,* 343–360.

———, and PALEY, EVELYN. Development of cognitive controls in children. *Child Develpm.,* 1964, *35,* 949–959.

SCARFE, N. V. Play is education. *Childh. Educ.,* 1962, *39,* 117–121.

SCHACHTEL, E. G. On memory and childhood amnesia. In P. Mullahy (Ed.), *A study of interpersonal relations.* New York: Hermitage Press, 1949.

SCHAEFER, E. S., and BAYLEY, NANCY. Maternal behavior, child behavior, and their intercorrelations from infancy through adolescence. *Monogr. Soc. Res. Child Develpm.,* 1963, *28,* No. 3 (Whole No. 87).

SCHAEFFER, M. S., and GERJUOY, IRMA R. The effect of stimulus naming on the discrimination learning of kindergarten children. *Child Develpm.,* 1955, *26,* 231–240.

SCHOPLER, ERIC. Visual versus tactual receptor preference in normal and schizophrenic children. Unpublished doctoral dissertation, University of Chicago, 1964.

SCHUSTERMAN, R. J. Strategies of normal and mentally retarded children under conditions of uncertain outcome. *Amer. J. ment. Defic.,* 1964, *69,* 66–75.

SCOTT, J. P. Critical periods in behavioral development. *Science,* 1962, *138,* 949–958.

SEARS, PAULINE S., and DOWLEY, EDITH M. Research on teaching in the nursery school. In N. L. Gage (Ed.), *Handbook of research on teaching.* Chicago: Rand McNally, 1963.

SEARS, R. R., WHITING, J. W. M., NOWLIS, V., and SEARS, PAULINE S. Some child-rearing antecedents of aggression and dependency in young children. *Genet. Psychol. Monogr.,* 1953, *47,* 135–234.

SELLARS, WILFRID. Imperatives, intentions and the logic of "ought." *Methodos,* 1956, *8,* 227–268.

SEMLER, I. J., and ISCOE, I. Comparative and developmental study of the learning abilities of Negro and white children under four conditions. *J. educ. Psychol.,* 1963, *54,* 38–44.

SHEPARD, WINIFRED O. Learning set in preschool children. *J. comp. physiol. Psychol.,* 1957, *50,* 15–17.

SHIELDS, J. Twins brought up apart. *Eugenics Rev.,* 1958, *50,* 115–123.

SHIPMAN, VIRGINIA C., and HESS, R. D. Children's conceptual styles as a function of social status and maternal conceptual styles. Paper read at Amer. Psychol. Assn., Chicago, September, 1965.

————. The verbal nature of a "nonverbal" test of intelligence: implications for testing the culturally disadvantaged child. *Amer. Psychol.*, 1966, *21*, 614. (Abstract)

SHIRLEY, MARY M. *The first two years: a study of twenty-five babies.* Minneapolis: University of Minnesota Press, 1931–33. 2 vols.

SIEGEL, ALBERTA E. Aggressive behavior of young children in the absence of an adult. *Child Develpm.*, 1957, *28*, 371–378.

————, and HAAS, MIRIAM B. The working mother: a review of research. *Child Develpm.*, 1963, *34*, 513–542.

————, STOLZ, LOIS M., HITCHCOCK, ETHEL A., and ADAMSON, JEAN. Dependence and independence in the children of working mothers. *Child Develpm.*, 1959, *30*, 533–546.

SIGEL, I. E. How does a research point of view contribute to the nursery school teacher? *J. nursery Educ.*, 1957, *13*, 18–26.

————. Developmental considerations of the nursery school experience. Paper read at Conf. on Nursery Sch. Educ., Council of Child Develpm., New York, 1962.

————. How intelligence tests limit understanding of intelligence. *Merrill-Palmer quart.*, 1963, *9*, 39–56.

————. Modes of classification as a function of representation of items among lower-class children. Paper read at Amer. Psychol. Assn., New York, 1966.

————, ANDERSON, L. M., and SHAPIRO, H. Categorization behavior of lower- and middle-class Negro preschool children: differences in dealing with representation of familiar objects. *J. Negro Educ.*, 1966, *35*, 218–229.

————, and HOPPER, F. *Current research on Piaget's theory.* New York: Holt, Rinehart, 1967.

————, JARMAN, P., and HANESIAN, H. Styles of categorization and their perceptual, intellectual, and personality correlates in young children. *Human Develpm.*, 1967, *10*, 1–17.

————, and MERMELSTEIN, E. Effects of nonschooling on Piagetian tasks of conservation. Paper read at Amer. Psychol. Assn., Chicago, September, 1965, as "Ability to conserve (matter, weight, volume) and to categorize among severely educationally deprived children."

————, ROEPER, ANNEMARIE, and HOOPER, F. H. A training procedure for acquisition of Piaget's conservation of quantity: a pilot study and its replication. *Brit. J. educ. Psychol.*, 1966, *35* (Part 3), 301–311.

SIMMEL, G. *Georg Simmel, 1858–1918.* Collected essays. K. H. Wolff (Ed.) Columbus: Ohio State University Press, 1959.

SKEELS, H. M. Some Iowa studies of the mental growth of children in relation to differentials of the environment: a summary. *Yearb. nat. soc. Stud. Educ.*, 1940, *39*, Part II, 281–308.

————. Effects of adoption on children from institutions. *Children*, 1965, *12*, 33–34.

————, and DYE, H. B. A study of the effects of differential stimulation on mentally retarded children. *Proc. Amer. Assn. ment. Def.*, 1939, *44*, 114–136.

SKINNER, B. F. Are theories of learning necessary? *Psychol. Rev.*, 1950, *57*, 193–216.

SKODAK, MARIE, and SKEELS, H. M. A final follow-up study of one hundred adopted children. *J. genet. Psychol.*, 1949, *75*, 85–125.

SLAVINA, L. S. Specific features of the intellectual work of unsuccessful pupils. In B. Simon (Ed.), *Psychology in the Soviet Union*. Stanford: Stanford University Press, 1957.

SLOBIN, D. I. The acquisition of Russian as a native language. Paper read at the Conference on Language Development in Children, Old Point Comfort, Va., April 28, 1965. (a)

————. The role of imitation in early language learning. Paper read at the Society for Research in Child Development, Minneapolis, March, 1965. (b)

SMEDSLUND, J. Development of concrete transitivity of length in children. *Child Develpm.*, 1963, *34*, 389–405.

————. Concrete reasoning: a study of intellectual development. *Monogr. Soc. Res. Child Develpm.*, 1964, *29*, No. 2 (Whole No. 93).

————. The development of transitivity of length: a comment on Braine's reply. *Child Develpm.*, 1965, *36*, 577–580.

SMILANSKY, S. Progress report on a program to demonstrate ways of using a year of kindergarten to promote cognitive abilities, impart basic information and modify attitudes which are essential for scholastic success of culturally deprived children in their first two years of school. Paper read at Res. Conf. on the Educ. of the Culturally Deprived, Chicago, June, 1964.

SMILEY, T. J. Entailment and deducibility. *Proc. of the Aristotelian Soc.*, 1959, *59*, 233–254.

SONTAG, L. W., BAKER, C. T., and NELSON, VIRGINIA L. Mental growth and personality development: a longitudinal study. *Monogr. Soc. Res. Child Develpm.*, 1958, *23*, No. 2 (Whole No. 68).

SPEER, G. S. The intelligence of foster children. *J. genet. Psychol.*, 1940, *57*, 49–55.

SPIKER, C. C., and IRWIN, O. C. The relationship between IQ and indices of infant speech sound development. *J. Speech and Hearing Disorders*, 1949, *14*, 335–343.

————, and TERRELL, G. Factors associated with transportation behavior of preschool children. *J. genet. Psychol.*, 1955, *86*, 143–158.

SPITZ, R. A. Hospitalism: an inquiry into the genesis of psychiatric conditions in early childhood. *Psychoanal. Stud. of the Child*, 1945, *1*, 53–74.

————. Hospitalism: a follow-up report. In Ruth S. Eissler (Ed.), *Psychoanalytic study of the child*. Vol. 2. New York: International Universities Press, 1947.

STAATS, A. W., MINKE, K. A., FINLEY, J. R., WOLF, M., and BROOKS, L. O. A reinforcer system and experimental procedure for the laboratory study of reading acquisition. *Child Develpm.*, 1964, *35*, 209–231.

————, and STAATS, CAROLYN K. A comparison of the development of speech and reading behavior with implications for research. *Child Develpm.*, 1962, *33*, 831–846.

STANDING, E. M. *Maria Montessori: her life and work*. London: Hollis and Carter, 1957.

STERN, CAROLYN. Acquisition of problem-solving strategies in young children and its relation to verbalization. *J. educ. Psychol.*, in press.

————, and KEISLAR, E. R. Acquisition of problem solving strategies by young children, and its relation to mental age. *Amer. educ. Res. J.*, 1967, *4*, 1–12.

STEVENSON, H. W., and STEVENSON, NANCY G. Social interaction in an interracial nursery school. *Genet. Psychol. Monogr.*, 1960, *61*, 37–73.

STODOLSKY, SUSAN S. Maternal behavior and language and concept formation in Negro pre-school children: an inquiry into process. Unpublished doctoral dissertation, University of Chicago, 1965.

STOLZ, LOIS M. Effects of maternal employment on children. *Child Develpm.*, 1960, *31*, 749–782.

STRAYER, LOIS C. Language and growth: the relative efficacy of early and deferred vocabulary training, studied by the method of co-twin control. *Genet. Psychol. Monogr.*, 1930, *8*, 215–317.

STRODTBECK, F. L. The reading readiness nursery: short-term social intervention technique. Unpublished manuscript, University of Chicago, 1964.

STRONGIN, T. Japanese tutors young violinists. *New York Times*, February 28, 1964, *113* (38751), 31.

SUGIHARA, T. Strict implication free from implicational paradoxes. *Mem. faculty lib. arts, Fukui univer.*, 1955, series 1, 55–59.

SUTTON-SMITH, B. Piaget on play: a critique. *Psychol. Rev.*, 1966, *73*, 104–110.

SWIFT, JOAN W. Effects of early group experience: the nursery school and day nursery. In M. L. Hoffman and Lois W. Hoffman (Eds.), *Review of child development research*. Vol. 1. New York: Russell Sage Foundation, 1964.

TEMPLIN, MILDRED C. Certain language skills in children, their development and interrelationships. *Inst. Child Welf. Monogr.*, 1957, No. 26.

TERMAN, L. M. An experiment in infant education. *J. appl. Psychol.*, 1918, *2*, 219–228.

———. *Genetic studies of genius*. Vol. 1 of *Mental and physical traits of a thousand gifted children*. Stanford: Stanford University Press, 1925.

TERRELL, G., DURKIN, KATHRYN, and WIESLEY, M. Social class and the nature of the incentive in discrimination learning. *J. abnorm. soc. Psychol.*, 1959, *59*, 270–272.

THOMAS, H. Visual-fixation responses of infants to stimuli of varying complexity. *Child Develpm.*, 1965, *36*, 629–638.

THOMPSON, G. G. The social and emotional development of preschool children under two types of educational program. *Psychol. Monogr.*, 1944, *56*, No. 5 (Whole No. 258).

THOMSON, W. R., and HERON, W. The effects of restricting experience in dogs. *Canad. J. Psychol.*, 1954, *8*, 17–31.

TIKTIN, SUSAN, and HARTUP, W. W. Sociometric status and the reinforcing effectiveness of children's peers. *J. exp. Child Psychol.*, 1965, *2*, 306–315.

TODD, VIVIAN E., and HEFFERNAN, HELEN. *The years before school: guiding preschool children*. New York: Macmillan, 1964.

UPDEGRAFF, RUTH. *Practice in preschool education*. New York: McGraw-Hill, 1938.

———, HEILIGER, L., and LEARNED, JANET. The effects of training upon the singing ability and musical interests of three-, four-, and five-year-old children. *Univ. Iowa Study Child Welf.*, 1938, *14*, 83–131.

UZGIRIS, INA C. Situational generality of conservation. *Child Develpm.*, 1964, *35*, 831–841.

———, and HUNT, J. M. A scale of infant psychological development. Unpublished manuscript, University of Illinois, 1964.

VANCE, BARBARA J. Social learning theory and guidance in early childhood. *Young Child.*, 1965, *21*, 30–42.

VILDOMEC, V. *Multilingualism: a study in the psychology of language*. Leyden: A. W. Sythoff, 1963.

VYGOTSKII, L. S. *Thought and language.* Cambridge: M.I.T. Press, 1962.
WALLACH, M. A. Research in children's thinking. *Yearb. nat. soc. Stud. Educ.,* 1963, 62, Part I. Pp. 236–276.
WALTERS, J., PEARCE, DORIS, and DAHMS, LUCILLE. Affectional and aggressive behavior of preschool children. *Child Develpm.,* 1957, 28, 15–26.
WALTERS, R. H., PARKE, R. D., and CANE, VALERIE A. Timing of punishment and the observation of consequences to others as determinants of response inhibition. *J. exp. Child Psychol.,* 1965, 2, 10–30.
WANN, K. D., DORN, MIRIAM S., and LIDDLE, ELIZABETH A. *Fostering intellectual development in young children.* New York: Bureau of Publications, Teachers College, Columbia University, 1962.
WARNER, W. L., HAVIGHURST, R. J., and LOEB, M. B. *Who shall be educated?* New York: Harper, 1944.
WEIKART, D. P. *Preschool intervention: a preliminary report of the Perry preschool project.* Ann Arbor: Campus Publishers, 1967.
————, KAMII, CONSTANCE K., and RADIN, NORMA L. Perry Preschool Project progress report. Unpublished manuscript, Ypsilanti Public Schools, Ypsilanti, Michigan, 1964.
WEINBERGER, OTA. *Die Sollsatzproblematik in der modernen logik. Können sollsätze (imperative) als wahr bezeichnet werden?* Praha, 1958.
————. Theorie des propositions normatives. Quelques remarques au sujet de l'interprétation normative des systèmes K_1 et K_2 de M. Kalinowski. *Stud. logica,* 1960, 9, 7–21.
WEIR, M. W. Developmental changes in problem-solving strategies. *Psychol. Rev.,* 1964, 71, 473–490.
WEISBERG, P. Social and nonsocial conditioning of infant vocalizations. *Child Develpm.,* 1963, 34, 377–388.
WELCH, L. The development of discrimination of form and area. *J. Psychol.,* 1939, 7, 37–54. (a)
————. The development of size discrimination between the ages of 12 and 40 months. *J. genet. Psychol.,* 1939, 55, 243–268. (b)
————. The span of generalization below the two-year age level. *J. genet. Psychol.,* 1939, 55, 269–297. (c)
————. The genetic development of the associational structures of abstract thinking. *J. genet. Psychol.,* 1940, 56, 175–206. (a)
————. A preliminary investigation of some aspects of the hierarchial development of concepts. *J. genet. Psychol.,* 1940, 22, 359–378. (b)
————. The transition from simple to complex forms of learning. *J. genet. Psychol.,* 1947, 71, 223–251.
WELLMAN, BETH L. The effects of preschool attendance upon intellectual development. In R. G. Barker, J. S. Kounin, and H. F. Wright (Eds.), *Child behavior and development.* New York: McGraw-Hill, 1943.
————. IQ changes of preschool and non-preschool groups during the preschool years: a summary of the literature. *J. Psychol.,* 1945, 20, 347–368.
WENGER, M. A. Conditioned responses in human infants. In R. G. Barker, J. S. Kounin, and H. F. Wright (Eds.), *Child behavior and development.* New York: McGraw-Hill, 1943.
WERNER, H. Process and achievement: a basic problem of education and developmental psychology. *Harvard educ. Rev.,* 1937, 7, 353–368.
————. *Comparative psychology of mental development.* (2nd ed.) Chicago: Follett, 1948.
WEST, EDITH. Concepts, generalizations and theories. Unpublished manuscript, University of Minnesota, 1964.

WHITE, B. L., CASTLE, P., and HELD, R. Observations on the development of visually-directed reaching. *Child Develpm.*, 1964, *35*, 349–364.

WHITE, B. L., and HELD, R. Plasticity of sensorimotor development in the human infant. In Judy F. Rosenblith and W. Allinsmith (Eds.), *The causes of behavior: readings in child development and educational psychology*. (2nd ed.) Boston: Allyn and Bacon, 1966.

WHITE, R. W. Motivation reconsidered: the concept of competence. *Psychol. Rev.*, 1959, *66*, 297–333.

————. Competence and the psycho-sexual stages of development. In M. R. Jones (Ed.), *Nebraska symposium on motivation*. Vol. 8. Lincoln: University of Nebraska Press, 1960.

WHITE, S. H. Learning. *Yearb. nat. soc. Stud. Educ.*, 1963, *62*, Part I.

————. Evidence for a hierarchial arrangement of learning processes. In L. P. Lipsitt and C. C. Spiker (Eds.), *Advances in child development and behavior*. Vol. 2. New York: Academic Press, 1965.

————. Age differences in reaction to stimulus variation. In O. J. Harvey (Ed.), *Flexibility, adaptability, and creativity*. New York: Springer, 1966.

WHITEMAN, M., BROWN, B., and DEUTSCH, M. Some effects of social class and race on children's language and intellectual abilities. In *Studies in deprivation*. New York: Institute for Developmental Studies, 1966.

WIENER, N. *Ex-prodigy: my childhood and youth*. New York: Simon & Schuster, 1953.

WINER, B. J. *Statistical principles in experimental design*. New York: McGraw-Hill, 1962.

WITKIN, H. A. Heinz Werner: 1890–1964. *Child Develpm.*, 1965, *36*, 307–328.

————, DYK, R. B., FATERSON, H. F., GOODENAUGH, D. R., and KARP, S. A. *Psychological differentiation*. New York: Wiley, 1962.

WOHLWILL, J. F. Developmental studies of perception. *Psychol. Bull.*, 1960, *57*, 249–288 (a)

————. A study of the development of the number concept by scalogram analysis. *J. genet. Psychol.*, 1960, *97*, 345–377. (b)

————. From perception to inference: a dimension of cognitive development. *Monogr. Soc. Res. Child Develpm.*, 1962, *27*, No. 2, 87–107.

————, and LOWE, R. C. Experimental analysis of the development of the conservation of number. *Child Develpm.*, 1962, *33*, 153–167.

WOODS, J. Relevance. *Logique et analyse*, 1964, *27* n.s., 130–137.

WRIGHT, G. H. VON. Deontic logic. *Mind*, 1951, *60*, 1–15. (a)

————. *An essay in modal logic*. Amsterdam: 1951. (b)

————. A note on deontic logic and derived obligation. *Mind*, 1956, *65* n.s., 507–509.

————. Logical studies. London: Routledge and Kegan Paul, 1957.

————. A note on entailment. *Phil. quart.*, 1959, *9*, 363–365.

————. *Norm and action*. London: Routledge and Kegan Paul, 1963.

WRIGHT, J. C., and KAGAN, J. (Eds.). Basic cognitive processes in children. *Monogr. Soc. Res. Child Develpm.*, 1963, *28*, No. 2 (Whole No. 86).

WYLIE, RUTH C. Children's estimates of their schoolwork ability, as a function of sex, race, and socioeconomic level. *J. Pers.*, 1963, *31*, 203–224.

YARROW, L. J. Maternal deprivation: toward an empirical and conceptual reevaluation. *Psychol. Bull.*, 1961, *58*, 459–490.

YOST, PATRICIA A., SIEGEL, ALBERTA E., and ANDREWS, JULIA M. Nonverbal probability judgments by young children. *Child Develpm.*, 1962, *33*, 769–780.

YOUNISS, J., and FURTH, H. G. Discrimination shifts as a function of degree of training in children. *J. exp. Psychol.*, 1965, *70*, 424–427.

ZEAMAN, D., and HOUSE, BETTY J. The role of attention in retardate discrimination learning. In N. R. Ellis (Ed.), *Handbook of mental deficiency: psychological theory and research.* New York: McGraw-Hill, 1963.

ZIGLER, E., and BUTTERFIELD, E. Motivational factors and IQ-changes in culturally deprived children attending nursery school. Unpublished manuscript, 1967.

———, and KANZER, P. The effectiveness of two classes of verbal reinforcers on the performance of middle- and lower-class children. *J. Pers.*, 1962, *30*, 157–163.

ZIMILES, H. A note on Piaget's concept of conservation. *Child Develpm.*, 1963, *34*, 691–695.

———. *The development of differentiation and conservation of number.* Bank Street College of Education (U.S.O.E. Cooperative Research Project No. 2270), 1965.

———. The development and conservation and differentiation of number. *Monogr. Soc. Res. Child Develpm.*, 1966, *31*, No. 6 (Whole No. 108).

———. The differentiation and conservation of number. *Monogr. Soc. Res. Child Develpm.*, in press.

ZIMMERMANN, R. R., and TORREY, C. C. Ontogeny of learning. In A. M. Schrier, H. F. Harlow, and F. Stollnitz (Eds.), *Behavior of nonhuman primates.* Vol. 2. New York: Academic Press, 1965.

ZINOV'EV, A. A. O logike normativnyi predlozenii (on the logic of normative propositions.) *Vop. filo.*, 1958, *11*, 156–159.

INDEX

INDEX